KB262604

ONE SHOT VOCA

어원으로
배우는
영어
단어장

유니 YUNI

원
샷
VOCA

1945
MYM
문예림

초판 인쇄	2015년 2월 1일
초판 발행	2015년 2월 5일
지은이	유니 YUNI 지음
발행인	서덕일
펴낸곳	문예림
주소	서울 광진구 능동로29길 6, 문예하우스 101호
전화	02-499-1281
팩스	02-499-1283
홈페이지	www.bookmoon.co.kr
이메일	info@bookmoon.co.kr
출판등록	1962년 7월 12일 제2-110호
ISBN	978-89-7482-833-2 (13740)

잘못된 책은 구입하신 서점에서 교환하여 드립니다.

평생 하는 영어 공부, 어디서부터 어떻게 시작해야 할까요?

영어공부가 작심3일로 끝나는 가장 흔한 이유는 무엇일까요?
'무엇인가 하기는 해야 하는데 어떻게 시작해야 할지 막막하기만 하다.'
'막상 시작하면, 공부를 하면 할 수록 모르는 것이 더 많이 나오는 것 같다.'
이런 이유들로 영어공부를 지속하는 것이 쉽지 않기 때문에 우리는 종종 영어공부를 마치기 전에
영어책을 그냥 덮어 버리곤 하죠.
그래서 '남들처럼' 누군가의 도움을 받기 위해 학원을 다니게 되고 TOEIC이나 TOEFL 등의 영어시험을
위해서는 시험준비반을, 영어회화를 위해서는 원어민과의 회화반을 등록 하지만, 시험점수는 늘
제자리 걸음을 하는 듯하고 미드나 영화를 보면 모르는 단어들이 새록 새록 등장하고 뉴욕타임즈를
읽어 보려 해도 단어 찾기에 바빠 "내가 지금까지 영어공부를 제대로 하긴 한건가?"라는 생각을
하신 적이 있으실 것입니다.

무작정 '남들처럼'하는 것만으로는 '배우고 있다'는 만족감을 주지 못합니다.
그럼 과연 우리에게 만족감을 갖지 못하게 하는 것은 무엇일까요?
그것은 바로 '단어'입니다.

우리의 발목을 잡는 것은 그 무엇도 아닌 '단어'죠!
그래서 우린 "단어만 알면…"이란 말을 입에 달고 살죠. 그럼 지긋지긋하게 우리의 발목을 잡고 있는

'단어'를 어떻게 해결해야 할까요?
단어라는 것은 어느 반에서 어느 책으로 공부를 하던 오롯이 '나의 몫'으로 남겨지게 되는 부분이고,
이 문제가 해결되지 않으면 늘 제자리 걸음을 하는 듯한 느낌을 떨칠 수 없습니다. 이 문제를 한방에
해결해 드리기 위해 원샷 VOCA가 어원 풀이로 길잡이를 해드리겠습니다.

다른 언어들과 마찬가지로, 영어도 하나의 어원에서 많은 어휘들이 파생되었죠. 그래서 하나의 어원을
익히면 거기서 파생된 많은 어휘들을 보다 빨리 이해할 수 있게 됩니다. 보다 쉽게 어휘력을
확대시킬 수 있는 방법이죠. 그렇다고 해서 모든 어휘를 어원 중심으로 분류하는 것은 예상되는 것처럼
상당히 지루한 과정이기 때문에 영어를 공부하는 입장에서는 크게 도움이 되지 못합니다. 그래서
'모두'가 아닌 '중요한' 어원들을 정리하고, 거기에 하나씩 하나씩 살을 붙이는 방식으로 어휘를 체계적으로
늘려 나간다면, 그리고 보다 일상적인 어휘와 그렇지 않은 어휘를 분류하여 어휘를 암기해 나간다면,
그 많고 다양한 어휘들을 보다 쉽게 '나의 어휘'로 만들 수 있습니다. 이러한 요구에 순응하기 위해 원샷
VOCA는 3개의 파트(<파트별 사용법>은 다음 페이지에)로 나누어 3,088개의 어휘를 정리했습니다

원샷 VOCA로 한방에 회화(conversation, spoken English)는 물론이고,
영어 시험(TOEIC, TOEFL, OPIC, TEPS, IELTS, GRE 등등)을 공부하시는 분들에게 어휘를
보다 쉽게 정리할 수 있게 해드리겠습니다.
평생하고 있는 영어 공부 원샷 VOCA로 보다 재미있고 간단하게 마무리 지으세요!

What is one shot voca?
이 책의 특징

PART 1

수 많은 어원들 중에서 영어공부에 반듯이 필요한 주요 어원 107개를 선별해 거기에서 파생된 어휘들을 『어근중심』으로 정리하여 총 695개의 어휘를 정리했습니다. 107거의 어원은 각각 번호를 붙여, 그 아래에 어원풀이를 해놓았습니다. 거기서 파생된 어휘들은 한국어풀이와 영어풀이로 설명해 놓고, 이 풀이 아래쪽에 어휘의 어원을 보다 상세히 풀어 놓아 어휘의 의미를 포괄적으로 이해하는데 도움이 되게 정리해 놓았습니다.

PART 2

회회 수준의 어휘(conversatior, spoken English, TOEIC, OPIC, TEPS 등등)인 기본 영어단어 1243개를 정리하였습니다. Part 2의 어휘는 영어를 공부하는 사람이라면 이미 알고 있어야만 하는 『기본어휘』이기 때문에, 이미 익숙한 어휘는 휘리릭 확인만하고 넘어가시고, 혹시라도 잊었거나 아직 알고 있지 않다면 걸른 암기하세요.

PART 3

Part 1 『어근중심』 어휘와 Part 2 『기본어휘』에는 포함되지 않지만, 미드나 영화 등에 흔히 등장할 뿐만 아니라 소설이나 뉴욕타임즈 등을 읽을 때 사전을 찾게 만드는 단어들의 모음입니다. IELTS, GRE와 같은 고난이도의 시험에도 등장하는 좋은 어휘 1150개입니다. "그래도 난 미드나 영화는 자막 없이도 볼 수 있다'거나 "how are you? I'm fine, and you?"가 아닌 조금은 더 세련된 영어를 구사하그자 한다면 Part 3의 어휘는 반드시 필수입니다.

저자 소개

유니(YUNI)

이화여자대학교 국제대학원을 거쳐, New York University(NYU)에서 TESOL 석사를 마쳤고, 성균관대학교, 토피아, 파고다어학원 등의 국내 어학원과 뉴욕 맨하튼의 NYU의 ESL 프로그램인 ALI와 BMCC의 ESL 프로그램 등에서 conversation 뿐만 아니라 TOEIC, TOEFL, GRE 등의 수업을 가르친 경험을 통해 한국 학생들에게 보다 효율적인 영어 학습 방식을 연구하고 보급하고 있습니다.

제안 / 의견

✉ yunioneshotvoca@gmail.com

Contents

PART 1 ··· 007

PART 2 ··· 193

PART 3 ··· 321

PART 1

One shot voca

01 a / an

a/an ~이 없는=without
a/an는 '~이 없는(without)'의 의미를 단어에 부가해 줍니다.

---

abandon
[əbǽndən]

포기하다, 저버리다
to give up completely; to cease to support or look after
a=without: bandon=control

The power plant was abandoned for several years.
발전소는 몇 년 동안 버려져 있었다.

adamant
[ǽdəmənt]

단호한
refusing to be persuaded or to change one's mind
a=without: daman=tame

The scholars remain adamant that the committee shouldn't intervene.
학자들은 위원회가 개입하지 말아야 한다는 것에 단호하다.

anarchy
[ǽnərki]

무정부 상태
absence of any form of political authority
a=without: arkhos=chief/ruler

The anarchy of the Internet often leads the computer users to unexpected directions.
인터넷의 무정부 상태는 사용자들은 예측하지 못한 방향으로 종종 이끈다.

anomalous
[ənámələs]

변칙적인, 비정상의
deviating from what is standard, normal, or expected
a=without: homalos=even/same

Charlie's suggestion was anomalous to the basic premise.
찰리의 제안은 기본 전제에 대해 변칙적이었다.

anonymous
[ənánəməs]

이름을 모르는, 익명인
not identified by name; of unknown name
a=without: onoma= name

Once people got used to accessing the Internet, anonymous sources tended to multiply in news stories.
사람들이 인터넷 사용이 익숙해진 이래로 익경의 제보가 뉴스에 급증했다.

apathetic
[æpəθétik]

무감각한, 무관심한
showing or feeling no interest, enthusiasm, or concern
a=without: pathos=feeling/suffering

Pope expressed his outrage at the officials' apathetic approach to the tragedy.
교황은 그 비극에 대한 관리들의 넝담한 방식에 대해 격분을 표출했다.

atrophy
[ǽtrəfi]

(신체 기능 등의) 퇴화; 약화, 감소
a wasting or decrease in size of a body organ, tissue, or part owing to disease, injury, or lack of use; a wasting away, deterioration, or diminution
a=without: trophē=food

Muscle atrophy often resulted from not using the muscles enough.
근육 퇴화는 근육을 충분히 사용하지 않는 것으로 부터 종종 기인된다.

averse
[əvə́:rs]

몹시 싫어하여
having a feeling of opposition, distaste, or aversion; strongly disinclined
a=without: vertere=turn

Some researchers were averse to taking risks.
몇몇 연구원들은 위험을 무릅쓰는 것을 몹시 싫어했다.

02 *ab*

ab ~이 없는 = from/away/apart
ab는 '~이 없는/떨어져 있는(from/away/apart)'이란 의미를 단어에 부가해 줍니다.

abduct
[æbdʌ́kt]

유괴하다, 꾀어내다
to carry off by force; kidnap
ab=away/from: ducere=lead

After the 11-month nationwide search, the police found the abducted child.
11개월 동안 전국을 조사한 후, 경찰은 유괴되었던 아이를 찾았다.

abject
[æbdʒekt]

절망적인, 굴욕적인, 비참한
cast down in spirit; servile, spiritless; showing hopelessness or resignation
ab=away/from: jacere=throw

Eliminating the abject poverty is the priority for the incumbent governor.
비참한 가난을 근절하는 것이 현직 주지사의 최우선 과제이다.

abnegate
[æbnəgéit]

포기하다, 버리다
to give up (rights or a claim, for example); renounce
ab=away/from: negare=deny

Jennifer had to abnegate the privilege as the chairman.
제니퍼는 의장으로써의 특권을 포기해야만 했다.

abnormal
[æbnɔ́:məl]

정상에서 벗어난, 비정상적인
not typical, usual, or regular; not normal; deviant
ab=away/from: norma=rule

Abnormal behavior of captive animals can be identified in several ways.
포획된 동물들의 비정상적인 행동들은 몇가지 방법으로 확인될 수 있다.

abrogate
[ǽbrəgèit]

공식적으로 폐지하다, 철폐하다
to repeal or do away with (a law, right, or formal agreement)
ab=away/from: rogare=ask

Due to the recently passed bill, some protections might be abrogated.
최근에 통과된 법안 때문에 몇몇 보호책은 폐지될 수 있다.

abrupt
[əbrʌ́pt]

갑작스런, 돌연한
unexpectedly sudden
ab=away/from: rumpere=break

The conversation came to an abrupt end when the phone rang.
전화가 왔을 때, 대화는 돌연 끝났다.

absolve
[æbzálv]

죄를 사하여 주다, 용서해 주다
to free (someone) from blame, guilt, or responsibility
ab=away/from: solver=loosen

The manager attempted to absolve herself of the crime regardless of others' opinions.
매니져는 다른 사람들의 의견과는 구관하게 자신을 범죄로부터 면제하려고 시도했다.

abstain
[əbstéin]

삼가다, 절제하다
to restrain oneself from coing or enjoying something
ab=away/from: tenere=hold

Are there any unexpected benefits related to abstaining from drinking coffee?
커피를 마시는 것을 삼과하는 것과 관련된 어떤 예측치 못한 이익이 있습니까?

abstemious
[əbstíːmiəs]

절제 있는, 금욕적인
eating and drinking in moderation
ab=away/from: temetum= liquor

After the 45 day alcohol abstemious period, the participant claimed his sound heath condition.
45일간 금주 후, 지원자는 자신이 건강한 상터라고 주장했다.

abuse
[əbjúːz]

남용, 악용; 악용하다, 남용하다
to use wrongly or improperly; misuse
ab=away/from: uti=use

Abuse of authority may be the prime source of corruption.
권력 남용은 부패의 주 원인일 수 있다.

03 ac/acr

ac, acr 날카로운 =sharp/harsh/sour
ac/acr는 '날카로운(sharp/harsh/sour)'이란 의미를 단어에 부가해 줍니다.

---

acerbic
[əsə́ːrbik]

신랄한, 신, 쓴
sharp and forthright; tasting sour and bitter
acerbare/acerbus=harsh

Because of his acerbic attitude, some future employers turned him down.
그의 신랄한 태도 때문에 몇몇 예비 고용주들이 그를 거절하게 했다.

acid
[ǽsid]

산성의, 매서운, 신랄한
a substance having a sour taste
acere=be sour

Tommy advised me to ignore Jane's acid tone.
타미는 내게 제인의 신랄한 말투를 무시하라고 조언했다.

acrid
[ǽkrid]

매운, 신, 신랄한
unpleasantly sharp, pungent, or bitter to the taste or smell;
caustic in language or tone
acer/acri=sharp

After the accident, the building was filled with an acrid smell of burning.
사고 후 건물은 화재의 매운 냄새로 가득 찼다.

acrimonious
[æ̀krəmóuniəs]

톡 쏘는, 신랄한
caustic, biting, or rancorous especially in feeling, language, or manner
acer/acri=sharp

Children often witness the acrimonious split of their parents.
아이들은 부모의 험악한 이혼의 종종 목격한다.

acumen
[əkjú:mən]

명민함, 통찰력, 총명함
the ability to make good judgments and quick decisions
acuere=sharpen

The new manager seems to have business acumen.
새로 온 매니져는 사업에 관한 통찰력을 가진 듯하다.

acute
[əkjú:t]

예각의, 예리한, 심각한, 급성인
very bad, serious, painful; perceptive, sensitive
acuere=sharpen

Of all managers, Rose had the most acute insight.
모든 매니져들 중, 로즈가 가장 예리한 통찰력을 가졌다.

04 *ad / a*

ad, a ~을 향하여 =to/toward
ad/a는 '~을 향하여(to/toward)'란 의미를 단어에 부가해 줍니다.

abase
[əbéis]

강등시키다, 낮추다
to reduce or lower the rank, office, reputation of; degrade
a=to/toward: baissier=lower

It's not difficult to see people abase themselves before the mighty.
권력 앞에서 자기 자신을 낮추는 사람들을 보는 것은 어렵지 않다.

abate
[əbéit]

줄이다, 감소시키다, 줄어들다, 완화되다
to reduce or lower the amount of; to become less intense or widespread
a=to/toward: batre=beat

According to the weather forecast, the tornado will abate soon.
일기예보에 따르면 토네이도는 곧 약화될 것이다.

abet
[əbét]

부추기다, 지원하다
to encourage and assist to do something wrong
a=to/toward: beter=bait

Jack was not guilty of misdemeanor, but guilty of abetting others.
잭이 비행에 대해 책임이 있는 것은 아니지만 다른 사람들을 부추긴 것에 대해서는 책임이 있다.

acclimate
[ǽkləmèit]

적응시키다, 적응하다
to become accustomed to a new climate or to new conditions
a=to/toward: climat=climate

Becky had difficulty in acclimating herself to urban life.
베키는 도시 생활에 적응하는데 어려움을 겪었다.

accost
[əkɔ́:st]

접근하다
to approach and speak to in an aggressive
a=to/toward: costa=side

A ragged man accosted me in the street.
어떤 누더기를 걸친 남자가 길거리에서 내게 접근해 왔다.

accrete
[əkrí:t]

점진적으로 증가하다
to grow by accumulation or coalescence
a=to/toward: crescere=grow

He is planning to have an exhibition with his accreted antiques.
그는 모아온 골동품 갖고 전시회를 열 예정이다.

adherent
[ædhíərənt]

추종자, 지지자
someone who supports a particular party, person, or set of ideas
a=to/toward: haerere=stick

Sandra expressed her opinions as an adherent of education reform.
산드라는 교육개혁의 지지자로서 그녀의 의견을 표현했다.

adore
[ədɔ́:(r)]

깊이 흠모하다, 숭배하다, 몹시 좋아하다
to worship as God or a god
a=to/toward: orare=speak/pray

He adored his children.
그는 그의 아이들을 몹시 사랑했다.

advent
[ǽdvent]

출현, 도래, 시작
the arrival of a notable person, thing, or event
a=to/toward: venire=come

The advent of the Internet changed our life dramatically.
인터넷의 출현은 우리 삶을 극적으로 변화시켰다.

adverse
[ǽdvə́:rs]

반대하는, 적의를 품은, 불리한
acting or serving to oppose; antagonistic
a=to/toward: vertere=turn

The research was hindered by the adverse weather conditions.
연구는 좋지 않은 날씨에 의해 지연되었다.

affable
[ǽfəbl]

사귀기 쉬운, 붙임성이 있는, 상냥한
friendly, good-natured, or easy to talk to
a=to/toward: fari=speak

The new executive turned out to be an affable and courteous gentleman.
새로온 간부는 친절하고 예의바른 신사로 판명되었다.

affiliate
[əfílièit]

친분관계를 맺다, 교제하다, 합병하다
to bring or receive into close connection as a member or branch
a=to/toward: filius=son

The department of Education has four affiliated schools for its research.
교육부는 연구를 위해 4개의 제휴학교가 있다.

affirm
[əfə́:rm]

단언하다, 확언하다
to confirm, assert, claim
a=to/toward: firmus=strong

The committee refused to affirm that this work is genuine.
위원회는 그 작품이 진품이라고 확인해 주기를 거부했다.

aggravate
[ǽgrəvèit]

악화시키다, 화나게 하다
to make (a problem, injury, or offense) worse or more serious; to annoy or exasperate persistently
a=to/toward: gravis=heavy

His sudden decision might aggravate the current bad situation.
그의 급작스런 결정이 현재의 나쁜 상황을 악화시킬 수 있다.

allocate
[ǽləkèit]

할당하다, 분배하다, 배치하다
to distribute (resources or duties) for a particular purpose
a=to/toward: locus=place

News media disclosed crucial information about allocating Federal Funds.
뉴스는 연방정부 예산 분배에 대한 중요한 정보를 폭로했다.

allude
[əlúːd]

넌지시 말하다, 암시하다
to make indirect reference
a=to/toward: ludere=play

The political scandal alluded to the governor's immorality.
그 정치 의혹은 주지사의 부도덕성을 암시했다.

arrest
[ərést]

막다, 저지하다, 이목을 끌다, 주의를 끌다, 체포하다, 검거하다
to stop or check (progress or a process); to attract the attention of (someone)
a=to/toward: restare=remain/stop

The natural tranquil surroundings arrested his attention.
자연의 고요한 상황이 그의 주의를 끌었다.

05 ambi / amphi

ambi, amphi 둘의 =both
ambi/amphi는 '둘의(both)'란 의미를 단어에 부가해 줍니다.

---

ambidextrous
[ǽmbidékstrəs]

양손잡이의, 재주가 많은, 교활한
able to use both hands with equal facility
ambi=both: dexter=right/handed

Surprisingly, nobody ensured what makes people ambidextrous.
놀랍게도, 어느 누구도 어떻게 양손잡이가 되는지에 확실하게 알지 못했다.

ambient
[ǽbiənt]

주변의, 둘러싸듯이 있는, 끊임 없이 움직이는
surrounding; encircling
ambi=both: ire=go

The paper is about how the ambient noise affects sleep.
보고서는 주변의 소음이 어떻게 잠에 영향을 미치는지에 관한 것이다.

ambiguous
[æmbígjuəs]

몇가지로 해석되는, 모호한
(of language) open to more than one interpretation, unclear or inexact
ambi=both: agree=drive

We need to eliminate several ambiguous provisions.
우리는 몇몇 모호한 조항들을 없앨 필요가 있다.

ambivalent
[æmbívələnt]

양면가치의, 상반된 감정이 있는
having mixed feelings or contradictory ideas about something or someone
ambi=both: valere=worth

As long as people wanted to be accepted, ambivalent attitudes looked more susceptible.
사람들이 인정 받고 싶어하는 한, 양면가치의 태도는 보다 쉽게 받아들여지는 듯이 보인다.

06 ambl / ambul

ambl, ambul 걷다 =walk
ambl/ambul은 '걷다(from/away/apart)'이란 의미를 단어에 부가해 줍니다.

---

amble
[ǽmbl]

천천히 걷다
to walk or move at a slow, relaxed pace
ambulare=walk

People and their dogs ambled along the riverside.
사람들과 그들의 개들은 강변을 따라 한가롭게 걸었다.

ambulatory
[ǽmbjələtɔ:ri]

보행의, 돌아다니는, 이동성의
of, relating to, or adaptec for walking
ambulare=walk

The ambulatory clinic offers a variety of medical services to
children in need.
이동 병원은 도움을 필요로 하는 아이들에게 다양한 의술을 제공한다.

preamble
[pri:ǽmbl]

서문, 머리말
a preliminary statement, especially the introduction to a formal
document that serves to explain its purpose
pre=before: ambulare=walk

Patrick advised the students to use the handout on the preamble
of the regulation.
패드릭은 학생들에게 규율의 서문에 대한 유인물을 이용하라고 조언했다.

07 anim

anim 정신 =mind/spirit/soul/life
anim은 '정신(mind/spirit/soul/life)'이란 의미를 단어에 부가해 줍니다.

animadvert
[ǽnəmædvə́:rt]

비난하다, 나무라다
to remark or comment critically, usually with strong disapproval or censure
animus=mind: ad=towards: vertere=turn

The scholars have animadverted upon the economic reform plans.
학자들은 경제 개혁 계획에 대해 비난했다.

animate
[ǽnəméit]

생명을 주다, 활기를 주다
to give life to; fill with life
anima=life/soul

Many industries with difficulties might be animated by the government subsidies.
어려움을 겪고 있는 많은 산업들은 정부보조에 의해 활성화 될 수 있다.

animosity
[ǽnəmásəti]

악의, 적의, 증오
bitter hostility or open enmity; active hatred
animus=spirit/mind

Because of his unfair dismissal, he bears animosity towards his former employer.
부당한 해고 때문에 그는 고용주에 대한 적대감이 있다.

pusillanimous
[pjù:səlǽnəməs]

소심한, 심약한, 우유부단한
showing a lack of courage or determination; timid
pusillus=very small: animus=mind

The journalist took a pusillanimous way of accepting his responsibility.
그 언론인은 자신의 책임을 인정하는 면에서 우유부단한 방식을 택했다.

unanimous
[ju:nǽnəməs]
만장일치의, 의견이 일치한
(of two or more people) fully in agreement
unus=one: animus=mind

Unanimously, the members approved the resolution.
만장일치로 회원들은 결의를 승인 했다.

08 ant / ante

ant, ante 이전의 =prior to/before
ant/ante는 '이전의(prior to/before)'란 의미를 단어에 부가해 줍니다.

antedate
[ǽntidèit]
선행하다, 앞서서 일어나다
to date as of a time prior to that of execution
ante=prior to/before: date=give

Before announcing the merge, the companies antedated the
publication of the reorganization plan.
합병을 발표하기 이전에 그 회사들은 개편 계획을 공표를 선행했다.

antediluvian
[æntidilú:viən]
노아의 대홍수 이전의, 태고적의, 고풍의, 구식의
extremely old and antiquated
ante=prior to/before: diluvium=deluge

New theories about the antediluvian animals will be added to the
new edition.
고대 동물에 대한 새로운 이론들이 이번 개정판에 추가될 것이다.

anterior
[æntiriə(r)]
보다 앞의, 이전의, 앞선
occurring before in time; earlier
ante=prior to/before

Harry was interested in the history of ancient America, anterior
to the time of Columbus.
해리는 콜럼버스 이전 시기인 고대 미국사에 흥미를 갖고 있었다.

anticipatory
[æntísəpətɔ́:ri]

예상한, 예기되는, 미리 내다본, 선구적인
expectant
ante=prior to/before: capere=take

Unfortunately, Jane seems to lose the anticipatory excitement of the party.
불행스럽게도 제인은 파티에 대해 예상되었던 흥미를 잃은 듯이 보였다.

09 anti / ant

anti, ant ~에 반대하는 =against/opposite
anti/ant는 '~에 반대하는(against/opposite)'이란 의미를 단어에 부가해 줍니다.

---

antagonistic
[æntægənistik]

상반되는, 대립하는, 적개심을 품은
being hostility that results in active resistance, opposition, or contentiousness
ant=against: agōnizesthai=struggle

The senator was concerned about the antagonistic opinions on his energy policies.
상원의원은 그의 에너지 정책에 대한 적대적인 의견을 염려하였다.

antidote
[æntidòut]

해독제, 방어수단
a medicine taken or given to counteract a particular poison
anti=against: didonai=give

What can be the best antidotes for stress?
스트레스에 대한 최선의 방어수단을 무엇이 될 수 있을까요?

antithetical
[æntəθétik(əl)]

대조법의, 정반대의
directly opposed or contrasted; mutually incompatible
ant=against: thé=set

Although the experiment was expected to work, the results were antithetical to the hypothesis.
실험이 잘 진행될 것으로 예측되었음에도 불구하고 결과는 가설과는 정반대였다.

10 *bell / belli*

bell, belli 전쟁 =war
bell/belli는 '전쟁(war)'이란 의미를 단어에 부가해 줍니다

---

antebellum
[æntibelám]

미국 남북전쟁(1861-1865) 이전의
belonging to the period before a war, especially the American Civil War
ante=prior to/before: bellum=war

To understand antebellum America, you need the in-depth study.
남북전쟁 이전의 미국을 이해하기 위해서, 당신은 심도 깊은 연구를 해야한다.

bellicose
[bélikòus]

호전적인, 싸우기 좋아하는
demonstrating aggression and willingness to fight
bellum=war

The talk show host did not hesitate to use bellicose language.
토크쇼 사회자는 호전적인 언어를 사용하는 것을 주저하지 않았다.

belligerent
[bəlídʒərənt]

호전적인, 전쟁중에 있는
hostile and aggressive; engaged in a war or conflict
bell=war: gerere=make

As long as both parties do not end belligerent approach, the failure of the negotiation cannot be prevented.
양당이 호전적인 방식을 끝내지 않는 한, 협상의 실패는 막아 질 수 없을 것이다.

rebel
[rébəl]

반항하다, 도전하다
to resist authority, control, or convention
re=again: bellum=war

The study explained why some children resented their parents and rebelled against them.
연구는 아이들이 그들의 부모에 대해 분노하고 반항하는 이유를 설명했다.

11 *ben / bene*

ben, bene 좋은 =good/well
ben/bene는 '좋은(good/well)'이란 의미를 단어에 부가해 줍니다.

---

benediction
[bènədíkʃən]

축복, 축도
the utterance or bestowing of a blessing, esp. at the end of a
religious service
bene=well: dicere=say

The service was closed, saying benediction.
축복을 말하며 예식은 끝났다.

benefactor
[bènəfǽktər]

은혜, 후원자
one that gives aid, especially financial aid
bene=well: facere=do

Generous contributions from our benefactors supported the
project.
후원자로 부터의 관대한 기부가 프로젝트를 지원했다.

beneficent
[bənéfəsənt]

선을 행하는, 자비심이 많은, 인정이 많은
generous or doing good
bene=well: facere=do

Irene still believes there are more beneficent citizens in society.
아이린은 우리 사회에 인정이 많은 시민이 더 많다고 여전히 믿는다.

beneficiary
[bènəfiʃiéri]

이익을 받는 사람, 수익자, (보험금 등의) 수취인
one that receives a benefit
bene=well: facere=do

If your minor children are the direct beneficiary of an insurance
policy, it will be necessary to name a guardian.
미성년 자녀가 보험의 수혜자인 경우, 보호자를 지정할 필요가 있다.

benevolent
[bənévələnt]

자비심 많은, 자선을 행하는, 호의적인
well meaning and kindly serving a charitable rather than a profit-making purpose
bene=well: velle=wish

We could see Benedict's benevolent smile when he entered the room.
베니딕트가 방에 들어왔을 때, 우리는 그의 자비로운 미소를 볼 수 있었다.

benign
[bináin]

친절한, 상냥한, 유리한, 온화한
gentle; kindly
bene=well: genus=born

The new manager was well liked because of his benign attitude toward colleagues.
동료에 대한 상냥한 태도 때문에 사람들은 새로온 매니져를 상당히 좋아했다.

benignant
[binígnənt]

친절한, 다정한, 유익한
kindly and benevolent; having a good effect; beneficial
bene=well: genus=born

People described Jack as dreamy-looking man with a benignant expression.
사람들은 잭을 다정한 말투를 갖고 있는 꿈을 꾸는 듯한 외모의 남자로 묘사했다.

12 ced / cess

ced, cess 양보하다, 가다 =yield/stop/go
ced/cess는 '양보하다/가다(yield/stop/go)'란 의미를 단어에 부가해 줍니다.

accede
[æksíːd]

동의하다, 따르다
to assent or agree to a demand, request, or treaty
a=to/toward: cedere=give way/yield

The committee did not accede to the members' request to change the format.
위원회는 형태를 바꾸자는 회원들의 요구에 동의하지 않았다.

ancestor
[ǽnsestər]

조상, 선조, 선구자
a person from whom one is descended, especially if more remote than a grandparent; a forebear
ante=before: cedere =go

The current research will help you trace your ancestors' records.
최근 연구는 당신이 선조의 기록을 추적하는 것을 도울 것이다.

antecedent
[ǽntisidənt]

전의, 앞선, 선행하는
going before; preceding
ante=before: cedere=go

Probabilities based on antecedent events projected meaningful consequences.
선행한 사건에 근거한 가능성은 의미있는 결과를 산출해냈다.

cede
[síːd]

포기하다, 양도하다, 할양하다
to give up (power or territory)
cedere=yield

There are still numerous small islands which are not ceded to the country.
그 나라에게 할양되지 않은 섬들이 아직 많이 있다.

cessation
[seséiʃən]

끝, 중지
a ceasing, an end, a pause or interruption
cessare= yield/stop

According to the research, smoking cessation is associated with improvements in mental health.
연구에 따르면 금연은 정신건강 향상과 관련이 있다.

concede
[kənsí:d]

시인하다, 인정하다, 양보하다
to admit that something is true or valid after first denying or resisting it, to admit (defeat); to surrender, yield
con=completely: cedere=yield

Jason conceded his victory against Mary.
제이슨은 메리의 경쟁에서 그의 승리를 양보했다.

exceed
[iksí:d]

한계를 넘어서다, 초과하다
to be greater than; surpass
ex=out: cedere=go

The court said that the bank had exceeded its powers in managing the financial crisis.
법원은 그 은행이 재정 위기를 관리할 능력이 충분히 있었다고 말했다.

precede
[prisí:d]

선행하다, 앞서다
to come, exist, or occur before in time
prae=before: cedere=go

Explosions in the tower's basement preceded collapses.
타워 지하에서의 폭발은 붕괴 보다 이전에 일어났다.

secede
[sisí:d]

탈당하다, 탈퇴하다
to withdraw formally from membership in an organization, association, or alliance
se=apart: cedere=go

The new chairman was appointed before the former chairman seceded.
이전의 의장이 탈퇴하기 이전에 새로운 의장이 지명되었다.

succeed
[səksíːd]

성공하다, 성취하다
to come next in time or succession; follow after another, replace
another in an office or a position
sub=close to: cedere=go

Brendan's team succeeded in winning for the first time.
브랜든의 팀은 처음으로 승리하는데 성공했다.

13 celer

celer 속도 =speed
celer은 '속도(speed)'란 의미를 단어에 부가해 줍니다.

accelerate
[æksélərèit]

가속화하다, 촉진하다
to increase the speed of
ad=towards: celer=swift

As soon as the car started, it accelerated rapidly.
그 차는 시동을 걸자 마자 급속히 가속했다.

celerity
[səlérəti]

신속함, 기민함
swiftness of action or motion; speed
celer=swift

Unlike most engineers, some engineers like to work at celerity.
대부분의 엔지니어들과는 다르게, 몇몇은 신속하게 일하는 것을 좋아한다.

14 *chron*

chron 시간 =time
chron은 '시간(time)'이란 의미를 단어에 부가해 줍니다.

anachronistic
[ənǽkrənístik]

시대 착오적인, 시대에 맞지 않는
having an error in chronology; of a thing that is conspicuously; no longer in use or vogue
ana=backwards: khronos=time

An anachronistic interpretation of the ancient city's history always has been historians' dilemma.
고대 도시의 역사를 시대 착오적으로 해석하는 것은 항상 역사학자들의 딜레마였다.

chronic
[krá:nik]

여러 해 전부터의, 끊임없는, 상습적인, 버릇이 된
of long duration; continuing
khronos=time

When you have chronic disease, the first thing you need to do is changing your diet.
만성병이 있을 때, 첫번째로 해야할 일은 식습관을 바꾸는 것이다.

chronicle
[kránikl]

연대기, 역사
an extended account in prose or verse of historical events, sometimes including legendary material, presented in chronological order and without authorial interpretation or comment
khronos=time

It appeared that his massive knowledge did not affect his contribution to the chronicles.
그의 많은 지식은 연대기에 대한 그의 공헌에 영향을 미치지 못한 것처럼 보였다.

chronological 연대순의, 날짜순의
[kránəládʒikl] arranged in order of time of occurrence
khronos=time

Unfortunately, the last chapter of the book did not follow a
chronological order.
불행스럽게도 그 책의 마지막 장은 연대기순을 따르지 않았다.

synchronize 동시에 일어나다, 일치시키다
[síŋkrənáiz] to occur at the same time; be simultaneous
syn=same: khronos=time

This program can be used for users to synchronize the content of
many folders recursively.
이 프로그램은 사용자들이 많은 폴더의 내용을 지속적으로 일치화시키는데 사용될 수 있다.

15 *circum*

circum 주변 =around
circum은 '주변(around)'이란 의미를 단어에 부가해 줍니다.

---

circumlocution 에두르기, 수다, 완곡한 표현
[sə́:rkəmloukjú:ʃən] the use of many words where fewer would do, esp. in a deliberate
attempt to be vague or evasive
circum=around: loqui=speak

The public called for the clear explanation rather than
circumlocution and euphemism.
대중은 에두르거나 완곡적인 표현 보다는 명확한 설명을 요구했다.

circumspect
[sə́:rkəmspèkt]

신중한, 주의깊은, 조심하는
wary and unwilling to take risks
circum=around: specere=look

Despite circumspect in his comments, they caused many controversies about the senator's candidacy.
상원의원은 비평을 하는데 신중했음에도 불구하고, 그의 비평은 그의 상원의원 출마에 대한 많은 논란을 만들어냈다.

circumstance
[sə́:rkəmstæns]

주위, 상황, 환경, 부수적인 문제
a condition or fact attending an event and having some bearing on it; a determining or modifying factor
circum=around: stare=stand

Concerning reporting suspicious circumstances, the committee encouraged the officials to focus on the details.
의심 가는 상황을 보고하는 것에 관하여, 위원회는 직원들에게 세부상황에 집중해 줄 것을 권했다.

circumvent
[sə́:rkəmvént]

피하다, 우회하다, 포위하다, 함정에 빠트리다
to find a way around (an obstacle)
circum=around: venire=come

The tutorial program showed how to circumvent possible problems with computer viruses.
안내 프로그램은 컴퓨터 바이러스와 관련된 문제들을 피하는 방법을 알려줬다.

16 co / col / com

co, col, com, con 함께 =together
co/col/com은 '함께(together)'란 의미를 단어에 부가해 줍니다.

---

coeducation
[kòuedʒukéiʃən]

남여공학
the system of education in which both men and women attend the same institution or classes
co=together: educere=lead out

According to the survey, coeducation has positive effects such as chances to learn the gender equality.
조사에 따르면 남녀공학은 성평등을 배울 기회와 같은 긍정적인 효과를 갖고 있다.

coherent
[kouhíərənt]

일관성 있는, 조리가 맞는, 긴밀히 결부된
(of an argument, theory, or policy) logical and consistent
co=together: haerere=stick

Small businesses tended to struggle with long-term coherent growth strategies.
작은 기업들은 장기간의 일관성있는 성장 전략을 세우는데 어려움을 겪는 경향이 있었다.

coincide
[kòuinsáid]

동시에 발생하다, 일치하다
to occur at or during the same time; to correspond in nature, tally
co=together: incidere=occur

The exhibition was set to coincide with the company's annual ceremony.
전시회는 그 회사의 연의식과 일치하게 계획되었다.

collaborate
[kəlǽbəréit]

공동작업하다, 협력하다, 공모하다
to work jointly on an activity, esp. to produce or create something; cooperate traitorously with an enemy
col=together: laborare=to work

Several novice artists have collaborated on the urban project.
몇몇의 신인 예술가들은 도시 프로젝트에 협력했다.

collapse
[kəlǽps]

붕괴; 무너지다, 붕괴하다
to fall down or inward suddenly
col=together: labi=fall

You can find more detailed information on structural failures and collapses through the fo lowing websites.
다음의 웹싸이트를 통해, 구조상 결점과 붕고 에 대한 보다 상세한 정보는 찾을 수 있다.

collude
[kəlúːd]

결탁하다, 공모하다
to cooperate with somebody secretly; conspire
col=together: ludere=play

Bureaucrats colluded to conceal information on bribes.
관료들은 뇌물에 관한 정보를 감추기로 공모했다.

commensurate
[kəménsərət]

동등한, 같은 크기의, 비례하는
corresponding in size or degree; in proportion, proportionate
com=together: mensurare=measure

The announcement says that the salary will be commensurate with experience and responsibilities.
공지에 따르면 봉급은 경험과 책임에 비례할 것이다.

compensate
[kámpənsèit]

보상하다, 보충하다, 상쇄하다
to offset; counterbalance
com=together: pensare=weigh

After the accident, employees expected the company to compensate for their loss.
사고 후에 직원들은 그들은 손실어 대해 회사가 배상할 것을 기대했다.

comprehend
[kàːmprihénd]

이해하다, 파악하다 , 포함하다, 함축하다, 의미하다
to take in the meaning, nature, or importance of; grasp
com=together: prehendere=grasp

Despite of the thorough observation, nobody seems to comprehend the complexity.
철저한 관찰에도 불구하고 아무도 그 복잡함을 이해하지 못하는 듯하다.

compromise
[kámprəmàiz]

타협하다, 위태롭게 하다, 훼손하다; 타협, 양보
to expose to suspicion, discredit, or mischief
com=together: pro=forward: mittere=send

J-Net announced that a number of users' e-mail accounts had been compromised by hackers.
J-Net은 해커들에 의해 많은 사용자들의 이메일이 노출되었다고 발표했다.

concert
[kánsərt]

협정하다, 타협하다, 계획하다; 음악회, 연주회; 일치, 협력
agreement in purpose, feeling, or action
con=together: cernere=discern

To win this election, they need to concert their tactics.
이번 선거에서 이기기 위해서, 그들은 그들의 전략을 협력할 필요가 있다.

concur
[kənkə́:r]

동의하다, 동시에 발생하다, 일치하다, 협동하다
to be of the same opinion; to agree; to happen or occur at the same time; coincide
con=together: currere=run

To pass the bill, we had to concur with the majority party.
법안을 통과시키기 위해서, 우리는 대수당과 협동을 해야만 했다.

condign
[kəndáin]

(형벌 등이) 타당한
deserved; adequate
con=together: dingus=worthy

The public called for condign punishment.
대중은 타당한 처벌을 요구했다.

condone
[kəndóun]

묵과하다, 용서하다
to accept and allow (behavior that is considered morally wrong or offensive) to continue
con=together: donare=give

The committee will not condone illegal activities relating with drug use.
위원회는 약물사용과 관련된 불법 행동을 묵과하지 않을 것이다.

conflict
[kənflíkt]

충돌하다, 모순되다, 싸우다, 다투다; 싸움, 투쟁, 언쟁; 부조화, 불일치
a state of open, often prolonged fighting; a battle or war
con=together: fligere=strike

The survey revealed conflicted public opinions about demolition of the historical buildings.
여론조사는 역사적인 건물 부수는 것에 대해 대중들이 서로 모순된 의견을 갖고 있다는 것을 보여줬다.

conform
[kənfɔ́ːrm]

따르다, 순응하다, 지키다
to comply with rules, standards, or laws con=together: formare=form

Each group has its own norms and rules for group members to conform.
각각의 그룹은 그 멤버들이 따르는 규범과 규정을 갖고 있다.

confound
[kanfàund]

혼돈시키다, 당황케하다
to cause surprise or confusion in (someone), esp. by acting against their expectations
con=together: fundere=pour/mix up

The audience seemed to be confounded at the last scene of the play.
청중은 연극의 마지막 장면에서 당황해 하는 듯이 보였다.

congruous
[káŋgruəs]

일치한, 조화된, 적합한
corresponding in character or kind; appropriate or harmonious
con=together: ruere=fall/rush

Individuals' behaviors are expected to be congruent to their own culture.
개인의 행동은 그들이 속한 문화에 적합할 것으로 기대된다.

conjecture
[kəndʒéktʃər]

추정, 추측; 추측하다
an opinion or conclusion formed on the basis of incomplete information
con=together: jacere=throw

Researchers conjectured the unfavorable outcomes concerning the international relations.
연구원들은 국제관계에 대한 불리한 결과를 추정했다.

conscientious
[kànʃiénʃəs]

양심적인, 진실한, 성실한
wishing to do what is right, esp. to do one's work or duty well and thoroughly
con=together: scire=know

Remy was conscientious and helpful all the times.
레미는 항상 양심적이고 도움이 되었다.

consensus
[kənsénsəs]

합의
general agreement
con=together: sentire=feel

In recent years, the effort has been made to achieve consensus on immigration issues.
최근 몇 년 동안, 이민 이슈에 대한 합의를 이뤄내기 위해 노력했다.

consolidate
[kənsálidèit]

합병하다, 굳건하게 하다, 강화하다
to make (something) physically stronger or more solid; to combine (a number of things) into a single more effective or coherent whole
con=together: solidare=make firm

The company needs to understand how to consolidate financial conditions in order to attract more investors.
회사는 더 많은 투자자를 유치하기 위해, 재정 상황을 강화하는 방법을 이해할 필요가 있다.

conspire
[kənspàiər]

공모하다
to make secret plans jointly to commit an unlawful or harmful act
con=together: spirare=breathe

Unfortunately, the proposal turned out to conspire with politicians against environmental groups.
불행스럽게도 그 제안은 환경단체에 대항하는 정치인들과의 공모의인 것으로 드러났다.

convergent
[kənvə́:rdʒənt]

한 점으로 향하는, 집중적인, 수렴성인
tending toward or approach an intersecting point
con=together: verger=incline

In convergent arguments, different premises always caused the exhausting discussion.
수렴이 되는 논의에서, 서로 다른 전제는 항상 지치는 토론을 하게 한다.

convert
[kənvə́:rt]

변형시키다, 바꾸다, 개종시키다
to cause to change in form, character, or function
con=together: vertere=turn

According to the local newspaper, some innovative college students succeeded in converting old standard cars into electric vehicles.
지역 신문에 따르면 몇몇 혁신적인 대학생들은 오래된 표준차는 전기차로
바꾸는데 성공했다.

convivial
[kənvíviəl]

명랑한, 사교적인
fond of feasting, drinking, and good company; sociable; merry
con=together: vivere=live

Nobody wanted to leave the convivial party.
아무도 그 사교적인 파티를 떠나고 싶어하지 않았다.

convoluted
[kánvəlù:tid]

복잡한, 난해한, 나선상의
(esp. of an argument, story, or sentence) extremely complex and difficult to follow
con=together: volvere=roll

To make a successful movie, convoluted plot is simply not enough.
성공적인 영화를 만들기 위해, 복잡한 줄거리만으로는 충분하지 않다.

17 contra / contro / counter

contra, contro, counter 대응하다 =opposing/against
contra/contro/counter은 '대응하다(opposing/against)'란 의미를 단어에 부가해 줍니다.

contradict
[kántrədíkt]

모순되다, 상반되다, 논박하다
to acquire or incur; to enter into or make an agreement
contra=against/opposing: dicere=speak

Jeremy criticized the book that contradicted his political opinions.
제레미는 그의 정치적인 의견과 상반되는 그 책을 비난 했다.

controversial
[kántrəvə́ːrʃəl]

논쟁적인, 토론을 좋아하는
giving rise or likely to give rise to public disagreement
contro=against/opposing: vertere=turn

Dr. Luke remained a controversial figure in the world of physics.
루크 박사는 물리학 분야에서 논쟁적인 인물로 남아 있었다.

counter
[káuntər]

받아치다, 논박하다; 반대의; 계산대, 카운터
to speak or act in opposition to, to respond to hostile speech or action
counter=against/opposing

The environmental group claimed that global warming already became increasingly difficult threats to counter.
환경 단체는 지구온난화가 이미 대응하기에 상당히 어려운 위협이 되었다고 주장했다.

counteract
[káuntərǽkt]

대항하다, 좌절시키다
to oppose and mitigate the effects of by contrary action
counter=against/opposing: act=do

The recent study may be helpful in order to counteract the city's poverty.
도시의 빈곤에 대항하기 위해, 최근 연구는 도움이 될것이다.

counterfeit
[káuntərfit]

위조하다, 위조품을 만들다, 뒤장하다; 가짜의, 위조의; 위조품
to make a copy of, usualy with the intent to defraud; forge
counter=against: facere=make

The con man was charged for counterfeiting authentic art works.
그 사기꾼은 진품들은 위조한 것으로 고발됐다.

counterpart
[káuntərpárt]

대응물, 동일한 것, 복사물
a person or thing holding a position or performing a function that
corresponds to that of another person or thing in another place
counter=against/opposing: partire=divide/share

The representatives of both parties wanted to talk with their
counterparts.
양당의 대표들은 상대 당의 대표들과 대화하기를 원했다.

encounter
[inkáuntər]

마주치다, 만나다, 대면하다
to meet as an adversary or enemy
in=in: counter=against/opposing

When you encountered problems during the online banking,
please let us know it ASAP.
온라상 은행업무 중 문제가 생기면 저희에게 가능한한 빨리 알려주세요.

18 cor / cord / card

cor, cord, card 심장 =heart
cor/cord/card는 '심장(heart)'이란 의미를 단어에 부가해 줍니다.

---

accord
[əkɔ́:rd]

조화를 이루다, 일치하다, 주다, 허용해주다
to bring into agreement; to grant or give especially as appropriate, due, or earned
ad=to: cor/cord=heart

The situation depended on how well the study's results accorded with its initial assumptions.
상황은 그 연구의 결과가 최초의 가정과 얼마나 잘 일치하느냐에 달려 있었다.

cardiac
[ká:rdiæk]

심장의; 심장병 환자, 강심제
of, near, or relating to the heart
kardia=heart

Unfortunately, he needed subsequent cardiac surgery.
불행스럽게도 그는 후속적인 심장 수술을 해야 했다.

concord
[kánkɔ:rd]

일치, 조화, 화합
agreement or harmony between people or groups
con=together: cor=heart

Joe defined happiness in terms of harmony and concord.
조는 행복을 조화와 화합의 관점에서 정의 내렸다.

19 cred

cred 신용 =trust/believe
cred는 '신용(trust/believe)'이란 의미를 단어에 부가해 줍니다.

---

credence
[krí:dəns]

신용, 신임
credibility, belief
credent=believing

After an hour-long discussion, the panel gave credence to the established theories.
한시간 동안의 토론 끝에, 패널은 이미 입증이 된 이론들을 신뢰했다.

credible
[krédəbl]

믿을 수 있는, 신용할 수 있는, 확실한
capable of being believed; plausible
credent=believing

There is only a little credible evidence.
믿을 만한 증거가 아주 조금 있다

credulous
[krédʒuləs]

잘 믿는, 잘 속아 넘어가는
showing too great a readiness to believe things; gullible
credent=believing

The released information seemed to mislead credulous consumers.
공개된 정보는 쉽게 잘 속아 넘어가는 소비자들을 오해하게 하는 듯이 보였다.

discredit
[diskrédit]

의심하다, 신용을 떨어뜨리다; 불신, 불명예
to damage in reputation; disgrace
dis=not: credent=believing

The false allegation is used to discredit the organization.
잘못된 주장은 그 단체에 대한 신용을 떨어뜨리는데 사용 되었다.

20 crypt

crypt 숨기다 =hide
crypt는 '숨기다(hide)'란 의미를 단어에 부가해 줍니다.

---

apocryphal
[əpákrəfəl]

저작자가 의심스런, 가짜의
of doubtful authenticity, although widely circulated as being true
apo=away from: kruptein= hide

In spite of some evidence, the stories about the governor's scandal seemed apocryphal.
몇몇 증거에도 불구하고 주지사의 스캔들에 대한 이야기들은 가짜인듯이 보였다.

cryptic
[kríptik]

숨은, 비밀의, 암호를 사용한
having a meaning that is mysterious or obscure
kruptein= hide

Although the public demanded clear explanation, the account of the crisis was rather cryptic.
대중이 명확한 설명을 요구 했음에도 불구하고 위기에 대한 그 설명은 오히려 모호했다.

encrypt
[énkript]

암호화하다
to put into code or cipher
en=make: kruptein=hide

The sale representative guaranteed that this service would keep all data encrypted.
판매원은 그 서비스가 모든 자료를 지속적으로 암호화 할것이라고 보증했다.

21 culp

culp 비난 = fault/blame
culp는 '비난(fault/blame)'이란 의미를 단어에 부가해 줍니다.

---

culpable
[kʌ́lpəbl]

과실이 있는, 비난 받을 만한
deserving of blame or censure as being wrong, evil, improper, or injurious
culpa=fault/blame

The governor was accused of bribery which was culpable violation of the Constitution.
주지사는 비난을 받을 만한 헌법 위반인 뇌물 수수로 고발되었다.

culprit
[kʌ́lprit]

범인, 범죄 용의자
one charged with an offense or crime
culpa=fault/blame: prit=ready

According to the report, the former CEO was the newly discovered culprit.
기사에 따르면, 전 CEO는 새롭게 드러난 범인이었다.

exculpate
[ékskʌlpèit]

혐의를 벗겨주다, 무죄로하다
to clear of guilt or blame
ex=out/from: culpa=blame

The senator who was accused of the illegal investment has been exculpated.
불법적인 투자로 비난 받았던 상원의원은 혐의가 벗겨졌다.

inculpate
[inkʌ́lpeit]

혐의를 씌우다, 죄를 씌우다
to incriminate
in=upon/towards: culpa=blame

Her statement clearly indicated that she had no inclination to inculpate her secretary.
그녀의 진술은 그녀가 비서에게 혐의를 씌우려는 의향이 없다는 것을 명확히 보여줬다.

22 *de*

de 벗어난, 낮아진 =down/low/out/away
de는 '벗어난/낮아진(down/low/out/away)'이란 의미를 단어에 부가해 줍니다.

---

debase
[dibéis]

(가치 등을) 저하시키다
to reduce (something) in quality or value; to degrade
de=down: base= low

Some people considered his remark debasing the dignity of God.
어떤 사람들은 그의 말이 신의 신성함을 저하시키는 것으로 고려했다.

debris
[dəbrí:]

파편, 잔해, (파괴물 등의) 부스러기
the scattered remains of something broken or destroyed; rubble or wreckage
de=down/away: debris=break down

According to the medical study, debris from the accident site tended to cause respiratory diseases.
의학연구에 따르면 사고현장으로 부터의 잔해들은 호흡기 질환을 기인하는 경향이 있었다.

decry
[dikrái]

비난하다
to denounce publicly
de=down: cry=cry out

Humanitarian groups have decried the increasing rate of violence against children.
박애주의 단체들은 아이들에게 일어나는 폭력의 급증하는 비율을 비난했다.

dehydrate
[di:háidreit]

건조시키다, 탈수시키다, 활기를 빼앗다
to cause (a person or a person's body) to lose a large amount of water
de=out: hudros/hudr=water

According to the study, drinking caffeinated drinks in moderation did not cause dehydration.
연구에 따르면 카페인이 들어간 음료를 적당량 마시는 것은 탈수를 기인하지는 않았다.

deject
[didʒékt]

낙담시키다, 기를 꺾다
to make sad or dispirited; depress
de=down: jacere=throw

The news stories about the war were so devastating that they dejected the public.
전쟁에 대한 소식들은 너무도 황폐했고, 그 결과 대중을 낙담시켰다.

delegate
[déligèit]

위임하다, 대표로 파견하다; 대리인
to entrust (a task or responsibility) to another person
de=down: legare=depute

The former manager's responsibilities should be delegated to the new one.
이전 매니져의 책임사항들은 새로온 매니져에게 위임되어야 한다.

delinquent
[dilíŋkwənt]

태만한, 의무를 게을리하는, 비행(자)의, 죄를 범한, 지급 기한이 지난
failing to do what law or duty requires
de=away: linquere=leave

Many teenagers tend to show various forms of delinquent behaviors during adolescence.
많은 10대 청소년들은 사춘기 동안 다양한 형태의 비행 행동을 보이는 경향이 있다.

demolish
[dimáliʃ]

파괴하다, 부수다
to destroy completely
de=down/out: moliri=construct

Each building should be demolished by using different techniques in order to reduce the subsequent demages.
연속적인 손실을 줄이기 위해서 각각의 건물들은 다른 방식으로 파괴되어야만 한다.

demoralize
[dimɔ́:rəlàiz]

사기를 꺾다, 용기를 꺾다, 의기소침하게 하다
to cause (someone) to lose confidence or hope
de=out: moral=moral

The government new policy has demoralized the trade unions.
정부의 새로운 정책은 노조의 사기를 꺾었다.

demote
[dimóut]

강등시키다, 지위를 낮추다
to give (someone) a lower rank or less senior position, usually as a punishment
de=down: mote=promote

The scandal finally caused the congressman to be demoted.
그 스켄들은 마침내 그 하원의원을 강등시켰다.

demur
[dimə́:r]

반대하다, 이의를 제기 하다; 이의 제기, 반대
to raise doubts or objections or show reluctance
de=away/completely: morari=delay

The representatives demurred about the committee's investigation.
대표자들는 위원회의 조사에 대해 이의를 제기했다.

denigrate
[dénigrèit]

중상하다, 헐뜯다, 손상시키다
to criticize unfairly; to disparage
de=away/completely: nigrare=black

The article said that the rumor might denigrate incumbent politicians.
그 기사는 루머가 현직 정치인들의 명성을 손상시켰을 것이라고 말했다.

depend
[dipénd]

믿다, 신뢰하다, 의존하다, 달려있다
to rely, especially for support or maintenance
de=down: pendere=hang

According to research, climate change clearly depended on a wide variety of factors.
연구에 따르면 기후 변화는 다양한 원인에 의해 좌우된다.

deport
[dipó:rt]

추방하다, 수송하다
to expel from a country
de=away: portare=carry

According to the record, the number of foreign citizens who were deported last year has increased dramatically.
기록에 따르면 지난해 추방된 외국인 숫자는 급증했다.

deprecate
[déprikèit]

비난하다, 반대하다
to express disapproval of; depreciate
de=away: precari=pray

Richard's article deprecating the political system got a lot of
attention from the public.
정치 시스템을 비난한 리차드의 기사는 대중들로부터 많은 관심을 얻었다.

depreciate
[diprí:ʃièit]

떨어뜨리다, 평가절하하다, 얕보다
to diminish in value over a period of time
de=down: pretium=price

Computer equipment depreciates quickly because of the
rapid technological development.
급속히 발전하는 기술 때문에 컴퓨터 장비들은 빨리 가치가 떨어진다.

descend
[disénd]

내려오다, 아래로 가다, 감소하다, 전해지다, 유전하다
to move from a higher to a lower place; come or go down
de=down: scandere=climb

When the rain descended, people at the festival started to
scatter in all directions.
비가 내렸을 때, 축제에 있었던 사람들은 사방으로 흩어지기 시작했다.

detach
[ditǽtʃ]

분리하다, 파견하다
to separate or unfasten; disconnect
de=away/out: attacher=attach

After the accident, the child is having difficulties in detaching her
emotions from her parents.
사고 후, 그 아이는 부모로부터 감정을 분리시키는데 어려움을 겪고 있다.

deter
[ditə́:r]

단념시키다
to discourage (someone) from doing something, typically by
instilling doubt or fear of the consequences
de=away: terrere=frighten

The strict regulations did not deter him from seeking justice.
엄격한 규율들은 그가 정의를 추구하는 것을 단념시키지 못했다.

detestable
[ditéstəbl]

증오할, 몹시 싫은, 진저리나는, 가증스러운
inspiring or deserving abhorrence or scorn
de=down: testari=witness

Despite of his fancy clothes, he seemed a man with detestable spirit.
그의 멋진 옷에도 불구하고 그는 증오할 만한 정신을 갖고 있는 사람 같이 보였다.

deviate
[díːvièit]

(표준, 기준에서) 벗어나다, 빗나가다
to depart from an established course
de=away: via=way

During the long journey, we were recommended not to deviate from the main course.
긴 여행 동안 우리는 주행로에서 벗어나지 말하는 권고를 받았다.

devoid
[divɔ́id]

~가 없는, 결여된
entirely lacking or free from
de=away: vacare=vacate

Larry was in shock and his voice sounded devoid of emotion.
래리는 충격을 받았고, 그의 목소리는 감정이 없는 듯이 들렸다.

23 *dic / dict / dit*

dic, dict, dit 말하다/단언하다 = declare/dictate/say
dic/dict/dit는 '단언하다/말하다(declare/dictate/say)'란 의미를 단어에 부가해 줍니다.

---

abdicate
[ǽbdəkèit]

사퇴하다, 사임하다, 포기하다, 버리다
to renounce one's thrown; fail to undertake or fulfill (one's responsibility or duty)
ab=away/from: dicare=say/declare

The public claims that the international community must not abdicate its responsibility to protect human rights.
국제사회는 인권을 보호할 책임을 버려서는 안된다고 대중들은 주장했다.

dictate
[díikteit]

지시하다, 명령하다, 받아쓰게 하다
to say or read aloud to be recorced or written by another
dicere=say/declare

The committee dictated how doctors should practice medicine.
위원회는 의사들이 약을 어떻게 다뤄야 하는 지를 지시했다.

indicate
[índikèit]

나타내다, 암시하다
to show the way to or the direction of; point out
in=towards: dicere=say/declare

The research indicated that consumer confidence was growing after the economic reform.
연구는 경제 개혁 이후로 시장의 소비자 확신이 성장했다고 나타냈다.

interdict
[íntərdikt]

금지하다; 금지 명령
to prohibit or place under an ecclesiastical or legal sanction
inter=between: dicere=say/declare

Participants were interdicted from consuming alcoholic beverages during the session.
행사기간 동안 참가자들은 알코올이 들어간 음료를 마시는 것이 금지 되었다.

predict
[pridíkt]

예언하다, 예시하다
to state, tell about, or make known in advance, especially on the basis of special knowledge
prae=beforehand: dicere=say/declare

The experts say that studying statistics can give you the power to predict election results.
전문가들은 통계를 분석하는 것이 선거결과를 예측할 수 있는 힘들 줄 수 있다고 말한다.

valedictory
[vǽlidiktəri]

작별인사의; 졸업생 대표의 고별 연설
a closing or farewell statement or address, especially one delivered at graduation exercises
vale=farewell: dicere=say/declare

We can easily find that a valedictory speech should differ from an informative address.
고별 연설이 정보를 주는 연설과 마땅히 달라야 한다는 것을 쉽게 알 수 있다.

verdict
[vǝ́rdikt]

평결, 판단, 결정
the finding of a jury in a trial
veir=true: dit=say/declare

Jordon showed no emotion as the verdicts were read.
조던은 평결이 읽켜지는 동안 감정을 드러내지 않았다.

dis, di 멀리하다/떨어뜨리다 =away/apart
dis/di는 '멀리하다/떨어뜨리다(away/apart)'란 의미를 단어에 부가해 줍니다.

---

disagreeable
[dìsəgríːəbl]

마음에 맞지 않는, 싫은, 불쾌한; 불쾌한 곳, 불쾌한 시점
not to one's liking; unpleasant or offensive
dis=away/apart: agreer=agree

When Patrick ran into someone who is disagreeable, he tended to be quiet.
패트릭은 마음이 맞지 않는 사람을 우연히 만나면 조용해 지는 경향이 있다.

disavow
[dìsəvàu]

부인하다, 거부하다
to disclaim knowledge of responsibility for, or association with
dis=away/apart: avouer=acknowledge

Mindy disavowed any responsibility for this issue.
민디는 이 문제에 대한 어떤 책임도 거부했다

discard
[diskàːrd]

버리다, 포기하다, 제외하다
to throw away; reject
dis=away/apart: khartēs=papyrus leaf

Before you discard the old batteries, you should find safer ways to do them.
오래된 건전지를 버리기 이전에, 보다 안전한 방식을 확인해야만 한다.

discern
[disə́ːrn]

알아보다, 이해하다, 분별하다
to perceive with the eyes or intellect, detect; to recognize or comprehend mentally; to perceive or recognize as being different or distinct, distinguish
dis=away/apart: cernere=separate

You need to discern that there might be differences between information and reality.
정보와 현실 사이에 차이가 있을 수 있다는 것을 인지할 필요가 있다.

discomfit
[dìskʌ́mfit]

완패하다, 의기를 꺾다, 당황 하다,
to make (someone) feel uneasy or embarrassed
dis=away/apart: conficere=put together

Sandra was discomfited when she heard that there was no support any more.
산드라는 더 이상 그녀를 지지하지 않는 다는 소식을 들었을 때 의기가 꺾였다.

disconcert
[dìskənsə́:rtid]

동요시키다, 혼란스럽게 하다
thrown into confusion, upset
dis=away/apart: concerter=bring together

The public was somewhat disconcerted by the sudden announcement.
대중은 갑작스런 발표에 다소 혼란스러워했다.

discourteous
[dìskə́:rtiəs]

무례한
lacking courtesy
dis=away/apart: corteis=yard

We easily see that a single discourteous conduct often becomes a blunder.
우리는 한번의 무례한 행동이 종종 큰 실수가 되는 것을 쉽게 본다.

discrepancy
[diskrépənsi]

불일치, 차이, 어긋남, 모순
a lack of compatibility or similarity between two or more facts
dis=away/apart: crepare=creak

The consumers required thoroughly fair methods of settling the discrepancies.
소비자들은 모순을 해결해줄 철저히 공정한 방식을 요구했다.

disdain
[disdéin]

경멸, 멸시, 모멸; 경멸하다
to look upon or treat with contempt; despise; scorn
dis=away/apart: dignari=consider worthy

The intolerant scholar had some disdain for mass entertainment.
그 편협한 학자는 대중연예에 대한 경멸감을 갖고 있었다.

disinterested
[disíntərèstid]

공정한, 냉담한
unbiased by personal interest or advantage; not influenced by selfish motives
dis=away/apart: inter=between: esse=be

As an arbitrator, I am supposed to give you disinterested advice.
중재인으로서, 나는 당신에게 공정한 충고를 줘야 한다.

dismay
[disméi]

쩔쩔매게 하다, 용기(열정)를 잃게하다, 움쯔리게하다; 경악, 당황, 낙담
to destroy the courage or resolution of by exciting dread or apprehension; alarm, upset
dis=away/apart: maier=be able to

His remark filled me with dismay.
그의 논평은 나를 경악하게 했다.

dismiss
[dismís]

일축하다, 해고하다, 해산시키다
to refuse to accept or recognize; reject
dis=away/apart: mittere=send

After Kate carefully reviewed all suggestions, she dismissed all of them.
케이트는 모든 제안을 조심스럽게 살펴본 후에, 모든 제안을 거절했다.

disparate
[díspærət]

본질적으로 다른
essentially different in kind; not allowing comparison
dis=away/apart: parare=prepare

There are extremely disparate ethnic groups in this county.
이 군에는 극단적으로 서로 다른 긴족 그룹들이 있다.

dispassionate
[dispǽʃənət]

감정에 휘둘리지 않는, 객관적인, 공정한
not influenced by strong emotion, and so able to be rational and impartial
dis=away/apart: passus=suffer

According to the statement, the committee is planning to hold a dispassionate debate on crimes.
성명서에 따르면 위원회는 범죄어 대한 공정한 토론회를 개최할 예정이다.

disregard
[disrigá:rd]

주의하지 않다, 무시하다
to pay no attention or heed to; ignore
dis=away/apart: re=backward, again: garder= guard

Joe received a lot of criticism for disregarding the rules.
조는 규정을 무시한 것에 대해 많은 비난을 받았다.

dissect
[disékt]

해부하다, 분석하다
to cut up (a body, part, or plant) methodically in order to study its internal parts
dis=away/apart: secare=cut

Jonathan learned how to dissect a frog in his biology classroom.
조나단은 생물학 수업에서 개구리 해부하는 방법을 배웠다.

divergent
[divé:rdʒənt]

분기하는, 다른, 불일치의, 벗어난
differing from each other or from a standard
dis=away/apart: verger=incline

Several studies provided divergent interpretations on the education reform policies.
몇몇의 조사는 교육 개혁 정책에 대한 서로 다른 해석을 했다.

25 dol

dol 슬퍼하다 =grieve
dol은 슬퍼하다(grieve)'란 의미를 단어에 부가해 줍니다.

---

condole
[kəndóul]

애도를 표하다, 위로하다
to express sympathy or sorrow
con=with/together: dolere=grieve/suffer

All members of the organization condoled with victims of the typhoon.
단체의 모든 멤버들은 태풍의 희생자들을 위로했다.

doleful
[dóulfəl]

슬픔에 잠긴, 침울한, 우울한
expressing sorrow; mournful; causing grief
dolere=grieve/suffer

Jane looked at the candle with doleful eyes.
제인은 슬픔에 잠긴 눈으로 양초를 바라보았다.

dolorous
[dóulərəs]

슬픔에 잠긴, 침울한, 우울한
marked by or exhibiting sorrow, grief, or pain
dolere=grieve/suffer

Jack did not want to hear the dolorous tale of that old man.
잭은 그 노인의 침울한 이야기를 듣고 싶지 않았다.

indolent
[índələnt]

게으른, 나태한
disinclined to exert oneself; habitually lazy
in=not: dolere=suffer/give pain

Zoe has the tendency to be indolent and complacent.
조이는 게으르고 자기만족을 하는 경향을 갖고 있다.

26 *duc / duct*

duc, duct 이끌다 =lead
duc/duct는 '이끌다(lead)'란 의미를 단어에 부가해 줍니다.

adduce
[ədjúːs]

증거로 제출하다, 인용하다
to offer as example, reason, or proof in discussion or analysis
ad=towards: ducere=lead

Meg will try to adduce further evidence.
맥은 더 많은 증가를 제출하려고 노력할 것이다.

conducive
[kəndjúːsiv]

공헌하는, 도움이되는
making a certain situation or outcome likely or possible
con=together: ducere=lead

The new system would be conducive to resolving current technical problems.
새로운 시스템은 현재 기술상의 문제를 해결하는데 도움이 될것이다.

deduce
[didjúːs]

추론하다
to arrive at (a fact or a conclusion) by reasoning
de=down: ducere=lead

The novice researcher's job was to deduce sensible conclusions from vague information.
신입 연구원의 일은 모호한 정보로부터 적절한 결론은 추론하는 것이었다.

ductile
[dʌ́ktail]

순종적인, 두드려 변형시킬 수 있는, 가소성의
docile, gullible; (of a metal) able to be drawn out into a thin wire, pliable, not brittle
ducere=lead

Due to her ductile personality, she seemed improper for the leader.
그녀의 순종적인 성격 때문에 그녀는 리더로써 부적절해 보였다.

educate
[édʒukèit]

교육하다, 훈육하다

to develop the innate capacities of, especially by schooling or instruction

e=out: ducere=lead

The program will provide students with more opportunities to be educated.

이 프로그램은 학생들에게 교육 받을 수 있는 더 많은 기회를 제공할 것이다.

seduce
[sidú:s]

꼬드기다, 유혹하다, 꾀다

to lead away from duty, accepted principles, or proper conduct

se=away, apart: ducere=lead

Due to the controversies, each was seduced into believing different things.

논쟁 때문에 개개인들은 서로 다른 것들은 믿게 유혹 되었다.

27 *dur*

dur 단단한, 오래 지속되는=hard/lasting
dur는 '단단한/오래 지속되는(hard/lasting)'이란 의미를 단어에 부가해 줍니다.

---

dour
[dàuər]

시무룩한, 뚱한, 우울한
relentlessly severe, stern, or gloomy in manner or appearance
durus=hard

Peter is a brilliant but dour man.
피터는 뛰어 났지만 무뚝뚝한 사람이다.

durable
[djúərəbl]

내구성이 있는, 튼튼한, 영속성 있는; 내구 소비재
capable of withstanding wear and tear or decay
durare=last

This study examined durable solutions to the poverty issue.
이 연구는 가난 문제에 대한 지속적인 해결책을 검토했다.

enduring
[indjúəriŋ]

영속적인
lasting, persistent
in=in: durus=hard

When you do business, having enduring relationships might be one of the most important things.
사업을 할 때 지속적인 관계를 갖는 것은 가장 중요한 것 중 하나일 것이다.

obdurate
[ábd:jurit]

고집센, 완고한
stubbornly refusing to change one's opinion
ob=in opposition: durare=harden

Chris was obdurate in supporting his conclusion although some of his colleagues challenged it.
크리스의 몇몇 동료들이 그의 결론에 도전했음에도 불구하고 자신의 결론을 옹호하는데 단호했다.

28 e / ec / ex

e, ec, ex 밖으로 =out/away
e/ec/ex는 '밖으로(out/away)'란 의미를 단어에 부가해 줍니다.

---

ebullient
[ibúljənt]

열광적인, 활력있는, 비등하는
cheerful and full of energy; boiling or agitated as if boiling
e=out: bullire=boil

The host of the welcome party was ebullient.
환영파티의 주최자는 열광적이었다.

---

eccentric
[ikséntrik]

별난, 엉뚱한
unconventional and slightly, peculiar, idiosyncratic
ek=out: kentron=centre

Amy said that, as children got older, eccentric behaviors tended to decrease.
에이미는 아이들이 나이가 들면서 엉뚱한 행동이 감소되는 경향이 있다고 말했다.

---

eclectic
[ikléktik]

여러가지 방법을 쓰는, 다양한, 절충주의의
composed of elements drawn from various sources
ek=out: legein=choose

Tom was eclectic when it came to methods for research.
연구 방식에 대해서, 탐은 절충주의적이었다

---

efface
[iféis]

삭제하다, 지워서 없애다, 눈에 띄지 않게 행동하다
to erase (a mark) from a surface; to act in an inconspicuous manner
e=away from: face=face

The signature on the envelope was effaced by heavy rain.
봉투 위의 서명은 폭우에 의해 지워졌다.

effete
[ifíːt]

활력없는, 쇠약한
no longer capable of effective action
ex=out: fetus=breeding

When Jack entered the room, he looked like an effete looking man.
잭이 방에 들어 왔을 때 그는 쇠약해 보이는 남자처럼 보였다.

elaborate
[ilǽbərət]

공들인, 복잡한, 정교한; 공들여 하다, 상술하다
planned or executed with painstaking attention to numerous parts or details; intricate, rich in detail
e=out: labor=work

Mary had to elaborate her economic policy in detail.
메리는 그녀의 경제 정책의 세부사항을 자세히 설명해야만 했다.

elated
[iléitid]

아주 즐거워하는, 기뻐하는
in high spirits; exultant or proud
ex=out/from: ferre=bear

When the prize was presented to her, Ellen seemed elated.
엘린은 상을 받았을 때 아주 기뻐하는 듯이 보였다.

eliminate
[ilíminèit]

없애다, 제거하다, 배제하다
to get rid of; remove
e=out: limen/limin=threshold

During the competition, participants will be eliminated one by one.
경쟁을 하는 동안에 참가자들은 한 명씩 떨어지게 될 것이다.

elude
[ilúːd]

잘 피하다, 회피하다, 교묘하게 벗어나다
to evade or escape from, as by daring, cleverness, or skill
e=out/away from: ludere=play

The main character tried to elude his pursuers in the middle of the night.
주인공은 한밤중에 추격자들을 회피하려 애썼다.

elusive
[ilúːsiv]

잡히지 않는, 이해하기 힘든, 정의하기 힘든
tending to evade grasp or pursuit; hard to comprehend or define
e=out/away from: ludere=play

The fisherman was patient with elusive fish.
그 어부는 잘 피하는 물고기에 대해 참을성을 갖고 있었다.

emaciated
[iméiʃièitid]

수척해진, 몹시 여윈
very thin especially from disease or hunger or cold
e=away from: macies=make think

After three month treatment, she looked emaciated.
3개월의 치료 후 그녀는 수척해 보였다.

emanate
[émənèit]

발산하다
to issue or spread out from (a source)
e=out: manare=flow

If noise has emanated from another part of the facility, we need to change the plans.
만약 소음이 시설의 다른 부분으로부터 발산된 것이라면 우리는 계획을 변경해야 한다.

emit
[imít]

내뿜다, 방출하다
to give or send out matter or energy
e=out: mittere=send

Carbon dioxide is the greenhouse gas emitted through human activities.
이산화탄소는 인간의 활동을 통해 방출되는 그린하우스 가스이다.

enervate
[énərvèit]

약화시키다, 무기력하게 하다
to cause (someone) to feel drained of energy or vitality; to weaken
e=out of: nervus=sinew

Although he is an elderly man, climbing mountain never enervates him.
비록 노년임에도 불구하고, 암벽등반은 그를 결코 무기력하게 만들지 않았다.

enunciate
[inʌnsièit]

명확히 설명하다, 명확히 발음하다
to express, say or pronounce clearly
e=out: nuntiare=announce

Due to her accent, she had to enunciate several words during the presentation.
그녀의 액센트 때문에 발표를 하는 동안에 그녀는 몇 개의 단어를 정확하게 발음해야 했다.

eradicate
[irædəkèit]

근절하다, 절멸하다
to do away with as completely as if by pulling up by the roots
e=out: radix/radic=root

Once a disease stops circulating in a region, people expect to eradicate the disease.
어떤 질병이 한 지역에서 더 이상 퍼지지 않으면 사람들은 그 병의 박멸을 예측한다.

evade
[ivéid]

피하다
to escape or avoid by cleverness or deceit
e=out: vadere=go

The perpetrator traveled to Asia several times in order to evade being arrested.
범인은 경찰에게 체포되는 것을 피하기 위해 아시아로 몇 차례 이동했다.

evasive
[ivéisiv]

책임 회피의, 회피적인
inclined or intended to evade
e=out: vadere=go

He was evasive about the questions related to the scandal.
그는 스캔들과 관련된 질문에 회피적이었다.

evict
[ivíkt]

퇴거시키다, 내쫓다
to expel (someone) from a property, esp. with the support of the law
e=out: vincere=conquer

The city development caused indigenous peoples to be evicted.
도시 개발은 토착민들을 몰아냈다.

evince
[ivíns]

나타내다, 명시하다, 증명하다
to show clearly
e=out: vincere=conquer

The city council has evinced interest in setting up offices in the downtown area.
시의회는 상업지역에 사무실을 설립하는 것에 관심을 표명했다.

exacerbate
[igzǽsərbèit]

악화시키다
to make (a problem, bad situation, or negative feeling) worse
ex=outside/out of/away from: acerbus=harsh/bitter

New environmental policies are expected to exacerbate the fertilizer industry.
새로운 환경 정책은 비료산업을 악화시킬 것으로 예상된다.

exacting
[igzǽktiŋ]

정확한, 엄격한
not approximated in any way; precise; tryingly or unremittingly severe in making demands
ex=thoroughly/out: agree=perform

When it comes to the distribution, Harold has very exacting standards.
분배에 관한한, 해롤드는 아주 정확한 기준을 갖고 있다.

exalt
[igzɔ́:lt]

칭송하다, 높이다, 고상하게 하다
hold (someone or something) in very high regard; think or speak very highly of; make noble in character, dignify
ex=out/upward: altus=high

After working for the company for 35 years, people finally exalted his achievement.
35년을 근무한 후에 사람들은 마침내 그의 성취를 격찬했다.

excerpt
[éksə:rpt]

발췌, 초록, 인용구; 발췌하다, 초록하다, 인용하다
to select or use (a passage or segment from a longer work)
ex=out of: carpere=pluck

According to the speaker, the following is an excerpt from Dr. Reese's first book.
연설자에 따르면 다음은 리스 박사의 첫번째 책의로 부터의 발췌이다.

excoriate
[ikskɔ́:rièit]

몹시 비난하다, 혹평하다, 껍질을 벗기다, 피부를 벗어지게 하다
to censure or criticize severely
ex=out/from: corium=skin/hide

The press openly excoriated the censorship.
언론은 검열을 공개적으로 비난했다.

execrate
[éksəkrèit]

혐오하다, 비난하다
to separate and discharge (waste matter) from the blood, tissues, or organs
ex=out: sacrare=consecrate

Since Jack was narrow-mined, he execrated all people who opposed him.
잭은 편협했기 때문에 그를 반대하는 모든 사람들을 몹시 싫어했다.

execute
[éksikjù:t]

수행하다, 행하다, 실행하다
to put into effect; carry out
ex=out: sequi=follow

Carter executed his strategic plans well.
카터는 그의 전략 계획을 잘 수행했다.

exhaustive
[igzɔ́:stiv]

포괄적인, 철저한, 고갈시키는
examining, including, or considering all elements or aspects; fully comprehensive
ex=out: haurire=draw/drain

During the session, the presenter explained the plan in exhaustive details.
회의 동안 발표자는 계획의 포괄적인 세부사항을 설명했다.

exile
[égzail]

국위 추방, 망명; 추방자; 추방하다, 망명하다
enforced removal from one's native country
ex=out: sedere=sit/live

James went into exile in order to save his own life and his family.
제임스는 그의 삶과 가족들을 보호하기 위허 망명했다.

exorbitant
[igzɔ́:rbətənt]

엄청난, 터무니없는, 과도한
exceeding the customary or appropriate limits in intensity, quality, amount
ex=out: orbita=course/track

The hotel was notorious for charging exorbitant rates for Wi-Fi.
그 호텔은 무선인터넷에 대해 터므니없는 요금을 부과하는 것으로 악명이 높았다.

expurgate
[ékspərgèit]

검열하여 삭제하다, 수정하다 정화하다
to remove matter thought to be objectionable or unsuitable from (a book or account)
ex=out: purgare=cleanse

As a novice editor, Lucy has difficulties in expurgating novels.
신출내기 편집장으로써, 루시는 소설들을 수정하는데 어려움을 겪고 있다.

extol
[ikstóul]

극찬하다, 격찬하다
to praise enthusiastically
ex=out/upward: tollere=raise

The magazine extolled the public park which was just built last month.
잡지는 지난달에 만들어진 공원을 격찬했다.

29 equ

equ 동일한 =equal
equ는 '동일한(equal)'이란 의미를 단어에 부가해 줍니다.

---

adequate
[ǽdəkwit]

충족시키는, 알맞은, 상당한
sufficient to satisfy a requirement or meet a need
ad=to: aequus=equal

The committee is having hard time to find an adequate replacement for the chairman.
위원회는 의장의 적당한 후임자를 찾는데 어려움을 겪고 있다.

equable
[ékwəbl]

침착한, 차분한, 한결같은, 안정된
not easily disturbed or angered; calm and even-tempered; not varying or fluctuating greatly
aequus=equal

The research claimed that the equable temperature of the island caused a wide variety of small tree species.
그 연구는 섬의 일정한 기온이 작은 나무 종들의 다양성을 기인했다고 주장했다.

equanimity
[ìːkwənímət̬i]

(마음의) 평정, 차분함
mental or emotional stability or composure, especially under tension or strain; calmness
aequus=equal: animus=mind

It was difficult to behave with equanimity when you heard such surprising news.
그런 놀라운 소식을 듣고 평정심을 갖고 행동하는 것은 어렵다.

equipoise
[ékwəpɔ́iz]

균형, 평형; 어울리다, 균형을 잡다
an equal distribution of weight; even balance
aequus=equal: pois=weight

George's behaviors seemed to be equipoised despite the bankruptcy.
파산에도 불구하고 조지의 행동은 균형이 잡힌 듯이 보였다.

equitable
[ékwətəbl]

공평한, 정당한
fair and impartial
aequus=equal

The proposal might result in equitable distribution of wealth in society.
이 제안은 사회의 부의 공평한 분배를 도출해낼 수 있다.

equivocate
[ikwívəkèit]

애매하게 둘러대다, 거짓 말하다
to use ambiguous language so as to conceal the truth or avoid committing oneself
aequus=equal: vocare=call

Whenever there are conflicts, Tom tends to equivocate.
탐은 논쟁이 있을 때 마다 말끝을 흐리는 경향이 있다.

30 err

err 배회하다 =wander/stray
err는 '배회하다(wander/stray)'란 의미를 단어에 부가해 줍니다.

aberrant
[əbérənt]

정도를 벗어난, 비정상의, 변종의; 괴짜, 기인, 변종, 돌연 변이
departing from an accepted standard; diverging from normal type
ab=away/from: errare=stray/wander

According to the study, parents shouldn't ignore children's aberrant behaviors.
연구에 따르면 부모들은 아이들의 정도를 벗어난 행동을 무시해서는 안된다.

errant
[érənt]

정도를 벗아난, 잘못된, 지방을 순회하는, 방황하는
straying from the proper course or standards
errare=stray/wander

It is obvious that Cindy's errant ways have rendered her a failure.
신디의 정도를 벗어난 방식이 그녀를 실패하게 만들었다는 것은 명백하다.

erratic
[irǽtik]

변덕스런, 일정하지 않은, 비정상적인; 별난 사람, 괴짜
having no fixed or regular course; wandering
errare=stray/err

His recent erratic behavior made his boss surprised.
최근 그의 변덕스런 행동은 그의 상사를 놀라게 했다.

erroneous
[iròuniəs]

잘못된, 틀린, 정도를 벗어난
containing or derived from error; mistaken
errare=stray/err

Unfortunately, erroneous assumptions led the experiment to failure.
불행스럽게도 잘못된 가설이 실험을 실패로 이끌었다.

31 eu

eu 좋은 =good/well
eu는 '좋은(good/well)'이란 의미를 단어에 부가해 줍니다.

eulogy
[júːlədʒi]

칭송, 찬양, 송덕문
a commendatory oration or writing especially in honor of one
deceased; high praise
eu=good/well: logia=logy

Teddy wrote eulogies for his grandfather.
테디는 할아버지를 위한 송덕문을 썼다.

euphemism
[júːfəmìzm]

완곡어법
the substitution of an agreeable or inoffensive expression for one
that may offend or suggest something unpleasant
eu=good/well: phēmē=speaking

We often use euphemisms to express what is socially difficult to
express in direct terms.
우리는 사회적으로 직접적인 표현이 어려운 상황을 표현할 때 완곡어법을 종종 사용한다.

euphonious
[júːfəniəs]

듣기 좋은, 음조가 좋은
pleasing or agreeable to the ear
eu=good/well: phōnē=sound

It is easy to say some euphonious phrases instead of proper
advice.
적절한 조언 대신에 듣기 좋은 말을 하기는 쉽다.

euphoria
[juːfɔ́ːriə]

행복감
a feeling or state of intense excitement and happiness
eu=good/well: pherein=bear

Exercising can be one way to induce a kind of euphoria.
운동을 하는 것은 행복감을 유발시키는 하나의 방법이다.

32 *fal*

fal 속이는 =deceive
fal은 '속이는(deceive)'이란 의미를 단어에 부가해 줍니다.

---

default
[difɔ́:lt]

의무불이행, 체납
failure to fulfill an obligation, esp. to repay a loan or appear in a
court of law
de=derived from/out of: faillir=deceive

Defaulting on a student loan in the United States can be a
potential economic issue.
미국 학생 융자 체납은 잠재적인 경제 문제가 될 수 있다.

fallacy
[fǽləsi]

잘못된 생각, 착오, 궤변
guile, trickery; a mistaken belief, esp. one based on unsound
argument
fallacy=deceiving

Since there are always nutrition fallacies, it is important to obtain
the accurate information.
영양에 대한 오해들이 늘 있기 때문에 정확한 정보를 얻는 것이 중요하다.

false
[fɔ:ls]

그릇된, 잘못된, 틀린
contrary to fact or truth
fallere=deceive

False allegations made by the congressman actually did hurt
Dean's candidacy.
하원의원에 의해 제시된 잘못된 주장은 딘의 입후보를 사실상 손상시켰다.

33 fern

fern 끓다 =boil
fern는 '끓다(boil)'란 의미를 단어에 부가해 줍니다.

---

effervescent
[èfərvésnsənt]

쾌활한, 활기찬, 기운이 넘치는, 부글 부글 끓는
of liveliness or exhilarat on
ex=out/up: fervescere=begin to boil

Effervescent people gathered in the park for the campaign.
홍보를 위해 활기찬 사람들이 공원에 모였다.

fervent
[fá:rvənt]

열렬한, 열심인
exhibiting or marked by great ir tensity of feeling
fervere=boiling

Larry was a fervent football supporter.
래리는 열렬한 풋볼 지지자였다.

fervid
[fá:rvid]

열렬한, 열의에 불타는
marked by great passion or zea
fervere=boil

As soon as Will joined t ne discussion, it became a fervid presentation.
윌이 토론에 참가를 하자 마자 토론은 열띤 발표회가 되었다.

fervor
[fá:rvər]

열성, 열렬, 열정
intense and passionate feeling
fervere=boil

When it comes to music, Jim talked with all the fervor.
짐은 음악에 대해선 열정적으로 이야기했다.

F

34 flagr / fulg / fulm

flagr, fulg, fulm 빛나다 =shine/light/burn
flagr/fulg/fulm은 '빛나다(shine/light/burn)'란 의미를 단어에 부가해 줍니다.

---

effulgent
[ifʌ́ldʒənt]

찬란히 빛나는, 눈부신
shining brilliantly; resplendent
ex=out: fulgere=shine

I could see effulgent light of the sun through the window.
나는 창을 통해 태양의 찬란히 빛나는 빛을 볼 수 있었다.

flagrant
[fléigrənt]

극악한, 악명 높은
(of something considered wrong or immoral) conspicuously or obviously offensive
fla=shine: grare=burn

The leader was accused of committing a flagrant breach of laws.
그 지도자는 법을 악명 높게 어진 것으로 비난 받았다.

fulminate
[fʌ́lmənéit]

굉장한 소리와 함께 폭발하다, 번쩍 빛나다, 격렬하게 비난하다
to issue a thunderous verbal attack or denunciation
fulminate=struck by lightning

The governor fulminated against the congress' plan to cut the budget.
지주사는 예산을 줄이려는 의회의 계획을 격렬하게 비난했다.

refulgent
[rifʌ́ldʒənt]

밝게 빛나는, 환희 빛나는
shining brightly
re=again: fulgere=shine

After passing through the darkness, there was refulgent light at the end of the tunnel.
어둠을 통과한 후에, 터널 끝에는 환히 빛나는 빛이 있었다.

35 *flect / flex*

flect, flex 구부리다 =bend/turn
flect/flex는 '구부리다(bend/turn)'란 의미를 단어에 부가해 줍니다.

---

flexible
[fléksəbl]

구부릴 수 있는, 휘기 쉬운, 유연한, 순응성 있는
capable of being bent or flexed; pliable
flectere= bend

It's always not easy to develop a flexible attitude toward different culture.
다른 문화에 대한 유연한 태도를 발달시키는 것이 늘 쉽지는 않다.

reflect
[riflékt]

반사하다, 비추다, 나타내다
to throw or bend back (light, for example) from a surface
re=back: flectere=bend

The teacher tried to reflect the cultural diversity in class.
선생님은 수업시간에 문화의 다양성을 반영하려고 노력했다.

36 gen

gen 낳다 =beget/produce/race/birth
gen은 '낳다(beget/produce/race/birth)'란 의미를 단어에 부가해 줍니다.

---

degenerate
[didʒénərèit]

퇴보하다, 타락하다, 퇴화하다
having declined, as in function or nature, from a former or
original state
de=away from: genus=race/kind

We often witness that a simple debate can easily degenerate into
blatant insults.
우리는 단순한 토론이 무례한 모욕주기로 쉽게 퇴보될 수 있다는 것을 종종 목격한다.

engender
[indʒéndər]

발생하게 하다, 생기다, 낳다
to bring into existence; give rise to
in=in: generare=beget

The economic policy has engendered controversies over the past
several years.
지난 몇 년 동안 경제 정책은 논쟁을 발생시켰다.

generous
[dʒénərəs]

관대한, 통이 큰, 풍부한
liberal in giving or sharing
genus/gener=stock/race

People were not aware that Alex was a generous benefactor to
many charities.
사람들은 알렉스가 많은 자선단체에 관대한 후원자라는 것을 몰랐다.

genesis
[dʒénisis]

기원, 발생
the coming into being of something; the origin
gignesthai=be born or produced

Whenever they gather, they talked about the oil genesis which
never come to a conclusion.
그들은 모일 때 마다, 결코 결론이 없는 기름의 기원에 대해 이야기 했다.

ingenious

[indʒíːnjəs]

독창적인, 정교한
(of a person) clever, original, and inventive
in=in: gignere=beget

The interior booklet shows 10 ingenious ways to make the most out of small spaces.
인테리어 책자는 작은 공간을 최대한 활용하는 10가지 창의적인 방법을 보여준다.

ingenuous

[indʒénjuəs]

순진한, 솔직한
innocent or childlike simplicity and candidness
in=in: gignere=beget

David gave an ingenuous statement concerning the current corruption situation.
데이비드는 현재 부패 상황에 대한 정직한 성명서를 발표했다.

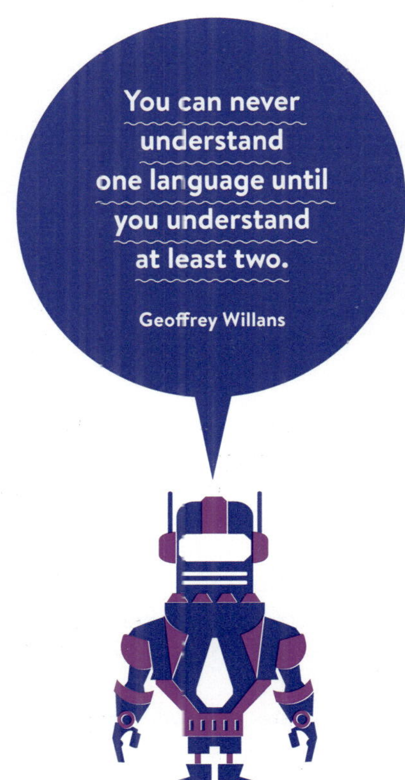

37 gni / gno / cogn / conn

gni, gno, cogn, conn 알다 =know
gni/gno/cogn/conn은 '알다(know)'란 의미를 단어에 부가해 줍니다.

---

cognizant
[kágnəzənt]

알고 있는, 지각하고 있는
having knowledge or being aware of
cognoscere=get to know

She looked cognizant at the podium while there was still chaos in audience.
청중들은 혼란스러워 하는 반면 그녀는 단상에서 자각한 하는 듯이 보였다.

---

diagnose
[dáiəgnòus]

진단하다, 원인을 규명하다
to identify the nature of (an illness or other problem) by examination of the symptoms
dia=apart: gignōskein=recognize/know

The doctor diagnosed Patrick as respiratory failure based on his medical history.
의사는 패트릭의 지금까지의 병력에 근간해, 그에게 호흡기가 제대로 작동하지 않는다는 것을 진단했다.

---

ignorant
[ígnərənt]

무식한, 무학의, 지식이 없는
lacking education or knowledge
in=not: gno=know

Teddy was ignorant in politics although he had a Ph.D degree in sociology.
테니는 사회학에 박사학위를 갖고 있었음에도 불구하고 정치학에는 무지했다.

---

prognosis
[pragnóusis]

예언, 예상
a prediction of the probable course and outcome of a disease
pro=before: gignōskein=know

To make an accurate prognosis, you need to reflect the effectiveness of current treatments.
정확한 예상을 하기 위해서 현재 치료의 효과를 반영할 필요가 있다.

recognize
[rékəgnáiz]

승인하다, 인정하다, 알아보다, 분간하다
to know to be something that has been perceived before
re=again: cognoscere= earn

Howard hardly recognized Betty because it had been almost 15 years not to see each other.
거의 15년간 서로 만나지 않았기 때문에 하-워드는 베티를 거의 알아보지 못했다.

reconnoiter
[rì:kənɔ́itər]

정찰하다, 조사하다, 답사하다
To make a preliminary inspection of, especially in order to gather military information
re=again: cognoscere=learn

Prior to anchoring, the boat reconnoitered the beach.
정박하기 이전에 보트는 해변을 정찰했다.

38 greg

greg 그룹, 무리 =group/ flock
greg은 '그룹/무리(group/flock)'이란 의미를 단어에 부가해 줍니다.

aggregate
[ǽgrigèit]

결합된, 총계의; 집단, 총계; 모으다
constituting or amounting to a whole; total
ad=towards: grex/greg=flock

The groups strive to aggregate people with similar kinds of hobbies.
그 그룹들은 유사한 취미를 갖은 사람들을 모으려고 노력했다.

congregate
[kɔ́ŋgrigèit]

모이다, 집합하다; 모인, 집합한
to bring or come together in a group, crowd, or assembly
con=together: grex/greg=flock

On Memorial Day, people from diverse background have congregated at the center.
전몰 장병 추도 기념일에 다양한 사람들이 센터에 모였다.

gregarious
[grigέəriəs]

사교적인, 군집성의, 무리의
seeking and enjoying the company of others; sociable
grex/greg=flock

Adnan was never gregarious but always discreet.
애드난은 사교적이지는 않지만 현명했다.

segregate
[ségrigeit]

분리하다, 격리하다, 차별하다; 분리된 사람, 차별된 집단
to separate or isolate from others or from a main body or group
se=apart: grex/greg=flock

Paul had to be segregated from the rest of members since he was under investigation.
폴은 조사 중이기 때문에 다른 회원들로 부터 격리되어야 했다.

39 hap

hap 우연 =by chance
hap은 '우연(by chance)'란 의미를 단어에 부가해 줍니다.

---

haphazard
[hæphǽzərd]

아무렇게나, 되는대로, 무작정의
dependent upon or characterized by mere chance
hap=chance: hasard= dice game

The performance was haphazard rather than creative.
그 공연은 창의적이라기 보다는 계획성 없이 마구잡이식이였다.

happen
[hǽpən]

일어나다, 생기다
to take place or occur by chance
hap=chance

What happened at the meeting was different from my expectations.
회의에서 발생한 일은 내가 기대했던 것과는 달랐다.

mishap
[míshæp]

불행한 일, 재난
bad luck
mis=badly: hap=chance

Several minor mishaps could hinder the research team from furthering their studies.
몇몇의 작은 안 좋은 일들은 연구팀이 그들의 연구를 발전시키는 것을 막을 수 있다.

40 hetero

hetero 다른 =other
hetero는 '다른(other)'이란 의미를 단어에 부가해 줍니다. (cf. home는 '동질의(same)'이란 의미)

---

heterogeneous
[hétərədʒíːniəs]

이질적인, 잡다한, 혼성의
Consisting of dissimilar elements or parts; not homogeneous
heteros=other: genos=kind

The exhibition was unique because the artist used heterogeneous materials.
예술가가 이질의 물질들을 사용했기 때문에 전시회는 독특했다.

41 icon

icon 우상, 상 =idol, image
icon은 '우상/상(idol/image)'란 의미를 단어에 부가해 줍니다.

---

iconoclastic
[aikanəklǽstik]

성상 파괴자의, 인습 타파론자의
being a person who attacks cherished beliefs or institutions
eikōn=likeness: klan=break

At first, his eccentricity drew attention but then his iconoclastic tendencies let people jaded.
처음에는 그의 독특함이 관심 끌었으나 곧 그의 인습 타파론자적 경향은 사람들을 싫증나게 했다.

42 il / im / in / ir

il, im, in, ir 아닌 =not
il/im/in/ir는 '아닌(not)'이란 의미를 단어에 부가해 줍니다.

---

illegible
[ilédʒəbl]

읽을 수 없는, 해독 불가한
not legible; indecipherable
il=not: legere=read

Although we found many records, most of them were illegible.
비록 많은 기록을 찾았지만 대부분은 읽을 수가 없었다.

illicit
[ilísit]

불법적인
not sanctioned by custom or law; unlawful
il=not: licite=be permitted

The brochure indicates a brief description for illicit drugs.
그 팜플렛은 불법적인 약에 대해 간략하게 묘사한다.

immaculate
[imǽkjələt]

더러워지지 않은, 순백의, 얼룩 하나 없이 깨끗한
impeccably clean; spotless
im=not: maculat=spotted

The police officer found the perpetrator's jacket in immaculate condition.
경찰은 손상되지 않은 상태의 범인의 자켓을 찾았다.

immature
[imətʃúər]

미완성의, (완전히) 발전하지 않은
not fully grown or developed
im=not: matures=timely/ripe

Tommy found an immature bird in the park.
타미는 공원에서 미숙한 새 한 마리를 발견했다.

immoderate
[imá:dərit]

중용을 잃은, 절도가 없는, 과도한, 터무니없는, 극단적인
exceeding normal or appropriate bounds; extreme
im=not: moderat=reduced/controlled

The committee decided to make the regulations concerning use of chemicals.
위원회는 화학 약품 사용에 대한 규율을 만들기로 결정했다.

impalpable
[impǽlpəbl]

손으로 만질 수 없는, 쉽사리 이해할 수 없는
not perceptible to the touch; intangible
im=not: palpare=feel/touch gently

Ben had impalpable senses of humor and it often made others uncomfortable.
벤은 쉽게 이해할 수 없는 유머감각을 갖고 있었고, 그것은 다른 사람들을 종종 불편하게 했다.

impartial
[impá:rʃəl]

치우치지 않는, 공평한, 편견이 없는
treating all rivals or disputants equally; fair and just
im=not: pars=part

We expect that a grand jury will be impartial.
우리는 배심원이 공평하기를 기대한다.

impeccable
[impékəbl]

결함없는, 완벽한
in accordance with the highest standards of propriety; faultless, perfect
im=not: peccare=sin

With my impeccable timing, I had arrived at the meeting.
나는 완벽한 타이밍으로 회의에 도착했다.

impenetrable
[impénətrəbl]

통과할 수 없는, 스며들 수 없는, 이해할 수 없는, 완고한
impossible to pass through or enter; impossible to understand
im=not: penetrate=placed/gone into

Colin was famous for using impenetrable jargon.
콜린은 이해할 수 없는 전문용어를 사용하는 것으로 유명했다.

impenitent
[ìmpénitənt]

(죄 등을) 뉘우치지 않는, 고집센, 완고한
not penitent; unrepentant
im=not: paenitent=repenting

Dan is one of the most narrow-minded and impenitent colleagues.
댄은 가장 편협하고 고집이 센 동료 중에 한 명이다.

imperceptible
[ìmpərséptəbl]

지각할 수 없는, 감지할 수 없는, 미세한, 경미한
impossible to perceive
im=not: percipere=seize/understand

Unfortunately, the impacts of the economic reform were imperceptible.
불행스럽게도 경제 개혁의 영향는 미비했다.

impermeable
[impə́:rmiəbl]

불침투성의
not allowing fluid to pass through
im=not: permeare=pass through

Dean's work will be the basic model for impermeable protective clothing.
딘의 작품이 불침투성 보호복의 기본 모델이 될 것이다.

imperturbable
[ìmpərtə́:rbəbl]

차분한, 동요하지 않는 냉정한
composed, calm, cool, and collected, coolheaded, self-controlled
im=not: per=completely: turbare=disturb

There was imperturbable tranquility which made Finch nervous.
핀치를 긴장하게 하는 냉정한 고요가 있었다.

impervious
[impə́:rviəs]

통과시키지 않는, 영향을 받지 않는, 둔감한
not allowing fluid to pass through; unable to be affected by
im=not: pervius=having a passage through

Dylan seemed impervious to criticism.
딜란은 비난에 영향을 받지 않는 듯이 보였다.

impious
[ímpiəs]

불경스런, 무례한, 적절하지 않은
exceeding the limits of propriety or good manners; improperly forward or bold: impertinent of a child to lecture a grownup; not pertinent; irrelevant
im=not: pius=dutiful/pious

Before entering the temple, Edie was wondering if his clothing was impious.
에디는 사원에 들어가기 전에 그의 복장이 불경스러운지 아닌지 궁금했다.

implausible
[implɔ́:zəbl]

정말 같지 않은, 믿기 어려운, 미심쩍은
difficult to believe; not plausible
im=not: plaus=applauded

All these dozen proposals seemed implausible.
모든 12개의 제안은 그럴듯해 보이지 않았다.

impotent
[ímpətənt]

무력한, 전혀 할 수 없는
lacking physical strength or vigor; weak
im=not: potent=being powerful/being able

After 3 hour long disputation, Eric felt impotent.
3시간 동안의 논쟁 후에 에릭은 무력하게 느꼈다.

improvident
[imprávədənt]

부주의한, 경솔한, 미래를 대비하지 않는, 낭비하는
not having or showing foresight; spendthrift or thoughtless
im=not: pro=forward: videre=see

Eva was accused of her improvident and undisciplined behaviors.
에바는 그녀의 부주의하고 부적절한 행동으로 비난 받았다.

imprudent
[imprú:dnt]

신중하지 못한, 경솔한, 무분별한
not showing care for the consequences of an action; rash
im=not: pro=forward: videre=see

Felix's imprudent mistake during the interview became a colossal blunder.
인터뷰를 하는 동안 페릭스의 경솔한 실수는 큰 실수 되었다.

impudent
[ímpjudnt]

무례한, 불손한, 건방진
not showing due respect for another person; impertinent
im=not: pudent=ashamed/modest

The manager was known for his impudent attitude.
그 매니져는 무례한 태도로 유명했다.

inadequate
[inǽdikwət]

부적절한, 불충분한
insufficient, deficient, poor, scant, scanty, scarce
in=not: ad=to: aequus=equal

When Garry accepted the money, he did not know that it was inadequate fund.
게리가 그 돈을 받았을 때 그는 그것이 부적절한 자금이라는 사실을 몰랐다.

inadvertent
[inədvə́:rtnt]

우연적인, 의도하지 않은, 경솔한, 태만한
unintentional, unintended, accidental, unpremeditated
in=not: advertent=turning the mind to

No matter how thoughtful you are, inadvertent errors might occur.
당신이 얼마나 신중한지와는 무관하게 의도하지 않은 실수는 일어날 수 있다.

incessant
[insésnt]

끊임없는, 계속적인
continuing without interruption
in=not: cessant=ceasing

We had to postpone the outdoor workshop because the rain fell incessantly throughout the day.
비가 하루 종일 끊임 없이 왔기 때문에 우리는 야외 웨크샵을 연기해야만 했다.

inconsequential
[inkà:nsikwénʃl]

중요하지 않은, 사소한, 논리적이 아닌, 엉뚱한
lacking importance; not following from premises or evidence; illogical
in=not: consequent=following closely

You can make your own decision but the choices based on the decision will not be inconsequential.
당신은 스스로 결정을 할 수 있으나 그 결정에 따른 선택을 사소한 것이 아닐 것이다.

indecorous
[indékərəs]

예절 없는, 거친, 천한, 보기 흉한, 꼴사나운
lacking propriety or good taste
in=not: decorus=seemly

The principal told the students that indecorous behaviors would be punished.
교장은 예절에 어긋난 행동은 벌을 받게 될것이라고 학생들에게 말했다.

indiscriminate
[indiskrímənət]

무차별의, 분간 없는, 무계획의
not making or based on careful distinctions; unselective
in=not: discriminate=distinguished between

Gordon warned that the indiscriminate use of antibiotics would cause unexpected results.
골든은 항생제를 무차별적으로 사용하는 것은 예측치 못한 결과를 기인할 것이라고 경고했다.

indispensable
[indispénsəbl]

필수불가결의
absolutely necessary
in=not: dispensare=continue to weigh out/ disburse

Nobody anticipated that Hamilton could become indispensable to his company.
아무도 해밀턴인 그의 회사에 필수불가결한 사람이 될 수 있다는 것을 예측하지 못했다.

ineffable
[inéfəbl]

말로 표현할 수 없는, 형언할 수 없는
incapable of being expressed; indescribable or unutterable
in=not: effari=utter

After the exhaustive research, Hank had to conclude that the truth was ineffable.
철저한 연구 후에 행크는 진실은 형언할 수 없는 것이라고 결론 내려야 했다.

ineluctable
[inilʌ́ktəbl]

피할 수 없는
unable to be resisted or avoided; inescapable
in=not: eluctari=struggle out

We had to admit the ineluctable outcome of war.
우리는 전쟁의 피할 수 없는 결과를 인정해야만 했다.

inept
[inépt]

서투른
having or showing no skill; clumsy
in=not: aptus=fitted

The press blamed Hugh for inept handling of the negotiation.
언론은 휴가 협상을 서툴게 처리했다고 비난 했다.

inexorable
[inéksərəbl]

설득할 수 없는, 막을 수 없는, 구자비한, 가차없는, 냉혹한
not to be persuaded, moved, or stopped; relentless
in=not: exorabilis=pliant

Isabel never expected to meet such inexorable opponents.
이자벨을 이런 무자비한 상대를 단날 것을 결코 예측하지 못했다.

innocuous
[inákjuəs]

무해한, 거슬리지 않는
not harmful or offensive
in=not: nocuus=injurious

Jane's criticism turned out to be one of the innocuous comments.
제인의 비난은 무해한 평가 중 하나인 것으로 드러났다.

inopportune
[inápərtjúːn]

(시기 등이) 부적절한, 시기를 놓친
inconvenient, unseasonable, unsuitable, malapropos, unfavorable, unfortunate
in=not: op=in the direction of: portus=harbor

Since Reese entered at the most inopportune moments, we had to take a break at the talk.
리스가 가장 부적절한 시기에 들어왔기 때문에 우리는 회의 중 휴식을 갖아야만 했다.

intolerant
[intálərənt]

결딜 수 없는, 관용이 없는, 편협한
unwilling to tolerate differences in opinions or beliefs, especially religious beliefs
in=not: tolerant=endurng

Jerry claimed that the society should not be intolerant of failure.
제리는 사회는 실패에 대해 편협해서는 안 된다고 주장했다.

intractable
[intræktəbl]

유순하지 않는, 다루기 힘든, 고집센
not easily governed, managed, or directed; not easily manipulated
in=not: tractare=handle

Kelly was willing to help members with some problems which seemed especially intractable.
켈리는 특히 다루기 어려워 보이는 문제들를 기꺼이 도왔다.

intrepid
[intrépid]

겁없는, 대담한
fearless; adventurous (often used for rhetorical or humorous effect)
in=not: trepidus=alarmed

Lee pretended to be an intrepid reporter.
리는 용감한 기자인척했다.

irreconcilable
[irékənsàiləbl]

화해할 수 없는, 대립하는
incompatible, conflicting, uncompromising, inflexible
ir=not: re=back: conciliare=bring together

At the beginning, the conflicts seemed irreconcilable but, fortunately, we could come to harmonious conclusion.
처음에 충돌은 화해할 수 없는 차이처럼 보였으나 행운스럽게도 우리는 조화로운 결론을 낼 수 있었다.

irrefutable
[iréfjutəbl]

논박할 수 없는
impossible to refute; incontrovertible
ir=not: refutare=repel/rebut

Wendy claims that this flooding is irrefutable evidence that global warming is in progress.
웬디는 이번 홍수가 지구온난화가 진행되고 있다는 확실한 증거라고 주장한다.

irrelevant
[iréləvənt]

관련없는, 타당하지 않은
not connected with or relevant to something
ir=not: relevant=raising up

Liz was annoyed by irrelevant and inappropriate comments.
리즈는 무관하고 부적절한 의견 때문에 짜증이 났다.

irreproachable
[ìripróutʃəbl]

비난의 여지가 없는, 흠잡을 데 없는
beyond criticism; faultless
ir=not: reprochier=near

As a presidential candidate, Luke's private life was irreproachable.
대통령 후보로써, 루크의 사생활은 흠잡을 게가 없었다.

irresolute
[irézəljúːt]

결단력이 없는, 우유부단한
unsure of how to act or proceed; undecided
ir=not: re=backward: solver=loosen

Maggie was an irresolute woman who always hesitated what to say.
메기는 무엇을 말해야 할지를 항상 망설이는 우유부단한 여자였다.

43 im / in.i

im, in, i 안의 =in, into
im/in/i는 '안의(in/into)'란 의미를 단어에 부가해 줍니다.

---

imbibe
[imbáib]

마시다, 쭉 들이켜다, 흡수하다
to drink
in=in: bibere=drink

As soon as he entered a bar, he imbibed alcohol.
그는 바에 들어오자 마자 술을 쭉 들이켰다.

immerse
[imə́:rs]

푹 담그다, 열중케 하다, 몰두시키다
to submerge; to involve deeply
in=in: merger=dip

This bar will provide you with a space to immerse yourself in jazz performance.
이 바는 당신이 째즈에 몰입할 수 있는 공간을 제공해 줄 것이다.

immigrate
[íməgrèit]

이주하다, 와서 살다
to enter and settle in a country or region to which one is not native
in=into: migrare=migrate

According to the record, Karl immigrated to USA in 1998.
기록에 따르면 칼은 1998년에 미국으로 이주했다.

immure
[imjúər]

감금하다, 가두다, 제한하다
to enclose or confine (someone) against their will
in=in: murus=wall

When Kent woke up, he found himself immured in a dark room.
켄트가 잠에서 깼을 때 그는 자신이 어두운 방에 감금되었다는 것을 알았다.

implant
[implǽnt]

심다, 가르쳐주다, 불어넣다, 이식하다
to insert or fix (tissue or an artificial object) in a person's body, esp. by surgery
in=into: plantare=plant

The scholar said that the first sound babies heard might be implanted in their brain.
그 학자는 아기들이 처음 듣는 소리가 그들의 뇌에 각인될 수 있다고 말했다.

incarcerate
[inɔ́ːspíʃəs]

투옥시키다, 감금시키다, 가두어 넣다
to imprison, confine in a particular place
in=into: carcer=prison

The number of people incarcerated in the city prisons is getting increased.
이 도시의 감옥에 투옥된 사람의 수는 계속 증가하고 있다.

incorporate
[inkɔ́ːrpərèit]

법인으로 만들다, 포함하다, 구체화하다
include, subsume, assimilate, integrate, take
in in=into: corporare=form into a body

The new proposal should incorporate statistical variations in order to represent the realistic perspectives.
현실적인 관점을 반영하기 위해서 새로운 제안은 통계상의 변수들을 포함해야 한다.

indigenous
[indídʒənəs]

고유한, 토종인, 토착인
originating and growing or living in an area or environment
indi=into: gignere=beget

The goal of this study is accounting the accurate number of indigenous people in this state.
이 연구의 목적은 이 주의 토착민의 수를 정확하게 산출하는 것이다.

inherent
[inhíərənt]

본질적인, 타고난
existing in something as a permanent, essential, or characteristic attribute
in=in/towards: haerere=stick

Liam argued that storing nuclear waste entailed inherent dangers.
리암은 핵폐기물을 저장하는 것은 본질적인 위험을 수반한다고 주장했다.

instill
[instíl]

(점차적으로) 주입하다, 서서히 스며들게 하다
to establish gradually but firmly (an idea or attitude, esp. a desirable one) in a person's mind; put (a substance) into something in the form of liquid drops
in=into: stillare=drop

Max tried to instill his thoughts into his poetry.
맥스는 그의 생각을 그의 시에 주입시키려고 노력했다.

inter
[inté:r]

매장하다
to place (a corpse) in a grave or tomb, typically with funeral rites
in=into: terra=earth

After the funeral, people were watching how the body was interred.
장례식 후에 사람들은 시신이 어떻게 매장되는지를 보고 있었다.

intricate
[íntrikət]

복잡한, 얽힌
very complicated or detailed; elaborate
in=into: tricae=tricks/perplexities

These intricate designs implied how much efforts he put into the project.
이 복잡한 디자인들은 그가 얼마나 많은 노력을 프로젝트에 들였는지 암시해 주었다.

inured
[injúər]

(안좋은 것에) 익숙해진, 단련된
accustomed to accept something undesirable
in=in: euvre=work

After working in a hospital for more than 20 years, Morgan was inured to death.
20년 이상을 병원에서 일한 후 모건은 죽음에 대해 단련됐다.

irrigate
[írəgéit]

관개하다, 물을 대다
to supply (dry land) with water by means of ditches, pipes, or streams; water artificially
in=into: rigare=moisten/wet

Irrigating properly is one of the most vital things in farming.
관개를 적절하게 하는 것은 농업에서 제일 중요한 것 중 하나이다.

44 *it / iter*

it, iter 길, 여행 =way/journey/go
it/iter은 '길/여행(way/journey)'이란 의미를 단어에 부가해 줍니다.

---

circuitous
[sərkjú:itəs]

우회로의, 에두르는, 완곡한
Being or taking a roundabout, lengthy course
circum=around: ire=go

The breaking news advised to take a circuitous route in order to avoid the accident site.
속보는 사고현장을 피하기 위해 우회도로를 사용할 것을 권했다.

initiate
[iníʃièit]

시작하다, 개시하다, 일으키다, 창시하다; 개시된, 초기의; 신참자
to set going by taking the first step; begin
it=go

In order to initiate discussions, Nate turned on the microphone.
토론을 시작하기 위해 네이트는 마이크를 켰다.

itinerant
[aitítənənt]

순회하는, 떠돌아다니는
traveling from place to place, especially to perform work or a duty
iter/itiner=journey/travelling/road

Pat, as an itinerant trader, had to travel over the world all the times.
떠돌아 다니는 무역업자로서, 팻은 항상 전세계를 여행해야만 했다.

45 joc

joc 농담 =joke
ant/ante는 '이전의(prior to/before)'란 의미를 단어에 부가해 줍니다.

jocose
[dʒoukóus]

익살맞은, 웃기는
playful or humorous
jocus=jest/wordplay

Randi tried to express his opinions in a jocose way.
랜디는 그의 의견을 익살맞은 방식으로 표현하려고 애썼다.

jocular
[dʒákjulər]

익살맞은, 까부는
fond of joking; humorous or playful
jocus=jest/wordplay

Although Polly looked serious, her voice sounded jocular.
폴리는 심각해 보였지만 그녀의 목소리는 일살맞게 들였다.

jocund
[dʒákənd]

쾌활한
cheerful and lighthearted
jocus=jest/wordplay

Everyone at the party was in a jocund mood.
파티에 있는 모든 사람들은 쾌활했다.

46 jure

jure 맹세하다 =swear
jure는 '맹세하다(swear)'란 의미를 단어에 부가해 줍니다.

---

abjure
[æbdʒúər]

맹세코 버리다, 부인하다, 취소하다
to abstain from; avoid
ab=away: jurare=swear

Because of the recent scandal, he had to abjure fealty to his religion.
최근 스캔들 때문에 그는 그의 종교에 대한 충성을 부인해야만 했다.

adjure
[adʒúər]

명하다, 간청하다, 부탁하다
to command or enjoin solemnly, as under oath
ad=to: jurare=swear

Ricky adjured me to tell him the progress in person.
리키는 진행상황을 그에게 개인즈으로 말해달라고 부탁했다.

jury
[dʒúəri]

배심원단, 심사원
a body of persons sworr to judge and give a verdict on a given matter, especially a body of persons summoned by law and sworn to hear and hand down a verdict upon a case presented in court
jurare=swear

Before the jury delivered the verdict, a series of careful questions was followed.
배심원 판결이 발표되기 이전에 일련의 조슨스런 질문을 했다.

J

47 *jur*

jus 법 =law
jur는 '법(law)'이란 의미를 단어에 부가해 줍니다.

---

judicious
[dʒuːdíʃəs]

현명한
having or exhibiting sound judgment; prudent
jus=law: dicere=say

James was famous for his judicious use of business tactics.
제임스는 사업 전술을 현명하게 사용하는 것으로 유명했다.

judge
[dʒʌdʒ]

재판관, 법관, 심사원
one who makes estimates as to worth, quality, or fitness
jus=law: dicere=say

Russ will be a head of judges to select the winning team.
루스는 승리하는 팀을 선택하는 심사위원단의 리더가 될 것이다.

jurist
[dʒúərist]

변호사, 법관, 법학도
one who has thorough knowledge and experience of law,
especially an eminent judge, lawyer, or legal scholar
jus/jur=law

The jurist issued a ruling keeping commercial areas from expanding.
법관은 상업지역이 확대되는 것을 막는 판결을 발표했다.

prejudice
[prédʒədis]

편견, 선입견
an adverse judgment or opinion formed beforehand or without
knowledge or examination of the facts
prae=in advance: jus=law: dicere=say

The prejudice against public nurseries might be hurting some
children who would be better off with good childcare from them.
공공 보육원에 대한 부정적인 편견은 그 시설로 부터 좋은 어린이보호를 받아 더 잘 살수
있는 아이들에게 나쁜 영향을 미칠 수 있다.

48 *laud*

laud 칭찬 =praise
laud는 '칭찬(praise)'이란 의미를 단어에 부가해 줍니다.

applaud
[əplɔ́:d]

박수 갈채하다, 칭찬하다
to express approval, especially by clapping the hands
ad=to: plaudere=clap

When Sally entered the auditorium, she was applauded by the audience.
샐리가 강당에 들어왔을 때 청중은 그녀를 박수갈채로 환호했다.

laud
[lɔ:d]

칭찬하다, 찬양하다; 칭찬, 찬양, 찬가
to praise (a person or their achievements) highly, esp. in a public context
laud=praise

Journalists lauded her as one of the most influential writers of the 21th century.
언론인들은 그녀를 21세기 가장 영향력있는 작가 중 한명이라고 칭찬했다.

laudatory
[lɔ́:dətɔ:ri]

칭찬하는, 찬양하는
expressing or conferring praise
laudat=praised

Sean published laudatory articles on the grassroots movement.
숀은 민중활동에 대해 칭찬을 하는 기사를 발행했다.

plaudit
[plɔ́:dit]

박수, 갈채, 찬양
praise, applause
plaudere=applaud

Sydney should deserve plaudits for her contribution.
시드니는 그녀의 공헌에 대해 마땅히 칭찬받아야 한다.

plausible
[plɔ́:zəbl]

그럴듯한, 정말 같은
(of an argument or statement) seeming reasonable or probable; believable, likely
plaus=applauded

Ralph, as a former pilot, gave the most plausible explanation for the missing airline.
파일럿이었던 랄프는 행방불명된 비행기에 대한 가장 그럴듯한 설명을 해줬다.

49 lec / leg / lex

lec, leg, lex 읽다 =read
lec/leg/lex는 '읽다(read)'란 의미를 단어에 부가해 줍니다.

dialect
[dáiəlékt]

방언, 지방어, 사투리
a regional variety of a language distinguished by pronunciation, grammar, or vocabulary, especially a variety of speech differing from the standard literary language or speech pattern of the culture in which it exists
dia=through: legein=speak

The linguistic team examined regional dialects for the past 6 months.
어학팀은 지난 6개월간 지역의 사투리를 조사했다.

lecture
[léktʃər]

강연; 강연하다
an exposition of a given subject delivered before an audience or a class, as for the purpose of instruction
lect=read/chosen

When you have difficulties in using the sofeware, you can use supporting lectures and tutorials online.
소프트웨어를 사용하는데 어려움이 있다면, 온라인 상의 지원 강의와 지도서를 사용할 수 있다.

legible
[lédʒəbl]

읽을 수 있는
possible to read or decipher
legere=read

The research team finally found the original manuscript but it was hardly legible.
조사팀은 최초의 필사본 마침내 찾았으나 거의 읽을 수가 없었다.

lexicon
[léksəkán]

사전, 어휘집
a dictionary
legein=speak

In order to understand the origin of words, you need to use a proper lexicon.
어원을 이해하기 위해서 적절한 사전을 사용해야 한다.

L

50 lev

lev 밝히다/가볍게해주다 =light/raise
lev는 '밝히다/가볍게해주다(light/raise)'란 의미를 단어에 부가해 줍니다.

---

alleviate
[əlíːvièit]

경감하다, 완화하다
to make (pain, for example) more bearable
ad=to: levare=raise/light

The public was not sure if the strategies would alleviate unemployment.
대중은 그 전략이 실업률을 경감시켜 줄 것인지에 대해 확신하지 못했다.

elevate
[éləvèit]

들어올리다, 고양하다
to move (something) to a higher place or position from a lower one; lift
e=out/away: levare=lighten

In case of arm injuries, try to keep your broken arm elevated above the level of the heart.
팔이 다쳤을 경우 부러진 팔을 심장 높이 보다 높게 유지해야 한다.

lever
[lévər]

지레로 움직이다; 지레, 지렛대
to move or lift with or as if with a lever
lever=lift

When you handle the lids of these hazardous chemicals, the lids should is levered off slowly.
위험한 화학약품의 뚜껑을 다룰 때, 뚜껑은 천천히 움직여져야 한다.

levy
[lévi]

징수, 소집군대, 징병한 병사; 징수하다, 할당하다
to impose or collect (a tax, for example)
lever=raise/light

IRS has a levy power, enabling it to seize your property.
IRS는 당신의 재산을 압류할 수 있는, 징수의 법적 권한을 갖고 있다.

51 *liber*

liber 자유 =free
liber는 '자유(free)'란 의미를 단어에 부가해 줍니다.

liberal
[líbərəl]

인색하지 않은, 풍부한, 편견0 없는, 자유개혁주의의
not limited to or by established, traditional, orthodox, or
authoritarian attitudes, views, or dogmas; free from bigotry
liber=free

Stacey has liberal views on gun control.
스테이시는 총기 규제에 대한 자유주의적 관점을 갖고 있다.

liberate
[líbərèit]

자유롭게 하다, 해방하다; 석방하다
to set free, as from oppression, confinement, or foreign control
liber=free

Susan was finally liberated from the constraints of her job
responsibilities.
수잔은 그녀의 직업에 대한 책임의 속박으로부터 마침내 자유로워졌다.

libertine
[líbərtìːn]

난봉꾼, 방탕자, 도덕적으로 속박되지 않은 사람; 방탕한, 자유사상의
a person, esp. a man, who behaves without moral principles or a
sense of responsibility, esp. in sexual matters
liber=free

Tate was known as a delinquent libertine.
테이트는 태만한 방탕자로 알려져 있었다.

license
[láisəns]

허락, 허가, 자유, 방종; 허가하다, 인가하다
to permit or authorize especially by formal license; allow
licentia=freedom

The principal was criticized for his excesses license.
교장은 그의 무제한적인 방종 때문에 비난 받았다.

licentious
[laisénʃəs]

음탕한, 방탕한, 부도덕한, 방종한
promiscuous and unprincipled in sexual matters
licentia=freedom

The general has failed to control the solder's licentious behaviors.
대령은 그 군인의 부도덕한 행동을 단속하지 못했다.

52 loq / loqu

loq, loqu 말하다 =speak/talk/thought/reason
loq/loqu는 '말하다(speak/talk/thought/reason)'란 의미를 단어에 부가해 줍니다.

colloquial
[kəlóukwiəl]

구어의, 회화체의, 격식을 차리지 않는
characteristic of or appropriate to the spoken language or to
writing that seeks the effect of speech; informal
col=together: loqui=speak

You should remember that the use of colloquial language can be
impolite in some cases.
회화체의 언어를 사용하는 것이 때때로 무례해질 수 있다는 것을 기억해야 한다.

eloquent
[éləkwənt]

(글, 문장 등이) 설득력있는, 웅변력있는
characterized by persuasive, powerful discourse
e=out: loqui=speak

Troy often uses eloquent speeches that raise serious
philosophical issues.
트로이는 심각한 철학적 문제를 제기하는 유창한 연설을 종종 한다.

grandiloquent
[grǽndíləkwənt]

과장된, 허풍떠는
pompous or extravagant in language, style, or manner, esp. in a
way that is intended to impress
grandis=grand: loqui=speak

The misunderstanding probably resulted from the grandiloquent
language Vera used.
아마도 그 오해는 베라가 사용했던 과장된 표현에서 기인한듯 했다.

logic
[lάdʒik]

논리, 이론, 추론
the study of the principles of reasoning, especially of the
structure of propositions as distinguished from their content and
of method and validity in deductive reasoning
logikē=reason/word

During the discussion, Will tried to find errors in logic.
토론을 하는 동안, 윌은 논리에 있는 실수를 찾으려고 노력했다.

loquacious
[loukwéiʃəs]

수다스런, 말하기를 좋아하는, 장황한, 지루한
very talkative; garrulous
loquax/loquac=talk

Zac's loquacious personality often gets on my nerves.
책의 수다스런 성격을 종종 내 신경을 건드린다.

obloquy
[ɔ́bləkwi]

불명예, 오명, 비난, 욕설
abusively detractive language or utterance; calumny
ob=against: loqui=speak

Adam had to endure months of obloquy during the trial.
재판을 하는 몇 달 동안, 아담은 비난을 참아야만 했다.

L

53 *luc / lux*

luc, lux 빛나다 =light
luc/lux는 '빛나다(light)'란 의미를 단어에 부가해 줍니다.

elucidate
[ilúːsədèit]

명료하게 하다, (명확히) 설명하다
to make clear or plain, especially by explanation; clarify
e=out: lucidus=lucid

The recent research is elucidating some of the clinical aspects of the disease.
최근 연구는 그 병에 대한 임상적인 관점에 대해 명료하게 설명한다.

lucid
[lúːsid]

명백하여 이해하기 쉬운, 명석한, 투명한
expressed clearly; easy to understand
lucere=shine

The exhibition gave the public a complete and lucid explanation of the artist.
전시회는 작가에 대한 철저하고 명확한 설명을 대중들에게 해주었다.

luster
[lʌ́stər]

광택
a gentle sheen or soft glow, esp. that of a partly reflective surface
lustrare= make bright/light

As Abby became unhealthy, she lost her hair as well as its luster.
에비가 병약해지면서, 그녀는 머리카락의 광택뿐만 아니라 머리카락도 잃었다.

pellucid
[pəlúːsid]

투명한, 맑은, 명료한, 명백한
admitting the passage of light; transparent or translucent
per= through: lucere=shine

The trees reflected in the pellucid water.
나무는 맑은 물에 비쳤다.

translucent
[trænspέərənt]

반투명인, 명쾌한, 맑은, 투명한
transmitting light but causing sufficient diffusion to prevent perception of distinct images; clear, lucid
trans=through: lucere=shine

The room is screened from the entry by a translucent glass wall.
방은 반투명한 유리 벽에 의해 입구로부터 가려졌다.

54 *mag / max / maj / mas*

mag, max, maj, mas 위대한 =great
mag/max/maj/mas는 '위대한(great)'이란 의미를 단어에 부가해 줍니다.

---

magnanimous
[mægnǽnəməs]

관대한, 도량이 넓은, 배포가 큰
generous in forgiving; eschewing resentment or revenge; unselfish
magnus=great: animus=soul

The press applauded the manager's magnanimous decision.
언론은 매이져의 관대한 결정을 칭찬했다.

magnificent
[mægnífisənt]

웅장한, 화려한, 고귀한
splendid in appearance; grand
magnus=great

Agatha was overwhelmed by magnificent mountains.
아가타는 웅장한 산에 의해 압도되었다.

magnify
[mǽgnəfai]

크게보이게 하다, 확대하다, 과장하다
to make greater in size; enlarge
magnus=great

According to the analyst, financial risks inherent in taking the banking procedure were magnified.
분석가에 따르면 은행 업무 절차에 내제된 재무상 위험은 과장되어 있었다.

magniloquent
[mægnílǝkwǝnt]

호언 장담하는
lofty and extravagant in speech; grandiloquent
magnus=great: loquus=speaking

Alan's promise sounded like such a magniloquent speech.
알랜의 약속은 일종의 호언 장담처럼 들렸다.

magnitude
[mǽgnǝtjúːde]

규모, 크기, 중요성
a number assigned to a quantity so that it may be compared with other quantities
magnus=great

When I understood the magnitude of the task, it was already too late to handle it on my own.
내가 일의 규모를 이해 했을 때는 이미 나 혼자 일을 처리하기에는 늦었었다.

55 mal

mal 나쁜 =bad
mal은 '나쁜(bad)'이란 의미를 단어에 부가해 줍니다.

---

maladroit
[mǽlədrɔit]

솜씨없는, 서투른
ineffective or bungling; clumsy
mal=bad: à=toward: droit=right/properly

Alton handled the conf icts in a very maladroit way.
알튼은 분쟁을 아주 서툰 방식으로 다뤘다.

---

malaise
[mæléiz]

초조, 불안, 불편, 불쾌
a general feeling of discomfort, illness, or uneasiness whose exact cause is difficult to identify
mal=bad: aise=ease

Dr. Kimberly said that any serious health condition could result in a feeling of malaise.
킴벌리 박사는 심각한 건강 상타는 불편함을 느끼게 할 수 있다고 말했다.

---

malcontent
[mǽlkəntent]

불만이 있는, (사회 체제 등어) 비판적인; 불만을 품은 사람
dissatisfied with existing conditions
mal=badly/ill: content=pleased

As a leader, Andre had to recognize and handle all malcontents from the groups.
리더로서, 안드레는 그룹으로부터의 불만을 품은 사람들을 인지하고 해결해야 했다.

M

---

malediction
[mælidíkʃən]

저주, 욕설, 중상
a curse
mal=bad: dicere=speak

When Pat finished her parts, I had to share the managers' muttered maledictions with her.
팻이 그녀의 파트를 마쳤을 때, 나는 매니져들이 중얼거렸던 욕설을 그녀와 공유해야 했다.

malefactor
[mǽləfæktər]

범인, 악인
one that has committed a crime; a criminal
mal=bad: facere=do

The evidence in crime scene investigations suggested several potential malefactors.
범죄 현장 조사에서의 증거는 몇 명의 잠재적인 범인들을 암시했다.

malevolent
[məlévələnt]

악의적인, 사악한
having or showing a wish to do evil to others
male=ill: volent=wishing

The teacher worried about Ashlee's malevolent influence on her little sisters.
선생님은 애슐리가 여동생들에게 미치는 악영향에 대해 걱정했다.

malicious
[məlíʃəs]

악의 있는, 적의 있는, 심술궂은
characterized by malice; intending or intended to do harm
malus=bad

We often don't know that accidental damage can be malicious in a long term.
우리는 우연한 손상이 장기적으로 악의적일 수 있다는 것을 종종 간과한다.

malign
[məláin]

욕설하다, 해를 끼치다; 악의 있는, 악성의
to speak about (someone) in a spitefully critical manner
malus=bad

During the campaign, politicians tend to malign opponents.
선거유세기간 동안 정치인들은 그들의 상대를 욕하는 경향이 있다.

malignant
[məlígnənt]

극히 해로운, 악의에 찬, 악성인, 유해한
highly injurious; pernicious
malus=bad

The study explained how a simple infection might cause malignant diseases.
그 연구는 간단한 감염이 어떻게 치명적인 병을 기인할 수 있는 지를 설명했다.

malodorous
[mælóudərəs]

악취가 나는
smelling very unpleasant
malus=bad: odorus=fragrant

According to the instruction, you need to use a special material to minimize malodorous gas of an old building.
설명서에 따르면 오래된 건물의 악취가 나는 가스를 최소화 하기 위해서는 특별한 물질을 사용해야 한다.

56 man / manu

man, manu 손 =hand
man/manu는 '손(hand)'이란 의미를 단어에 부가해 줍니다.

---

emancipate
[imǽnsipeit]

해방하다, (지배, 속박, 인습 등에서) 해방하다, 자유롭게 하다
to free from bondage, oppression, or restraint; liberate
e=out: manus=hand: capere=capture

Because there were still many things to be solved, Jane was far from being emancipated.
아직도 많은 것들이 해결되어야 했기 때문게 제인은 자유롭지 않았다.

manacle
[mǽnəkl]

수갑, 속박; 속박하다, 족쇄를 채우다
a device for confining the hands, usually consisting of a set of two metal rings that are fastened about the wrists and joined by a metal chain
manus=hand

When we arrived at the police station, there were already 14 criminals manacled.
우리가 경찰서에 도착했을 때, 이미 수갑이 채워진 14명의 범인들이 있었다.

mandate
[mǽndeit]

명령, 요구, 위임; 요구하다
to make mandatory; order
manus=hand: dare=give

Derek clarified the public library's mandate to provide a learning environment to the public.
데릭은 대중에게 배울 수 있는 환경을 제공해 줘야 하는 공공도서관의 위임을 명확히 했다.

maneuver
[mənú:vər]

교묘한 책략, 술책; 책략으로 움직이다, 조종하다, 교묘히 시키다
to make a controlled series of changes in movement or direction toward an objective
manus=hand: operari=work

Chuck was blamed because he used several maneuvers that made his life easier.
척은 자신의 삶을 좀 더 용이하게 만들었던 술책들을 썼기 때문에 비난 받았다.

manifest
[mǽnəfèst]

뚜렷한, 명백한; 명백히 하다, 적하 목록에 기재하다; 적하목록, 승객명단
clear or obvious to the eye or mind
manus=hand

The interviewer was impressed by Clive's manifest appeal and resume.
면접관은 크리브의 명백한 매력과 이력서에 감동 받았다.

manipulate
[mənípjulèit]

교묘하게 다루다, 조종하다
to change by artful or unfair means so as to serve one's purpose
manipulus=handful

Colin manipulated the details of the negotiation without any approval.
콜린은 어떤 승인도 받지 않은 상태로 협상의 세부사항을 교묘히 조종했다.

manumit
[mǽnjumít]

해방하다
to release from slavery; to set free
manus=hand: mittere=send

The history book explained how slaves were manumitted.
그 역사책을 어떻게 노예들이 해방 되었는지 설명했다.

manuscript
[mǽnjəskript]

필사본, 손으로 쓴 책, 원고
a book, document, or other composition written by hand
manus=hand: scriptus=written

The archeologists discovered the manuscripts in ancient Hebrew.
고고학자들은 고대 히브루어로 씌어진 필사본을 발견했다.

57 mand / mend

mand, mend 명령하다 =order/command/commit
mand/mend는 '명령하다(order/command/commit)'란 의미를 간어에 부가해 줍니다.

---

command
[kəmǽnd]

명령하다, 지배하다; 명령, 지휘, 통솔
to direct with authority; give orders to
com=together: mandare=commit/command

Dalton commanded that the researching team should investigate the issue.
달튼은 조사팀은 문제는 철저히 즈사해야 힌다고 명령했다.

M

commend
[kəménd]

칭찬하다, 추천하다
to express approval of; praise
com=together: mandare=commit/entrust

Darcy was commended by his generous behaviors.
달시는 그의 관대한 행동 때문에 칭찬받았다.

demand
[dimǽnd]

요구, 청구; 요구하다, 청구하다
to ask for urgently or peremptorily
de=formally: mandare=order

The official demanded that each group should submit their policy.
그 관리는 각각의 단체에게 그들의 정책을 계출해야 한다고 요구했다.

recommend
[rekəménd]

추천하다, 천거하다, 충고하다, 매력적으로 만들다
to praise or commend (one) to another as being worthy or desirable
re=again: commendare=commit/ command

When I was looking for the replacement for Dion, Penny was recommended by one of most reliable colleagues.
내가 디온의 후임자를 찾고 있었을 때, 가장 믿을 만한 동료 중 한명은 페니를 추천했다.

reprimand
[réprimænd]

질책, 비난; 질책하다, 비난하다
to reprove severely, especially in a formal or official way
re=again: premere= press: mand=command/commit

The candidate was reprimanded for a breach of the regulations.
그 후보는 규율을 위만한 것으로 비난 받았다.

58 *medi*

medi 중간의 =middle
medi는 '중간의(middle)'이란 의미를 단어에 부가해 줍니다.

---

immediate
[imí:dət]

즉시, 바로 이웃의, 직접적인
occurring at once; instant
in=not: mediates=intervening/middle

The governor issued immediate actions for the crisis.
주지사는 위기에 대한 즉각적인 행동을 발표했다.

---

mediate
[mí:dièit]

성립시키다, 조정하다, 중재하다; 조정의, 중재의, 간접의
to resolve or settle (differences) by working with all the
conflicting parties
medius=middle

Dustin tried to mediate between the warring parties.
더스틴은 싸우고 있는 당들을 중재하려고 노력했다.

---

medieval
[mi:dí:vəl]

중세의, 중세적인
relating or belonging to the Middle Ages
medium=middle

The article said that the first medieval castles were made of
wood.
그 기사는 최초의 중세 성은 나무로 지어졌다고 했다.

---

mediocre
[mì:dióukər]

평범한, 보통의, 2류의
moderate to inferior in quality; ordinary
medius=middle: ocris=rugged mountain

Edward was an honest person but a mediocre novelist.
에디워드는 정직한 사람이었지단 2류의 그저 그런 소설가였다.

59 *mis*

mis 잘못된 =badly/wrongly
mis는 '잘못된(badly/wrongly)'이란 의미를 단어에 부가해 줍니다.

---

misconstrue
[mìskənstrúː]

뜻을 잘못 해석하다, 오해하다
to mistake the meaning of; misinterpret
mis=badly, wrongly: con=together: struere=pile/build

Unfortunately, Eliot's intent was misconstrued.
불행스럽게도 엘리어트의 의도는 잘못 받아들여졌다.

misdemeanor
[mìsdimíːn]

나쁜 행동, 악행, 비행, 경범죄
to behave badly
mis=badly, wrongly: demeanor=behavior

The congressman was criticized for his latest misdemeanor.
하원의원은 최근의 잘못된 행실에 대해 비난 받았다.

mislead
[mislíːd]

속이다, 오도하다, 잘못 이끌었다
to cause (someone) to have a wrong idea or impression about someone or something
mis=badly, wrongly: leden=way/course

The report on the economic policy misled the public into believing its impacts.
경제 정책에 대한 기사는 대중이 이 정책의 영향을 믿게 끔 잘못 이끌었다.

misnomer
[misnóumər]

오명, 잘못 붙여진 이름
a use of a wrong or inappropriate name
mis=badly, wrongly: nommer=name

Elias's misnomer in his article was overlooked by the editor.
편집장은 일라이어스의 기사에 사용된 오명을 간과했다.

60 moll

moll 부드러운 =soft
moll은 '부드러운(soft)'이란 의미를 단어에 부가해 줍니다.

---

emollient
[imáljənt]

완화하는, 달래는, 부드럽게하는
making less harsh or abrasive; mollifying
e=out: mollis=soft

Emollient creams can be bought at any store in town.
연화제는 도시 내 어떤 가게에서도 구매 가능하다.

mollify
[máləfài]

달래다
to calm in temper or feeling; soothe
mollis=soft

The governor's statement obviously mollified public concerns.
주지사의 발표는 확실히 대중의 우려를 누그려뜨렸다.

molly-coddle
[málikɔdl]

응석받이; 응석을 받아 주다
to be overprotective and indulgent toward
molly=the name Molly, nickname for Mary: coddle= treat
indulgently

Since Erin was molly-coddled at home, she didn't know what to
do with her classmates.
집에서 에린의 응석을 다 받아줬기 때문에 그녀는 급우들과 어떻게 지내야 할지 몰랐다.

61 mor / mort

mor, mort 죽음 =death
mor/mort는 '죽음(death)'이란 의미를 단어에 부가해 줍니다.

---

amortize
[ǽmərtaiz]

청산하다, 상환하다, 양도하다
to liquidate (a debt, such as a mortgage) by installment payments or payment into a sinking fund
ad=to/at: mors/mort=death

The budget will be used to amortize the public debt.
그 예산은 공공부채를 청산하는데 쓰일 것이다.

immortal
[imɔ́:rtəl]

불사신의, 불후의, 불변의
not subject to death
im=not: mors/mort=death

The mystery novel provides readers with very fascinating stories about immortal souls.
그 미스터리 소설은 독자들에게 불멸의 영혼에 관한 매우 흥미로운 이야기들을 소개했다.

moribund
[mɔ́:rəbʌ̀nd]

다죽어가는; 기력없는
approaching death; about to die
mori=death

The surgeon was asked to operate a moribund patient.
의사는 죽어가는 환자를 수술해 달라고 요청을 받았다.

mortality
[mɔ:rtǽləti]

대규모의 사망, 사망률, 사망자 수
the quality or condition of being mortal
mors/mort=death

According to the research, reducing car accidents is one way to lower child mortality.
연구에 따르면 자동차 사고를 줄이는 것이 아동 사망률을 줄이는 한 가지 방식이다.

mortify
[mɔ:rtifái]

굴욕감을 주다, 분하게 하다
to cause to experience shame, humiliation, or wounded pride;
humiliate
mors/mort=death

Evan was mortified to hear his sudden dismissal.
에반은 그의 급작스런 해고 소식에 굴욕감을 느꼈다.

62 mut

mut 변하다 =change
mut는 '변하다(change)'란 의미를 단어에 부가해 줍니다.

---

commute
[kəmjú:t]

바꾸다, 변화시키다, 통근하다
to travel as a commuter; to make substitution or exchange
com=altogether: mutare=change

Harold commuted from Fort Lee to the Upper East Side.
해롤드는 포트리에서 어퍼이스트 사이드로 통근했다.

M

immutable
[imjú:təbl]

불변의
unchanging over time or unable to be changed
im=not: mutare=change

Although there are controversies, Fallon's findings are immutable
scientific facts.
논쟁이 많음에도 불구하고 팰론의 발견은 블변의 과학적 사실이다.

mutate
[mjú:teit]

변화하다, 변화시키다
change or cause to change in form or nature
mutare=change

The party on Saturday soon mutated into chaos.
토요일 파티는 곧 혼란상태로 변해다.

mutual
[mjú:ʃtuəl]

상호간의, 서로의, 공통의
having the same relationship each to the other
mutare=change

To settle the problem, we have to increase mutual understanding between the party and the public.
문제를 해결하기 위해서 우리는 당과 대중 간의 상호 이해를 높여야 한다.

63 masc/nat/gna

nasc, nat, gna 출생 =birth
nasc/nat/gna는 '출생(birth)'이란 의미를 단어에 부가해 줍니다.

---

innate
[inéit]

타고난, 자연스런, 본질적인
possessed at birth; inborn
in=into: nasci=be born

Some linguists insist that people have an innate capacity for langue.
몇몇의 어학자는 인간은 언어에 대한 타고난 능력이 있다고 주장한다.

nascent
[næsnt]

지금 막 생겨난
coming into existence; emerging
nascent=being born

There are many indicators to show nascent signs of global warming.
지구 온난화의 초기 증후를 보여주는 지표가 많다.

native
[néitiv]

타고난, 천부의, 토착의; 원주민, 본토박이
being such by birth or origin
nat=born

You can get more information about local native birds online.
지역 토착 새들에 대한 더 많은 정보를 온라인상에서 얻을 수 있다.

pregnant
[prégnənt]

임신한, 충만한, 풍만한
carrying developing offspring w thin the body
prae=before: gnasci=be born

According the news, smoking makes it harder for a woman to get pregnant.
뉴스에 따르면 흡연은 여성이 임신하기 어렵게 만든다고 한다.

64 neo / nov

neo/nov 새로운 =new
neo/nov는 '새로운(new)'이란 의미를 단어에 부가해 줍니다.

innovate
[inəvéit]

쇄신하다, 혁신하다, 처음으로 채용하다
to begin or introduce something new
in=into: novare=make new

The managers contemplated how they can continue to innovate on the company.
매니저들은 어떻게 회사를 지속적으로 혁신시킬 수 있는지를 심사숙고했다.

neolithic
[niːəliθik]

신석기의
of or relating to the cultural period beginning around 10,000 B.C. in the Middle East and later elsewhere, characterized by the development of agriculture and the making of polished stone implements
neo=new: lithos=stone

The color of the local pottery is characterized by Neolithic distinction.
이 현지 도자기의 색깔은 신석기시대의 특징을 보인다.

neologism
[niá:lədʒizəm]

신조어, 새 표현, 신조어 사용
a new word, expression, or usage
neo=new

As online communities have become a very popular way of interaction between people, understanding online neologisms is getting difficult.
온라인상의 대중들의 상호관계의 인기 있는 방법이 되면서, 온라인상의 신조어를 이해하는 것은 점점 어려워 진다.

neophyte
[ní:əfàit]

초심자, 신출내기, 신개종자
a person who has just started learning or doing something
neos=new: photon=plant

As a neophyte researcher, Barry has some difficulties in conducting field observations.
신출내기 연구원으로써, 베리는 현장 관찰을 하는데 어려움이 있다.

novelty
[návəlti]

새로움, 참신함, 혁신
a beginner or novice
novel=new/fresh

People often confuse novelty with creativity.
사람들은 새로운 것과 창의적인 것을 종종 혼돈한다.

novice
[návis]

초보자
a person new to or inexperienced in a field or situation
novus=new

The manual is especially for novice staff.
매뉴얼은 초보 직원들을 위한 것이다.

renovate
[renəvéit]

다시 새롭게해다, 다시 혁신하다, 활기를 불어넣다
to restore to an earlier condition, as by repairing or remodeling
re=back/again: novus=new

The pre-war building was newly renovated.
1930년대의 건물은 새롭게 수리되었다.

65 null

null 무 =nothing
null은 '무(nothing)'란 의미를 단어에 부가해 줍니다.

---

annul
[ənʌ́l]

무효로하다, 취소하다, 폐지하다
to declare invalid (an official agreement, decision, or result)
ad=to: nullum=nothing

Congress annulled the decision to raise the general tax.
의회는 일반 세금을 올리려던 결정을 폐기했다.

---

nullify
[nʌ́ləfài]

무효화하다
to make legally null and void; to invalidate
nullum=nothing

Based on the Constitution, there is nothing Congress can do to nullify a Supreme Court ruling.
헌법에 근간하면 의회는 대법원의 판결을 무효화 할 수 없다.

N

66 ob

ob 순종하는 =obeying
ob는 '순종하는(obeying)'이란 의미를 단어에 부가해 줍니다.

---

obedient
[əbíːdiənt]

순종하는, 충실한, 유순한, 얌전한, 말을 잘 듣는
dutifully complying with the commands, orders, or instructions of one in authority
obedient=obeying

Beckett wanted her dog to be obedient.
베킷은 그녀의 개가 순종적이기를 바랬다.

obeisant
[oubéisənt]

정중한
showing deferential respect
obeissant=obeying

When Bert encountered me, he gave an obeisant nod of the head.
벌트가 나를 우연히 만났을 때, 그는 정중한 머리인사를 했다.

obsequious
[əbsíːkwiəs]

아부하는, 추종하는
obedient or attentive to an excessive or servile degree
ob=obeying: sequi=follow

Brenda was reluctant to give any opinion on the obsequious manager, Mr. Warren.
브랜다는 아부하는 매니져인 워렌씨에 대한 어떤 의견도 말하는 것을 꺼렸다.

67 ob

ob 반대의 =against, in opposition
ob는 '반대의(against/in opposition)'란 의미를 단어에 부가해 줍니다.

---

obliterate
[əblítərèit]

완전히 제거하다, 지우다
to destroy utterly; to wipe out
ob=in opposition: littera=letter

After the accident, Cal seemed to obliterate the painful memories.
사고 후에 칼은 고통스런 기억을 지워버린 듯이 보였다.

object
[ábdʒikit]

반대하다, 싫어하다 ; 물건, 다상, 목표
to present a dissenting or opposing argument; raise an objection
ob=in opposition: jacere=throw

Residents objected any construction in this area since it was the historical area.
주민들은 이 동네가 역사적인 장소이기 때문에 근처의 어떤 건축공사도 반대했다.

obstacle
[ábstəkl]

장애, 방해
one that opposes, stands in the way of, or holds up progress
ob=against: stare=stand

According to the political research, politicians' corruption is a major obstacle to economic development.
정치연구에 따르면 정치인들의 부정부패가 경제 발전의 제일 큰 장애물이다.

obstreperous
[əbstrépərəs]

통제가 안되는, 시끄러운, 떠들석한
noisy and difficult to control
ob=against: strepere=make a noise

Carmen was having trouble with several obstreperous customers.
카르멘은 몇몇 다루기 어려운 고객 때문에 어려움을 겪고 있었다.

obstruct
[əbstrʌkt]

막다, 방해하다
to block or fill (a passage) with obstacles or an obstacle
ob=against: struere=build/pile up

The summer travel was obstructed by the hurricane.
여름 여행은 허리케인 때문에 방해받았다.

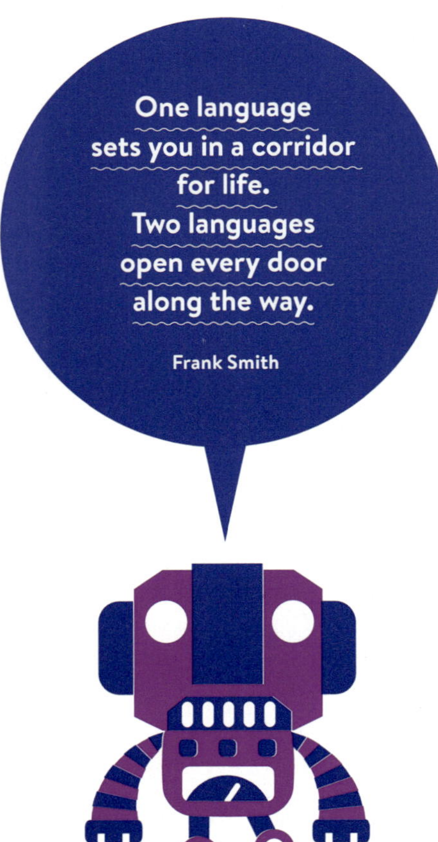

68 oner

oner 짐 =burden
oner는 '짐(burden)'이란 의미를 단어에 부가해 줍니다.

---

exonerate
[igzánərèit]

용서하다, 면제하다; 면제, 면책
to absolve (someone) from blame; release from duty
ex=from; onus/oner=burden

Chelsea was exonerated while her manager took the blame.
첼시는 매니져가 비난을 받을 동안에 비난으로부터 자유로웠다.

힘든, 성가신, 귀찮은
(of a task, duty, or responsibility) involving an amount of effort
and difficulty that is oppressively burdensome
onus/oner=burden

After the promotion, it was inevitable that Chloe should finish
the onerous tasks.
승진 후에 클로이가 어려운 직무를 마쳐야 한다는 것을 확실했다.

onus
[óunəs]

무거운짐, 부담, 책임, 의무
a difficult or disagreeable responsibility or necessity; a burden or
an obligation
onus/oner=burden

The scholar said that parents should stop putting the onus on
teachers in order to make school work well.
그 학자는 학교가 잘 운영되기 위해선 학부모들이 선생님들에게 책임을 부여하는 것을
멈춰야 한다고 말했다.

69 pan / pant

pan, pant 모두 =all
pan/pant는 '모두(all)'란 의미를 단어에 부가해 줍니다.

---

panacea
[pǽnəsìːə]

만병통치약, 모든 문제의 해결책
a remedy for all diseases, evils, or difficulties; a cure-all
pan=all: akos=remedy

The owner of the company should know that firing employees will be no panacea for any problems.
회사의 소유주는 해고가 문제를 해결하는 해결책이 아니라는 것을 알아야 한다.

pandemic
[pændémik]

(병이) 전국이나 전세계적으로 퍼지는; 전국적 유행병
(of a disease) prevalent over a whole country or the world; an outbreak of such a disease
pan=all: dēmos=people

Because of the weakness of human immunity, human beings are vulnerable to an influenza pandemic.
인간의 면역체계가 약하기 때문에 인간은 인풀루엔자의 전국적 유행병에 노출되어 있다.

panegyric
[pænədʒírik]

칭송, 찬양
a public speech or published text in praise of someone or something
pan=all: aguris=agora/assembly

The article was covered with panegyrics on Kate's paintings.
기사는 케이트의 그림에 대한 칭찬으로 가득했다.

panorama
[pænəræmə]

전경, 파노라마, 연속적으로 변해가는 광경
an unbroken view of an entire surrounding area
pan=all: horama=view

You can see an amazing panorama of the town from the rooftop.
옥상으로부터 도시의 놀랄 만한 전경을 볼 수 있다.

70 path

path 느끼다 =feel/suffer
path는 '느끼다(feel/suffer)'란 의미를 단어에 부가해 줍니다.

---

antipathy
[æntípəθi]

반감, 혐오
a deep-seated feeling of dislike; aversion
anti=against: pathos=feeling

The author of the book expressed some antipathy to capitalism.
그 책의 저자는 자본자의에 대한 반감을 표출했다.

apathy
[ǽpəθi]

무관심, 무감정
lack of interest or concern, especially regarding matters of
general importance or appeal; indifference
a=without: pathos=suffering

One of the consistent problems in U.S. politics has been voter apathy.
미국 정치의 지속적인 문제 중 하나가 유권자들의 무관심이다.

empathy
[émpəθi]

공감, 이해
identification with and understanding of another's situation,
feelings, and motives
em=in: pathos=feeling

Carter was criticized for his lack of empathy.
카터는 그의 공감력 부족으로 비난 받았다.

pathetic
[pəθétik]

불쌍한, 측은한, 감동적인
arousing or capable of arousing sympathetic sadness and
compassion
pathos=suffering

When we entered the center, there were a lot of exhausted and
pathetic refugees.
우리가 센터에 들어갔을 때, 거기에는 지치고 측은한 난민들이 많이 있었다.

sympathy
[símpəθi]

공감, 호의, 동정
a relationship or an affinity between people or things in which whatever affects one correspondingly affects the other
sym=with: pathos=feeling

Since Debra returned from the camp, she had more sympathy for the war victims.
캠프에서 돌아온 후로, 데브라는 전쟁 피해자들을 더 공감했다.

71 pec

pec 돈 =money
pec는 '돈(money)'란 의미를 단어에 부가해 줍니다.

impecunious
[ìmpikjú:niəs]

무일푼의
lacking money; penniless
in=not: pecunious=having money/wealthy

After the bankruptcy, Kate, as the impecunious person, still bears some responsibilities.
파산 후에, 무일푼인 케이트는 아직도 책임을 갖고 있다.

pecuniary
[pikjú:nieri]

금전에 의한, 재정상의
of or relating to money
pecunia=money

Desmond was trying to obtain a pecuniary advantage by M&A.
데스몬드는 합병으로 재정적인 이익을 얻으려고 애썼다.

ped 교육 =education
ped는 '교육(education)'이란 의미를 단어에 부가해 줍니다.

---

pedagogy
[pédəgòudʒi]

교육(학)
the art or profession of teaching; preparatory training or
instruction
pais/paid=boy; agōgos=guide

It's time to answer whether we need an online pedagogy.
온라인 교육학이 필요한지 아닌지에 대해 다답해야할 때이다.

pedantic
[pədǽntik]

현학적인, 아는척하는, 규칙에 목메는
of or like a pedant (a person who is excessively concerned
with minor details and rules or with displaying academic learning)
pais/paid=boy; agōgos=guide

Denzel was the most pedantic and meticulous writers I have ever
encountered.
덴젤은 내가 만났었던 가장 현학적이고 지나치게 꼼꼼한 작가였다.

P

73 *plac*

plac 즐겁게해주다, 가라앉히다 =please/clam/appease
plac은 '즐겁게해주다/가라앉히다(please/clam/appease)'란 의미를 단어에 부가해 줍니다.

---

complacent
[kəmpléisənt]

자기만족의, 기뻐하고 있는
contented to a fault; self-satisfied and unconcerned
com=together: plac=please

Although most were dissatisfied with their presentation, Joss seemed complacent.
대부분이 발표에 불만족했음에도 불구하고 조스는 만족스런 듯이 보였다.

implacable
[implǽkəbl]

달랠 수 없는, 냉혹은, 무자비한
impossible to placate or appease
in=not: placare=appease/please

The government faced implacable opposition on the issue of nuclear waste.
정부는 핵폐기물에 대한 냉혹한 반대에 직면했다.

placate
[plǽkeit]

달래다
to allay the anger of, especially by making concessions; appease
placat=appeased

The proposal was designed to placate warring activists.
제안서는 투쟁 중인 활동가들을 달랠 목적으로 계획되었다.

placebo
[pləsí:bou]

위약(僞藥), 일시적인 위안의 말 또는 행위, 위로, 발림말
a substance containing no medication and prescribed or given to reinforce a patient's expectation to get well
placer=please

Drake studied how a placebo for a painkiller actually works.
드레이크는 진통제에 대한 위약이 실제로 어떻게 작용하는 지를 연구했다.

placid
[plǽsid]

평온한, 고요한
undisturbed by tumult or disorder; calm or quiet
placer=please

Duncan relished the placid waters of the lake.
던컨은 호수의 평온한 물을 즐겼다.

74 ple / plen / plet

ple, plen, plet 채우다 =full/fill
ple/plen/plet은 '채우다(full/fill)'란 의미를 단어에 부가해 줍니다.

accomplish
[əkámpliʃ]

수행하다, 성취하다, 완성하다
to succeed in doing; bring to pass
ad=to: com=together: plere=fill

Ed's New York exhibition will offer his most accomplished works of recent years.
에드의 뉴욕 전시회는 최근 그의 작품 중 최고의 작품을 보여줄 것이다.

complement
[kámpləmənt]

보충물; 보완하다, 보충하다, 온전하게 하다
something that completes, makes up a whole, or brings to
perfection; to serve as a complement to
com=together: plere=fill

Edison's suggestions clearly complemented the ramifications of the policy.
에디슨의 제안들은 정책의 세부사항을 확실혀 보완했다.

complete
[kəmplíːt]

완결하다, 완전히 갖추다; 완전한, 완결된
having all necessary or normal parts, components, or steps; entire
com=together: plere=fill

Elaine never completed her dissertation although she spent 7 years at graduate school.
일레인은 7년간 대학원에 있었지만 논문을 마치지 못했다.

deplete
[diplíːt]

고갈시키다
use up the supply of; exhaust the abundance of
de=out/down: plere=fill

The research team tried to clarify how human activities made ground water depleted.
연구 팀은 어떻게 인간의 활동이 지하수를 고갈시켰는 지를 명확히 설명하려고 애썼다.

implement
[ímpləmənt]

이행하다, 실행하다; 도구, 용구, 수단
to put (a decision, plan, agreement, etc.) into effect
in=in: plere=fill

Because the current student loan system has many problems, we need to implement the new program.
현재 학생 융자 시스템이 문제를 많이 갖고 있기 때문에 우리는 새로운 프로그램을 이행할 필요가 있다.

plenitude
[plénətjùːd]

풍성함, 완전함
the quality or state of being full; abundance
plenus=full

Before Alexia started her thesis, she tried to gather a plenitude of information on the topic.
알렉시아는 논문를 시작하기 전에 주제에 관한 많은 정보를 모으려고 노력했다.

plenty
[plénti]

많음, 충분, 다수, 풍부함, 넉넉함; 풍부한, 많은
a full or completely adequate amount or supply
plenus=full

We have plenty of time to deal with the problem.
우리는 문제를 해결할 충분한 시간을 갖었다.

plethoric
[pləθɔ́:rik]

과다한, 과장된
excessive in quantity; superabundant
plenus=full

Despite the plethoric production, the works in the exhibition are not actually creative at all.
다량의 작품에도 불구하고 전시회의 작품들은 사실상 전혀 창의적이지 않았다.

replete
[riplí:t]

충분한, 가득한
abundantly supplied; abounding
re=back/again: plere=fill

Peter's report was replete with errors.
피터의 보고서는 실수로 가득차 있었다.

supplement
[sʌ́pləmənt]

보충, 추가; 보완하다, 보충하다
something added to complete a thing, make up for a deficiency, or extend or strengther the whole
sub=from below: plere=fill

Pam was looking for a part-time job to supplement her income.
팸은 자신의 수입을 보충하기 위해 시간제 일을 찾고 있었다.

75 pre

pre 이전의 =before
pre는 '이전의(before)'란 의미를 단어에 부가해 줍니다.

---

precaution
[prikɔ́:ʃən]

예방조치, 조심, 경계; 미리 경고하다, 경계시키다
an action taken in advance to protect against possible danger or failure; a safeguard
prae=before: cavere=take heed/beware of

Taylor wanted to ask the doctor about other precautions before leaving the clinic.
테일러는 병원을 떠나기 전에, 의사에게 다른 조심해야 할것들에 대해 묻고 싶었다.

precipitate
[prisípətèit]

급경사의, 성급한; 촉발하다, 재촉하다
to cause to move suddenly and with force; done, made, or acting suddenly or without careful consideration
prae=before: caput=head

The journalists criticized the governor because his actions were too precipitate.
언론인들은 주지사의 행동이 너무 성급했기 때문에 그를 비난했다.

preclude
[priklú:d]

배제하다, 막다
to exclude or debar from something; to prevent from happening; make impossible
prae=before: claudere=shut

Tera said that while early treatment was valuable it should not preclude the need of careful examination.
테라는 초기 치료가 중요하지만, 조심스런 진찰을 배제해서는 안된다고 말했다.

precocious
[prikòuʃes]

조숙한

manifesting or characterized by unusually early development or maturity, especially in mental aptitude

prae=before: coquere=cook

Claudia explained that there were certain characteristics of intellectually precocious children.

클라우디아는 지적으로 조숙한 아이들은 특정한 특징이 있다고 설명했다.

precursor
[priké:rsər]

선구자, 선행하는 것

a person or thing that comes before another of the same kind; a forerunner

prae=before: currere=run

The TI art museum, a precursor of the modern museum, was built in 1978.

현대 박물관의 선구자인 TI 예술 박물관은 1978년에 설립되었다.

predetermine
[prì:dité:rmin]

미리 결정하다, 선결하다

to determine, decide, or establish in advance

prae=before: determinare=lim t/settle

Based on predetermined criteria, the regulations will be revised.

이미 결정된 규정에 근거해 규율은 수정될 것이다.

predict
[pridíkt]

예보하다, 예언하다, 예시하다

to state, tell about, or make known in advance, especially on the basis of special knowledge

prae=before: dicere=say

Based on the string of the experiments, researchers tried to predict the result.

일련의 실험에 근거해서 연구원들은 결과를 예측하려고 노력했다.

predominant
[pridámənèit]

우세한, 탁월한
having superior strength, influence, or authority; prevailing; being most frequent or common
prae=before: dominus=lord/master

Tom's invention became the predominant force in his field.
톰의 발명은 그의 분야의 탁월한 영향력을 갖게 되었다.

preempt
[priːémpt]

선제적으로 막다, 선취하다, 선점하다
to take action in order to prevent (an anticipated event) from happening; to acquire or appropriate (something) in advance
prae=before: emere=buy

When we got the restaurant, all tables by the windows were already preempted.
우리가 식당에 도착했을 때 모든 창가쪽 테이블은 이미 선점되었다.

preponderant
[pripándərənt]

능가하는, 압도하는, 우세하는
predominant in influence, number, or importance
prae=before: ponderare=weigh/consider

Experts said that various lobbyists wielded preponderant influence over the government.
전문가들은 다양한 로비스트들이 정부에 압도적인 영향력을 행사했다고 말했다.

pro 이전 =before
pro는 '이전(before)'란 의미를 단어에 부가해 줍니다.

---

problem
[prábləm]

문제, 과제, 다루기 어려운 일
a question to be considered, solved, or answered
pro=before: ballein=throw

The workshop is supposed to give you some tips to fix financial problems.
워크샵은 당신에게 재정상의 문제를 해결할 수 있는 정보를 줄 것으로 추정된다.

procedure
[prəsí:dʒər]

순서, 절차, 방식
a manner of proceeding; a way of performing or effecting something
pro=before

The manager wanted to review the whole procedures.
매지져는 전체 절차를 재검토 하그 싶어 했다.

proceed
[prəsí:d]

나아가다, 계속하다, 전진하다
to go forward or onward, especially after an interruption; continue
pro=before: cedere=go

Due to mistakes in the resume, I was not able to proceed with my application for an internship.
이력서의 착오 때문에 나는 인턴쉽 지원을 계속 할 수 없었다.

proclaim
[prəkléim]

선언하다, 공표하다
to announce officially and publicly; declare
pro=before: clamare=shout

The governor proclaimed a state of emergency on Friday.
주지사는 금요일에 응급상황을 공표했다.

proclivity
[prouklívəti]

성향, 경향
a natural propensity or inclination; predisposition
pro=before: clivus=slope

Tory had the proclivity to keep on using her cell-phone while working.
토리는 일하는 동안 지속적으로 휴대폰을 사용하는 경향이 있었다.

prohibit
[prouhíbit]

금지하다, 방해하다
to forbid by authority
pro=before: habere=hold

The regulation prohibited the use of the Internet on the 11th floor.
규정은 11층에서 인터넷 사용을 금지했다.

propensity
[prəpénsəti]

강한 기호, 경향
an inclination or natural tendency to behave in a particular way
pro=before: pendere=hang

It was clear that the media had a propensity for using the word "useful information."
언론이 "유용한 정보"라는 말을 사용하는 경향이 있다는 것은 명확했다.

prophetic
[prəfétik]

예언하는, 전조가 되는
of, belonging to, or characteristic of a prophet or prophecy
pro=before: phētēs=speaker

The documentary film seemed to be prophetic in terms of climate change.
다큐멘터리 영화는 기후 변화에 대해 예언적인 듯이 보였다.

propound
[prəpáund]

제안하다
to offer for discussion or consideration
pro=before: ponere=put

According to the review, the book propounded the classical theory of management.
논평에 따르면 그 책은 경영의 고전적인 이론을 제안했다.

prospect
[práspekt]

가망, 공산, 전망; 조사하다, 답사하다
to search for mineral deposits in a place, esp. by means of
experimental drilling and excavation
pro=before: specere=look

As soon as you participated in the program, you would be trained
to improve your job prospects.
이 프로그램에 참여를 하자마자, 직업 전망을 향상할 수 있도록 훈련 받을 것이다.

protest
[próutest]

항의, 이의제기, 항의하다, 이의를 제기하다
to object to, especially in a formal statement
pro=before: testari=assert

The large-scale protests against the war were held in many cities
throughout the country.
전쟁에 반대하는 대규모 항의가 전국적으로 많은 도시에서 일어났다.

provident
[právədənt]

미래를 대비하는, 검소한, 절약하는
making or indicative of timely preparation for the future; thrifty,
economical, frugal
pro=before: videre=see

The state government's announced plans must be good news for
provident home seekers.
주정부가 발표한 계획들은 미래를 대비하며 집을 사고자 하는 사람들에게 좋은
소식임에 틀림없다.

77 prope / prox

prope, prox 가까운 =near
prope/prox는 '가까운(near)'이란 의미를 단어에 부가해 줍니다.

---

approximate
[əprá:ksimət]

근접한, 가까운; 가까이 가다, 어림잡다.
(esp. of a cause of something) closest in relationship, immediate;
closest in space or time; nearly accurate, approximate
ad=to: proximus=very near

Olivia assumed the approximate time based on traffic condition.
올리비아는 교통상황에 근거해 대략의 시간을 예측했다.

propinquity
[prəpíŋkwəti]

(장소, 시간, 관계의) 가까움, 근접, (혈통의) 근친
proximity; nearness
prope=near to

The official stated that geographic propinquity provided the
most important information about current contagion.
관리는 지역적 근접함이 현재의 전염에 대한 가장 중요한 정보를 제공해 준다고 발표했다.

proximate
[práksəmət]

(관계, 원인, 장소, 시간 등이) 가장 가까운, 근사값의
closely related in space, time, or order; very near
proximus=very near

According to the investigation, Jacob's negligence was not the
proximate cause of the injury.
조사에 따르면 제이콥의 부주의가 부상의 직접적인 원인은 아니였다.

proximity
[pra:ksíməti]

(장소, 시간, 순서, 발생, 관계 등이) 가까움, 근접, 접근
the state, quality, sense, or fact of being near or next; closeness
proximus=very near

Unfortunately, you cannot operate any electronic devices in
close proximity to rivers.
불행스럽게도 강 근처에서는 전자 장비를 사용할 수 없다.

pug, pun 찌르다 =prick/fight
pug/pun은 '찌르다(prick/fight)'란 의미를 단어에 부가해 줍니다.

---

expunge
[ikspΛndʒ]

지우다, 삭제하다
to erase or strike out
ex=out: pungere=prick

Michael tried to have his criminal record expunged.
마이클은 그의 범죄 기록을 삭제하려 노력했다.

impugn
[impjúːn]

비난하다, 논박하다, 공격하다
to dispute the truth, validity, or honesty of (a statement or motive); to call into question
in=towards: pugnare=fight

Liam released the public statement of impugning the government's motives.
리암은 정부의 의도를 비난하는 공식 논평을 발표했다.

poignant
[pɔ́injənt]

통렬한, 마음에 사무치는, 마음에 강하게 호소하는, 감동적인
painfully affecting the feelings
pugnare=fight

The film critic stated that Emily's poignant drama gave a fresh approach on the commemorations of the war.
영화 비평가는 에밀리의 감동적인 드라마가 전쟁 기념에 대한 신선한 방식이었다고 발표했다.

pugnacious
[pʌgnéiʃəs]

호전적인
eager or quick to argue, quarrel, or fight; combative; belligerent
pugnare=fight

The pugnacious demeanor of politicians at the Tea Party Movement was out of control.
티파디 활동에서의 정치인들의 호전적인 행동은 수습할 수 없게 되었다.

punctilious
[pʌŋktíliəs]

세심한, 꼼꼼한
showing great attention to detail or correct behavior
pungere=prick/fight

William was punctilious about informing us of how the accident happened.
윌리엄은 그 사고가 어떻게 발생했는 지를 알려주는데 꼼꼼했다.

punctual
[pʌ́ŋktʃuəl]

시간을 엄수하는, 규칙적인
acting or arriving exactly at the time appointed; prompt
pungere=prick

Today Mia was punctual although she was known for her tardiness.
미아는 더딘 것으로 알려져 있었지만 오늘은 시간을 엄수했다.

punctuate
[pʌ́ŋktʃuèit]

구두점을 찍다, 중단 시키다, 강조하다
to provide (a text) with punctuation marks
pungere=prick

Sophia's badly punctuated letter caused the misunderstanding as well as business failures.
소피아의 잘못 구두점을 찍은 편지는 오해를 기인했을 뿐만 아니라 사업 실패도 기인했다.

pungent
[pʌ́ndʒənt]

찌르는 듯이 자극하는, 신랄한, 호소하는 듯한
affecting the organs of taste or smell with a sharp, acrid sensation
pungere=sting/prick

Madison explained that pungent criticisms of the program in the magazine might hurt the business.
메디슨은 잡지에 실린 프로그램에 대한 신랄한 비판이 사업을 손상시킬 수 있다고 설명했다.

repugnant
[ripʌ́gnənt]

혐오스런, 적대하는
arousing disgust or aversion; offensive or repulsive
re=again/back: pugnare=fight/prick

Judge Warren's judgment seemed repugnant to the democratic principles.
워렌 판사의 판결을 민주주의 원칙에 모순되는 듯이 보였다.

79 *quie / quit*

quie, quit 조용한 =quiet/rest
quie/quit는 '조용한(quiet/rest)'란 의미를 단어에 부가해 줍니다.

---

acquiescent
[ækwiésnt]

묵묵히 따르는, 순종하는
disposed or willing to acquiesce
ac=to/at: quiescere=rest

Bella was acquiescent to accept her employer's offer.
벨라는 그녀의 고용주의 제안을 묵묵히 받아들였다.

disquiet
[diskwáiət]

불안, 동요, 걱정
a feeling of uneasiness or anxiety
dis=not: quiet=repose/quiet

The newspaper said that there was widespread public disquiet about the education policy.
신문은 교육정책에 대한 넓게 퍼진 대중들의 불안이 있다고 말했다.

quiescent
[kwaiésnt]

조용한, 활발하지 않은, 가라앉은, 정지 중인
being quiet, still, or at rest; inactive
quies=quiet/rest

Emma mentioned that tuberculosis was one of the quiescent infections.
엠마는 결핵이 활발하지 않은 질병 중의 하나라고 언급했다.

quiet
[kwáiət]

고요함, 정적, 평화, 태평; 고요한, 평화로운
making no noise; silent
quies=quiet/rest

The salesman said that this lawn mower would be quiet.
판매원은 이 잔디깍는 기계가 조용할 것이라고 말했다.

quit
[kwit]

그만두다, 중지하다
to depart from; leave
quiet=rest

Manny thought about quitting the job after working for the company for 17 years.
매니는 17년 동안 근무한 후에 회사를 그만두는 것을 생각했다.

tranquil
[trǽŋkwil]

고요한, 평온한
free from commotion or disturbance
trans=through: quiet=rest

When you visit the public park, you will relish the lovely tranquil garden there.
공공 공원을 방문한다면, 그 곳의 사랑스럽게 고용한 정원을 즐길 수 있을 것이다.

80 rud

rud 가공되지 않은, 미완성인 =crude/rough

rud는 '가공되지 않은/미완성인(crude/rough)'란 의미를 단어에 부가해 줍니다.

---

erudite
[érjudàit]

박식한, 학구적인

having or showing great knowledge or learning

e=ex: rudis=rough

Whenever James leads the conversation, he tends to turn it into an erudite discussion.

제임스는 대화를 이끌 때 마다 대화를 학구적인 토론으로 바꾸는 경향이 있다.

rude
[rú:d]

무례한, 교양없는, 거친, 가공하지 않은, 조잡한

ignorant and educated; vigorous; roughly made or done; lacking subtlety or sophistication

rudis=rough

The study indicated that the rude behaviors among employees could negatively affect consumer perceptions.

연구는 직원들간의 무례한 행동이 소비자들의 인지에 부정적인 영향을 미칠 수 있다는 것을 보여줬다.

rudimentary
[rù:dəméntəri]

미발달의, 미성숙의, 기본적인

of or relating to an immature, undeveloped, or basic form, primitive

rudis=rough

The scholar said that children generally received their rudimentary education at home.

그 학자는 아이들이 일반적으로 가정에서 기본적인 교육을 받는다고 말했다.

81 sacer / sacr / sanct

sacer, sacr, sanct 신성한 =holy/sacred
sacer/sacr/sanct는 '신성한(holy/sacred)'이란 의미를 단어에 부가해 줍니다.

---

sacrifice
[sǽkrəfàis]

희생, 제물; 제물로 바치다, 희생하다, 버리다
the act of offering something to a deity in propitiation or homage, especially the ritual slaughter of an animal or a person
sacer=holy

Marc was willing to sacrifice everything for his children.
마크는 그의 아이들을 위해 어떠한 희생도 기꺼이 했다.

sacrilegious
[sæ̀krəlídʒəs]

신성을 더럽히는, 신앙심이 없는
of violation or misuse of what is regarded as sacred
sacer=sacred: legere=take possession of

Bishop denounced the sacrilegious acts and vandalism that occurred last week.
주교는 지난 주에 일어났던 신성모독 행동과 파괴주의에 대해 비난 했다.

sacrosanct
[sǽkrousæŋkt]

신성불가침의
regarded as too important or valuable to be interfered with
sacro=by a sacred rite: sanctus=holy

Mark argued that human rights must remain sacrosanct.
마크는 인권은 반듯이 신성불가침이어야 한다고 주장했다.

saint
[seint]

성자, 성인; 성인의 반열에 오르다
a person officially recognized, especially by canonization, as being entitled to public veneration and capable of interceding for people on earth
sanctus=holy

The official process for declaring someone a saint is called canonization.
누군가를 성인으로 선언하는 공식적인 과정을 '시성'이라 한다.

sanctimonious
[sǽŋktəmouniəs]

성인인체 하는, 신자인체 하는
feigning piety or righteousness
sanctus=holy

The article said that we could easily see sanctimonious hypocrites on Capitol Hill.
기사는 의사당에서 성인인척 하는 위선자들을 쉽게 볼 수 있다고 말했다.

sanction
[sǽŋktʃən]

허가, 인가, 구속력, 처벌; 인정하다, 비준하다
authoritative permission or approval that makes a course of action valid
sanctus=holy

Before they signed the agreement, they demanded official sanction for their principles.
그들은 합의에 서명하기 이전에 원칙에 대한 공식적인 허가를 요구했다.

sanctity
[sǽŋktəti]

거룩함, 고결함, 신성함
holiness of life or disposition; saintliness
sanctus=holy

There was a report that researchers discovered the site of the sanctity for the ancient society.
조사자들이 고대 사회의 신성한 장소를 발견했다는 보고가 있었다.

sanctuary
[sǽŋktʃuèri]

지성소, 피난처
a sacred place, such as a church, temple, or mosque; sanctum; a place of refuge or asylum
sanctus=holy

We often read stories that people take sanctuary in the church.
우리는 사람들이 교회를 피난처로 택하는 이야기를 종종 읽는다.

sanctum
[sǽŋktəm]

신성한 장소, 성지
a sacred place; a private place where one is free from intrusion
sanctus=holy

During the travel, I found the sanctum to be a proper place to meditate.
여행 동안에, 나는 그 성지가 명상을 하기에 적적한 장소라는 것을 알았다.

82 sag / sap / sav

sag, sap, sav 맛을 느끼다/분간하다, 생각하다 =taste/think/wise
sag/sap/sav는 '맛을 느끼다/분간하다, 생각하다(taste/think/wise)'란 의미를 단어에 부가해 줍니다.

insipid
[insípid]

맛없는, 재미없는, 지루한
lacking flavor or zest; not tasty
in=not: sapere=taste

Unfortunately, all works at the exhibition seemed insipid and conventional.
불행스럽게도 전시회의 모든 작품들은 지루하고 진부해 보였다.

sagacious
[səɡéiʃəs]

현명한, 기민한
having or showing keen mental discernment and good judgment; shrewd
sagax/sagac=wise

We hoped that the manager was sagacious enough to prevent employees' outage.
우리는 매니져가 직원들의 분노를 예방할 수 있을 만큼 충분히 현명하기를 바랬다.

sagacity
[səɡǽsəti]

현명, 기민
the quality of being discerning, sound in judgment, and farsighted; wisdom
sagax/sagac=wise

The incumbent governor was known for lacking political sagacity.
현직 상원의원은 정치적인 현명함이 부족한 것으로 일려져 있다.

sage
[séidʒ]

현인, 현자; 현명한, 박식한 체하는
a profoundly wise man, esp. one who features in ancient history or legend.
sapere=be wise

Because I had been watching how he handled the problem, I had to say that he was not a sage.
그가 문제를 어떻게 다루는 지를 봤기 때문에 나는 그가 현자는 아니라고 말해야만 했다.

sapient
[séipiənt]

슬기로운, 지혜로운
possessing wisdom and discernment; wise, sagacious
sapere=be wise

Sapient decision making depends on how accurately you understand the reality.
지혜로운 결정을 내리는 것을 현실을 얼마나 정확하게 이해 하느냐에 달려 있다.

savor
[séivər]

맛보다, 즐기다; 맛, 풍미, 특성, 특징
to taste or smell with pleasure; relish; to delight in; enjoy
sapere=taste

When the members got the beach, they were finally able to savor every moment.
멤버들이 해변에 도착했을 때, 그들은 마침내 매 순간을 즐길 수 있었다.

83 salu / slav

salu, slav 건강 =health, save
salu/slav는 '건강(health/save)'란 의미를 단어에 부가해 줍니다.

---

salubrious
[səlúːbriəs]

건강에 좋은, 유익한, 건강한
health-giving; healthy; not run-down
salus=health

The park has various spots where visitors can get fresh air and salubrious weather.
공원에는 방문자들이 신선한 공기와 건강에 좋은 날씨를 즐길 수 있는 많은 장소가 있다.

salutary
[sǽljutèri]

유익한
producing good effects; beneficial
salus=health

The article said that the actual salutary effects of the legislation were not substantial.
기사는 그 법안의 사실적인 유익한 효과는 충분하지 않다고 말했다.

salute
[səljúːt]

인사, 결례; 인사하다, 경의를 표하다
to greet or address with an expression of welcome, goodwill, or respect
salus=health

At the National Cemetery, there were many people and soldiers saluting the flag.
국립묘지에는 국기에 경의를 표하는 많은 사람들과 군인들이 있었다.

salvage
[sǽlvidʒ]

(난파선 등) 구조하다, 해난구조하다; 해난구조
to rescue (a wrecked or disabled ship or its cargo) from loss at sea
salvare=save

The rescue team tried a number of attempts to salvage refugees.
구조팀은 난민들을 구조하기 위해 여러 번 시도를 했다.

salvation
[sælvéiʃən]

(죄로 부터) 구원, (손상을) 구제
deliverance from sin and its consequences, believed by Christians to be brought about by faith in Christ; preservation or deliverance from harm, ruin, or loss
salvare=save

In the church yard, there were some prayers believing in salvation.
교회 안뜰에는 구원을 믿으며 기도를 하는 사람들이 있었다.

salve
[sæv]

연고, 위안, 달래주는 것; 달래다, 진정시키다
an analgesic or medicinal ointment
salvare=save

Gabriel was waiting until the doctor prescribed several salves.
가브리엘은 의사가 연고 몇 개를 처방해줄 따까지 기다렸다.

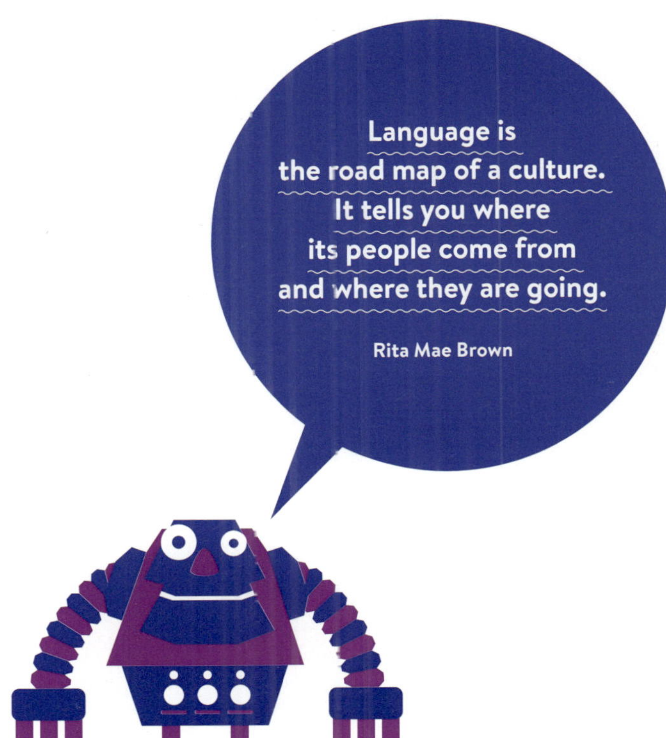

R

84 sang

sang 피 =blood
sang은 '피(blood)'란 의미를 단어에 부가해 줍니다.

---

sang-froid
[sǽŋfrwá:]

침착, 냉정
composure or coolness, sometimes excessive, as shown in danger or under trying circumstances
sang=blood: froid=cold

The police officer handled everything with the sang-froid at the crime scene.
범죄현장에서 경찰은 냉정하게 모든 일을 처리했다.

sanguine
[sǽŋgwin]

낙관적인, 쾌활한, 혈색이 좋은, 불그레한
cheerfully optimistic
sanguine=blood

Zoe was sanguine about prospects for her theory of climate change.
조이는 날씨 변화에 대한 그녀의 이론에 대한 예상에 낙관적이었다.

85 sat

sat 충분한 =enough
sat는 '충분한(enough)'이란 의미를 단어에 부가해 줍니다.

---

asset
[ǽset]

유용한것, 장점, 이점, 재산, 정보제공자
a useful or valuable quality, person, or thing; an advantage or a resource
ad=to: satis=enough

Lily was a valuable asset to this organization.
릴리는 이 단체의 가치있는 사람이었다.

insatiable
[inséiʃəbl]

만족할 줄 모르는, 한없는, 탐욕스런
(of an appetite or desire) impossible to satisfy
in=not: satis=enough

Insatiable scientific curiosity leads you to more innovations.
만족할 줄 모르는 과학적 호기심이 당신을 더 혁신적으로 만든다.

sate
[séit]

충분히 만족시키다
to satisfy (a desire or an appetite) to the full
satis=enough

To sate his curiosity, Joshua stayed the library until midnight.
조슈아는 그의 호기심을 만족시키 위해, 자정까지 도서관에 머물렀다.

satiate
[séiʃièit]

충분히 만족시키다, 물리게 하다
to satisfy (as a need or desire) fully or to excess
satis=enough

The main role of food is not only to satiate hunger but also to provide essential energy.
음식의 주 역할은 허기를 만족시키는 것 뿐만 아니라 기본적인 에너지를 제공하는 것이다.

satisfy
[sǽtisfài]

만족시키다, 충족시키다, 납득시키다
to gratify the need, desire, or expectation of
satis=enough: facere=make

The advisor knew how I felt because I was not satisfied with my job.
조언자는 내가 직업에 만족하지 못하기 때문에 어떻게 느끼는지 지를 알고 있었다.

saturate
[sǽtʃərèit]

흠뻑적시다, 열중하게 하다
to treat, furnish, or charge with something to the point where no more can be absorbed, dissolved, or retained
satis=enough

After the heavy rain, the soil was too saturated.
폭우 후에 땅은 너무 흠뻑 젖어 있었다.

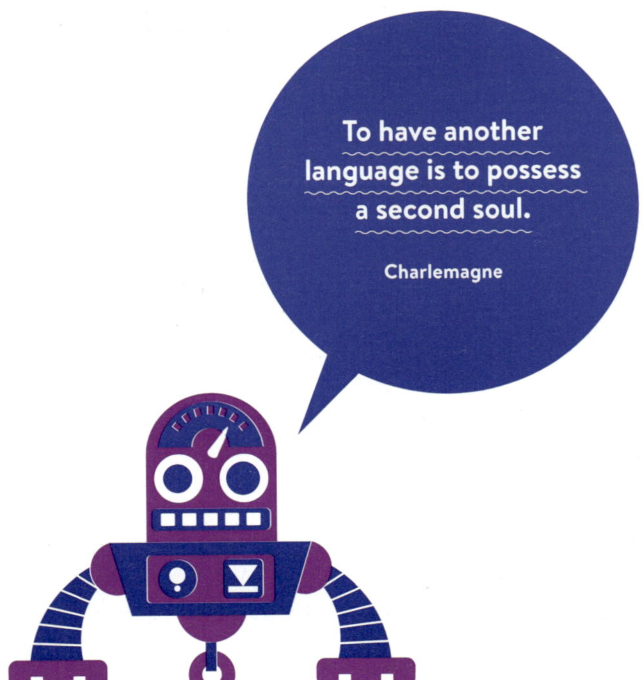

86 scribe / script / scriv

scribe, script, scriv 쓰다 =write
scribe/script/scriv는 '쓰다(write)'란 의미를 단어에 부가해 줍니다.

ascribe
[əskráib]

<A(원인, 동기, 기원 등)를 B(사물)에> 있다고 하다; <A(결과 등)를 B(사물)의> 탓으로 돌리다
To attribute to a specified cause, source, or origin
ad=to: scriber=write

The critic said that Luke should not ascribe his success to his partner.
비평가는 루크가 그의 성공을 파트너 덕이라고 해서는 안된다고 말했다.

circumscribe
[sə́:rkəmskráib]

제한하다, 경계를 정하다
To draw a line around; er circle
circum=around: scriber=write

The CEO's power should be circumscribed by the company regulations.
CEO의 힘은 회사 규율에 의해 계한 되어야만 한다.

describe
[diskráib]

기술하다, 표현하다, 묘사하다, 평하다
to give an account of in speech or writing
de=down: scriber=write

Before starting the experiment, Harold described the procedure to every researcher.
실험을 시작하기 이전에 해롤드는 모든 연구원들에게 과정을 설명했다.

inscribe
[inskráib]

쓰다, 적다, 새기다
to write, print, carve, or engrave (words or letters) on or in a surface
in=into: scriber=write

The back of the benches were inscribed with the donors' names.
벤치의 뒷면에는 기증자의 이름이 새겨져 있었다.

prescribe
[priskráib]

규정하다, 명하다, 처방하다
to lay down, in writing or otherwise, as a rule or a course of action to be followed; to appoint, ordain, or enjoin
prae=before: scriber=write

The doctor prescribed certain medicines to Allison after he reviewed her chart.
의사는 앨리슨의 차트를 검토하고 약을 처방해줬다.

proscribe
[prouskráib]

금지하다, 못하게하다, 비난하다
to forbid, esp. by law
pro=in front of: scriber=write

The manager clarified that the use of electronic devices would be proscribed during the session.
매니져는 회의 동안에 전자기기 사용이 금지 될 것이라는 것을 명확하게 했다.

subscribe
[səbskráib]

기부하다, 응모하다, 동의하다, 구독하다
to pledge or contribute (a sum of money) sub=under: scriber=write

Subscribe to the magazines today and receive special discounts.
오늘 잡지를 구독하고 특별 할인을 받으세요.

transcribe
[trænskráib]

필기하다, 베끼다, 나타내다
to make a full written or typewritten copy of (dictated material, for example)
trans=through: scriber=write

According to the ad, this system will transcribe your speeches automatically.
광고에 따르면 이 시스템은 연설을 자동으로 필기할 것이다.

87 sed / sid

sed, sid 앉다, 놓여있다 =sit
sed/sid는 '앉다/놓여있다(sit)'란 의미를 단어에 부가해 줍니다.

---

assiduous
[əsídʒuəs]

근면 성실한
showing great care and perseverance
ad=toward: sedere=sit

Mary was the most assiduous researcher who always had some solutions.
매리는 늘 해결책을 갖고 있는, 가장 성실한 연구원이었다.

dissident
[dísədənt]

의견을 반대하는 사람; 반대하는
disagreeing especially w th an established religious or political system, organization, or belief
dis=apart: sedere=sit

The leadership should listen to t ne voice of the dissident as well.
지도부는 의견을 달리하는 사람들의 의견 역시 들어야 한다.

insidious
[insídiəs]

남을 속이는, 교활한, 방심할 수 없는, 모르는 사이에 작용하는, 잠행성의
working or spreading harmfully in a subtle or stealthy manner
in=on: sedere=sit

Austin was ignorant of several insidious incidents and that caused bigger problems later.
오스틴의 몇몇 잠행성의 사건들을 인지하지 못했고 그것은 더 큰 문제를 기인했다.

preside
[prizáid]

의장을 하다, 사회를 하다, 관리하다
to hold the position of authority; act as chairperson or president
prae=before: sedere=sit

Parker, as a judge, presided over several cases.
판사로서 파커는 몇 개의 사건을 관리했다.

reside
[rizáid]

거주하다, 존재하다, 있다
to live in a place permanently or for an extended period
re=back: sedere=sit

When Ian resided in France, he met his fiancée.
이안이 프랑스에 거주할 때 그는 그의 약혼자를 만났다.

sedate
[sideit]

(사람, 태도, 빛깔 등이) 차분한, 온화한, 침착한, 수수한
serenely deliberate, composed, and dignified in character or manner
sedere=sit

Adam was so sedate that nobody recognized his anger.
아담이 너무 차분한 결과 아무도 그의 분노를 인지하지 못했다.

sedative
[sédətiv]

진정제; 진정시키는
having a soothing, calming, or tranquilizing effect; reducing or relieving anxiety, stress, irritability, or excitement
sedere=sit

Andrea asked the doctor for more effective sedative drugs.
앤드리아는 의사에게 더 효과적인 진정제를 요구했다.

sedentary
[sédntèri]

정주하는, 주로 앉아 있는; 앉아 지내는 사람, 앉아 일하는 사람
not migratory ; settled
sedere=sit

Because I'm the most sedentary person in this office, I need to exercise more regularly.
사무실에서 내가 제일 많이 앉아 있는 사람이기 때문에 나는 좀 더 규칙적인 운동이 필요하다.

subside
[səbsáid]

내려앉다, 가라앉다
to become less intense, violent, or severe
sub=below: sedere=sit

When the storm subsided, students were informed to leave the school.
학생들은 폭풍이 가라앉아졌을 때 학교를 떠나라는 공지를 받았다.

supersede
[sù:pərsí:d]

대신하다, 대체하다
to take the place of (a person or thing previously in authority or use); supplant
super=above: sedere=sit

I do not think that books can be superseded by computers.
나는 책이 컴퓨터에 의해 대체될 수 있다고 생각하지 않는다.

88 sem

sem 씨를 뿌리다 =seed
sem은 '씨를 뿌리다(seed)'란 의미를 단어에 부가해 줍니다.

---

disseminate
[disémənèit]

퍼뜨리다, 확산시키다
to disperse throughout
dis=abroad: semen/semin=seed

Before assessing proliferated information, it is more important to understand why it was disseminated in a given community.
확산된 정보를 평가하기 이전에, 왜 그 정보가 일정한 집단에 확산되었는지를 이해하는 것이 더 중요하다.

seminal
[sémənəl]

발생의, 씨종의, 발달 가능성이 있는, 미발달의
relating the power to originate; creative;
highly influential in an original way; constituting or providing a basis for further development
semen=seed

The prize was awarded to Alex due to his seminal work.
알렉스는 발전 가능성 있는 작업 덕분에 상을 받았다.

seminar
[sémənàːr]

세미나, 연구회
a small group of advanced students in a college or graduate school engaged in original research or intensive study under the guidance of a professor who meets regularly with them to discuss their reports and findings
semen=seed

During the seminar, Sara had to answer the phone.
사라는 세미나 동안에 전화를 받아야만 했다.

89 *sin / sinu*

sin, sinu 굽히다, 휘다 = bend/curve
sin/sinu는 '굽히다/휘다(bend/curve)'란 의미를 단어에 부가해 줍니다.

---

insinuate
[insínjuèit]

넌지시 말하다, 비추다
to introduce or insert (oneself) by subtle and artful means
in=in: sinuare=curve

Mandy insinuated that she was not involved in the scandal.
맨디는 그녀가 그 의혹과 관련이 없다는 것을 건지시 말했다.

sinuate
[sínjuèit]

꼬불 꼬불한
to bend or curve; wind in and out
sinuare=bend

Nick designed the pattern which was inspirited by sinuate leaves.
닉은 꼬불 꼬불한 잎의 선에 영감 받아 패턴을 디자인 했다.

sinuous
[sínjuəs]

꼬불꼬불한, 물결모양의
characterized by many curves or turns; winding
sinus=bend

We relished nature on the sinuous road to the castle.
우리는 성으로 가는 꼬불꼬불한 길에서 자연을 즐겼다.

soph 지혜 =wisdom/wise/deceive
soph는 '지혜(wisdom/wise/deceive)'란 의미를 단어에 부가해 줍니다.

---

philosopher
[filásəfər]

철학자, 현자
a student of or specialist in philosophy
philein=love: sophos=wise

Paul's professor is one of the world leading philosophers.
폴의 교수님은 전세계 선도하는 철학자 중의 한명이다.

sophism
[sófizəm]

궤변, 억지이론, 잘못된 이론
a plausible but fallacious argument; deceptive or fallacious argumentation
sophisma=clever device

Seth's theory sounded interesting but it was fundamentally a sophism.
세스의 이론은 흥미롭게 들렸지단 근본적으로 궤변이였다.

sophist
[sófist]

궤변론자
one skilled in elaborate and devious argumentation
sophizesthai=devise/become w se

Since everybody used the Internet, there have been many sophists online.
모든 사람들이 인터넷을 사용하거 된 이래토, 온라인상에는 많은 궤변론자가 있었다.

sophisticated
[səfistəkèitid]

세련된, 교양있는, 세상물정에 익숙한, 기교에 치우친
having acquired worldly knowledge or refinement; lacking natural simplicity or naiveté; very complex or complicated
sophos=clever

In order to minimize machines' failure rate, researchers must find more sophisticated methods.
기계의 고장률을 낮추기 위해서 연구자들은 보다 섬세한 방법을 찾아야만 한다.

sophistry
[sɔ́fistri]

궤변
plausible but fallacious argumentation
sophos=clever

Although Lucia tried to elaborate her argument, it was pure sophistry.
루이아가 그녀의 주장을 정밀하게 설명하려 노력했음에도 불구하고, 그녀의 주장은 단지 궤변이었다.

sophomoric
[sɔfəmɔ́rik]

2학년생의, 젠체하나 미숙한, 아는체하는, 건방진
conceited and overconfident of knowledge but poorly informed and immature
sophos=clever: moros=dull

Juliet's behaviors were nothing more than sophomoric.
줄리엣의 행동은 미숙했다.

91 spect / spic

spect, spic 보다 =look/see
spect/spic은 '보다(look/see)'란 의미를 단어에 부가해 줍니다.

---

aspect
[æspect]

외관, 모양, 측면, 견지
a particular look or facial expression; a way in which something can be viewed by the mind
ad=to/at: specere=look

Sierra said that recently she realized the importance of every aspect of life.
시에라는 최근에 인생의 모든 측면의 중요성을 인지했다고 말했다.

---

auspicious
[ɔːspíʃəs]

길조의, 유리한
conducive to success; favorable
avis=bird: specere=look

Because the manager was upset, Elliot tried to figure out the most auspicious moment to submit the proposal.
매니저가 화가 났기 때문에 엘리어트는 제안서를 제출해야 할 최상의 순간을 찾으려 노력했다.

---

conspicuous
[kənspíkjuəs]

잘 보이는, 눈에 잘 띄는, 알아보기 쉬운
easy to notice; obvious
con=direct: spicere=look at

Iris managed to make the statement conspicuous on the bulletin board.
아이리스는 게시판에 그 성명서가 눈에 잘 띄게 하려고 애썼다.

---

expect
[ikspékt]

예기하다, 기대하다, 당연한 것으로 생각하다
to look forward to the probable occurrence or appearance of
ex=out: spectare=look

The exhibition was expected to hold in 3 months.
그 전시회는 3개월 후에 열릴 것으로 예상되었다.

inspect
[inspékt]

점검하다, 정밀조사하다
to examine carefully and critically, especially for flaws
in=in: spectare=look

Recently, Phoebe had a property inspected by the state government.
최근에 피비는 주 정부로부터 그녀의 소유물을 점검 당했다.

perspective
[pərspéktiv]

관점, 시각, 전망
a mental view or prospect
per=through: specere=look

The book introduced three venues that provided unique perspectives on the island.
그 책은 섬에 대한 특별한 전망을 갖게 해주는, 3개의 장소를 소개했다.

perspicacious
[pə̀:rspəkéiʃəs]

통찰력 있는, 명민한
keen, shrewd; having clear vision
per=through: specere=look

Foster was known for the most perspicacious reporter in town.
포스터는 이 도시의 가장 통찰력 있는 기자로 알려져 있었다.

perspicuous
[pərspíkjuəs]

명확한, 명료한
clearly expressed and easily understood; lucid; (of a person) able to give an account or express an idea clearly
per=through: specere=look

Louis's explanation was sufficiently perspicuous to be understood by all members.
루이스의 설명은 모든 멤버들에 의해 이해될 수 있게 충분히 명료했다.

specious
[spí:ʃəs]

허울좋은, 겉만 번드르르한, 실제로는 잘못된
superficially plausible, but actually wrong
specere=look

There is the website which published specious arguments about the crime rate.
범죄율에 대한 잘못된 주장을 알리는 웹싸이트가 있다.

spectacle
[spéktəkl]

장관, 구경거리
something that can be seen or viewed, especially something of a remarkable or impressive nature
specere=look

The park was always filled with tourists because a public spectacle was taking place there.
공원은 눈에 띄는 구경거리들이 일어나기 떠문에 늘 관광객들로 붐볐다.

speculative
[spékjulətiv]

사색의, 이론적인, 추측에 의한, 투기의 위험한
something that can be seen or viewed, especially something of a remarkable or impressive nature
specere=look

Parker casted the speculative glance at his colleague.
파커는 그의 동료를 추측의 시선으로 보았다.

suspect
[səspékt]

알아채다, 수상하게 여기다
to surmise to be true or probab e; imagine
sub=below: specere=look

Ty can make a distinction between individuals based on what he suspected.
타이는 그가 알아챈 것에 근거해 사람들 간의 차이점을 알아낼 수 있다.

suspicious
[səspíʃəs]

의심을 일으키는, 수상한
arousing or apt to arouse suspicion; questionable
sub=below: specere=look

The police found three suspicious briefcases at the terminal.
경찰은 터미널에서 세개의 수상한 서류가방을 찾았다.

transpicuous
[trænspíkjuəs]

투명한
easily understood or seen through
trans= across/beyond/through: specere=look

The reporter strove to discover the transpicuous truth.
기자는 투명한 진실을 밝히려고 노력했다.

92 *sua*

sua 즐겁게해주다 =please/sweet/advise
sua는 '즐겁게해주다(please/sweet/advise)'란 의미를 단어에 부가해 줍니다.

---

assuage
[əswéidʒ]

달래다, 완화시키다, 만족시키다
to make (something burdensome or painful) less intense or severe
ad=to: suavis=sweet

Taylor's advice assuaged my fears of being fired.
테일러의 충고는 해고에 대한 나의 두려움을 완화시켰다.

dissuade
[diswéid]

설득하여 단념시키다
to deter (a person) from a course of action or a purpose by persuasion or exhortation
dis= do the opposite of: suadere=advise

The financial crisis couldn't dissuade citizens from investing.
그 금융 사건은 시민들이 투자하는 것을 단념시키지는 못했다.

persuade
[pərwéid]

설득하다, 재촉하여 시키다
to induce to undertake a course of action or embrace a point of view by means of argument, reasoning, or entreaty
per=through/completion: suadere=advise

Pablo believed that people tended to persuade others to do right things.
파블로는 사람들은 다른 사람들이 올바른 일을 하도록 설득하는 경향이 있다고 믿었다.

suave
[swa:v]

온화한, 점잖은, 세련된, 기분 좋은
smoothly agreeable and courteous
suavis=agreeable/sweet

Surprisingly, our suave manager was in her jogging pants when we arrived there.
놀랍게도, 우리가 도착했을 때 세련된 매니져는 운동복 차림이였다.

93 super / sur

super, sur 위의 =above
super/sur은 '위의(above)'란 의미를 단어에 부가해 줍니다.

---

superannuated
[sjù:pərǽnjuèitid]

노쇠한, 노후한, 낡은, 시대에 뒤진, 폐물이 된
outmoded; obsolete
super=above: annus=year

Since the machinery was superannuated, it was not easy to find adequate replacement of parts.
기계가 노후됐기 때문에 부품의 적절한 대체품을 찾기가 쉽지 않았다.

superb
[su:pə́:rb]

훌륭한, 우수한
marked to the highest degree by grandeur
superbus= above/proud/magnificent

The audience enthusiastically applauded the singer's superb performance at the concert.
공연에서 청중은 가수의 훌륭한 공연에 열정적으로 박수갈채를 보냈다.

supercilious
[sù:pərsíliəs]

거만한, 건방진
behaving or looking as though one thinks one is superior to others
super=above: cilium=lower eyelid

The athlete seemed supercilious during the interview.
그 운동선수는 인터뷰 동안 거만해 보였다.

superficial
[sù:pərfíʃəl]

피상적인, 깊이가 없는
existing or occurring at or on the surface; not thorough, deep, or complete; cursory
super=above: facies=face

Despite the accident, the car had only superficial damage.
사고에도 불구하고 차는 단지 피상적인 손상만 있었다.

superfluous
[suːpéːrfluəs]

잉여의, 여분의, 불필요한
unnecessary, esp. through being more than enough
super=above: fluere=flow

Liam wanted to change the front page because it had superfluous information.
리암은 표지가 잉여의 정보를 갖고 있어서 이것을 바꾸고 싶었다.

superior
[sjuːpíːerier]

높은, 상급의, 중요한, 뛰어난; 상사, 선배
higher than another in rank, station, or authority
super=above

The book explained how to use recruiting methods that would ensure superior hires.
그 책은 어떻게 탁월한 고용을 확실하게 해주는 채용 방식을 사용하는 지를 설명했다.

supernatural
[sjùːpərnǽtʃərəl]

불가사이한, 초자연적인, 이상한; 초자연적인 현상
of or relating to existence outside the natural world
super=above: natura=birth/nature/quality

According to the documentary film, there was the occurrence of supernatural events in Oklahoma.
다큐멘터리 영화에 따르면 오클라호마에 초자연적인 사건들이 발생했다.

supersede
[sùːpərsíːd]

대신하다, 대체하다
to take the place of; replace
super=above: sedere=sit

The article introduced an interesting story about why the telephone did not immediately supersede the telegraph.
기사는 왜 전화가 전보로 즉각적으로 대체되지 않았는지에 관한 흥미로운 이야기를 소개했다.

supervise
[sùːpərvàiz]

감독하다, 관리하다, 지시하다
to have the charge and direction of; superintend
super=above: videre=see

Managers were supposed to supervise all machinery for the safety.
매지져들은 안전을 위해 모든 기계를 관리할 것으로 추정됐다.

surfeit
[sə́:rfit]

과다, 과대한 양, 과식; 식상하게 하다, 과식하다
an excessive amount of something
super=above: facere=co

Michael was concerns about a surfeit of heating due to the cost.
마이클은 비용 때문에 과량의 난방에 대한 걱정했다.

surmise
[sərmàiz]

추측하다, 짐작하다
to suppose that something is true without having evidence to confirm it
super=above: mittere=send

Elle surmised that everybody must have been outside at the time.
엘리는 당시 모든 사람들이 밖에 있었을 것이라고 추측했다.

surmount
[sərmàunt]

극복하다, 오르다, 넘다
to overcome (a difficulty or obstacle)
super=above: mont=mountain

The book said that you could surmount the obstacles in your path if you were determined enough.
그 책은 당신이 충분히 단호하다면 인생의 장애물들을 극복할 수 있을 것이라고 말했다.

surpass
[sərpǽs]

능가하다, 보다 낫다, 초월하다
to exceed; to be greater than
super=above: passer=pass

Daniel was excited about the conference because the number of attendees surpassed the expectations.
다니엘은 컨퍼런스의 참가자수가 예측을 초과했기 때문에 활기차 있었다.

survey
[sə́:rvéi]

둘러보다, 개관하다, 조사하다, 측량하다; 개관, 조사, 측량
To examine or look at in a comprehensive way
super=above: videre=see

To make detailed plans, Anna's team started to survey the coasts and islands.
상세한 계획을 만들기 위해, 안나의 팀은 해변과 섬을 측량하기 시작했다.

94 *tacit*

tacit 고요한 =silent
tacit는 '고요한(silent)'이란 의미를 단어에 부가해 줍니다.

---

reticent
[rétəsənt]

과묵한, 삼가하는, 신중한
inclined to keep one's thoughts, feelings, and personal affairs to oneself
re=used as an intensive: tacere=silent

Victor was extremely reticent about her social life.
빅터는 사생활에 대해서는 상당히 과묵했다.

---

tacit
[tǽsit]

암묵적인, 무언의, 잠잠한
not spoken
tacere=silent

Both parties reached the tacit agreement on the environmental policy.
양당은 환경 정책에 대한 무언의 합의를 이뤘다.

---

taciturn
[tǽsitə:rn]

과묵한, 말수가 적은
habitually untalkative
tacere=silent

It was not easy for Jenna, a novice journalist, to interview the taciturn scientist.
초보 기자인 제나가 과묵한 과학자를 인터뷰하는 것은 쉽지 않았다.

95 tact / tag / tam / tang

tact, tag, tam, tang 손대다 =touch
tact/tag/tam/tang는 '손대다(tough)'란 의미를 단어게 부가해 줍니다.

---

contact
[cántækt]

접촉, 마주침, 교제, 교신; 접촉시키다, 연락하다
a coming together or touching as of objects or surfaces
con=together: tangere=touch

The statement said that incidents involving contact between heavy equipment and power-lines should be prevented.
성명서는 중장비와 전력선 간의 연결과 관련된 사고들은 방어되어야 한다고 말했다.

contagious
[kəntéidʒəs]

접촉 전염성의, 전염병을 감염시키는
transmissible by direct or indirect contact; communicable
con=together: tangere=touch

During the contagious disease outbreak, the university's emergency response teams will monitor the campus situation.
접촉 전염성 발생 동안, 대학 응급 대응 팀은 학내 상황을 지속적으로 관찰할 것이다.

contaminate
[kəntǽmənèit]

더럽히다, 불순하게 하다, 오염시키다
to make impure or unclean by contact or mixture
con=together: tangere=touch

A wide range of chemicals can easily contaminate our water or air, impacting the environment and our health.
다양한 종류의 화학물질들은 환경과 건강에 영향을 미치는 물과 공기를 쉽게 오염시킬 수 있다.

contiguous
[kəntígjuəs]

인접하는
sharing a common border; touching
con=together: tangere=touch

The article stated that it is important for towns to protect contiguous forest habitat.
기사는 도시들이 인접한 산림의 서식지를 보호하는 것은 중요하다고 상술했다.

contingent
[kəntíndʒənt]

우발적인, 우연의, 부수적인, 따르는
subject to chance; dependent on
con=together: tangere=touch

The company had many consultants who would function for its contingent condition.
회사는 우발적인 상황에 대해 활동할 수 있는 자문단을 갖고 있었다.

intact
[intǽkt]

손대지 않은, 손상되지 않은
untouched especially by anything that harms or diminishes
in=not: tangere=touch

The archeologist found a book in the site and its many parts remained intact.
고고학자는 현장에서 책을 한 권 발견했고 그 책의 많은 부분은 손상되지 않은 상태로 남아있었다.

intangible
[intǽndʒəbl]

만질 수 없는, 비물질적인, 불분명한
unable to be touched or grasped; not having physical presence
in=not: tangere=touch

This article reviewed the intangible factors that could influence the political environment.
그 기사는 정치에 영향을 미칠 수 있는 비물질적인 요소들을 검토했다.

tact
[tǽkt]

사람 혹은 상황을 잘 다루어 불쾌하지 않게 하는 센스, 재치
adroitness and sensitivity in dealing with others or with difficult issues
tangere=touch

James, as the leader, was behaving with tact and consideration.
제임스는 리더로서 재치와 신중함을 갖고 행동했다.

tactful
[tǽktfəl]

재치 있는, 약삭빠른
possessing or exhibiting tact; considerate and discreet
tangere=touch

Parents should talk about irritations with children with tactful words.
부모들은 재치있는 말로써 아이들이 화를 내는 것에 대해 아이들과 대화해야 한다.

tactless
[tǽktləs]

재치 없는, 외교적 수완이 없는, 무뚝뚝한
lacking or exhibiting a lack of tact; bluntly inconsiderate or indiscreet
tangere=touch

Accidently, I had made a tactless remark and, therefore, I wanted to leave the place.
우연히 말실수를 해서 나는 그 장소를 떠나그 싶었다.

96 tim

tim 두려움 =fear
tim은 '두려움(fear)'이란 의미를 단어에 부가해 줍니다.

---

intimidate
[intímədèit]

두려워하게 하다, 겁먹게 하다, 위협하다
to frighten or overawe (someone), esp. in order to make them do what one wants
in=in: timidus=fear

Carter was intimidated by his colleague's success.
카터는 동료의 성공에 겁을 먹었다.

timid
[tímid]

겁먹은, 소심한, 심약한
shy and fearful; showing a lack of courage or confidence; easily frightened
timidus=fear

Robert was too timid to have a successful job interview.
로버트는 너무 소심해서 성공적인 면접을 하지 못했다.

timorous
[tímərəs]

겁먹은, 소심한, 자신감이 없는
showing or suffering from nervousness, fear, or a lack of confidence
timidus=fear

Although Adam tried to appear confident, his voice clearly sounded timorous.
아담은 비록 자신감이 있어 보이려고 노력 했으나 그의 목소리는 확실히 자신감이 없이 들렸다.

97 *tor / torq / tort*

tor, torq, tort 꼬다 =twist
tor/torq/tort는 '꼬다(twist)'란 의미를 단어에 부가해 줍니다.

---

distort
[distó:rt]

왜곡하다, 곡해하다, 비틀다
to twist out of a proper or natural relation of parts; misshape
dis=apart: torquere=twist

Due to the lack of experience, the researcher let several errors distort the results.
경험 부족 때문에 연구원은 몇몇 실수가 결과를 왜곡하게 했다.

extort
[ikstó:rt]

강요하다, 강탈하다
to obtain from another by coercion or intimidation
ex=out: torquere=twist

Last month Michael Wren was found guilty of extorting money in return for approving liquor licenses.
지난달 마이클 워렌은 주류 허가를 승인해주는 대가로 돈을 강요한 것에 대해 유죄임이 드러났다.

torch
[tó:rtʃ]

횃불, 빛; 횃불처럼 타오르다, 토치램프로 가열하다
a portable light produced by the flame of a stick of resinous wood or of a flammable material wound about the end of a stick of wood; a flambeau
torquere=twist

While camping on the island, Lucy was in charge of lighting torches.
섬에서 캠핑을 하는 동안 루시는 횃불에 불을 밝히는 것을 담당했다.

torment
[tɔːrmént]

몹시 괴롭히다, 고통을 주다, 괴롭히다; 고통, 고통을 일으키는 것
to cause severe usually persistent or recurrent distress
torquere=twist

The book was helpful to stop mental torment.
그 책은 정신적 고통을 멈추게 하는데 도움이 되었다.

tortuous
[tɔ́ːrtʃuəs]

구불구불한, 에두르는, 솔직하지 못한
full of twists and turns; excessively lengthy and complex, devious
torquere=twist

Although Stella got the approval from the editor, it still seemed a tortuous route to publish her first novel.
비록 스텔라가 편집장으로 부터 승인을 받았지만 그녀의 첫 번째 소설을 출판하는 것은 구불구불한 길처럼 보였다.

torture
[tɔ́ːrtʃuər]

고문, 고통; 고문하다, 몹시 괴롭히다, 곡해하다
infliction of severe physical pain as a means of punishment or coercion
torquere=twist

In his memoir, Nolan depicted how he suffered from physical and mental torture.
놀란은 회고록에서 그가 어떻게 신체적 정신적인 고문으로 부터 고통을 겪었는지를 묘사했다.

trans 건너서, 저편에 =across/beyond/through
trans는 '건너서/저편에(across/beyond/through)'란 의미를 단어에 부가해 줍니다.

---

intransigent
[intrǽnsədʒənt]

비타협적인, 완고한
unwilling or refusing to change one's views or to agree about something
in=not: trans=across: agree=drive

Although they needed to reach a consensus, every participant was intransigent.
합의를 이뤄야 함에도 불구하고 모든 참가자들은 비타협적이었다.

transcend
[trænsénd]

초월하다
to be or go beyond the range or limits of (something abstract, typically a conceptual field or division)
trans=across: scandere=climb

Although every member had different opinions, Jacob tried to transcend the differences.
모든 멤버들이 다른 의견을 갖고 있음에도 불구하고 제이콥은 그 차이점을 초월하려고 노력했다.

transfer
[trænsfə́ːr]

옮기다, 이전하다, 양도하다, 바꾸다
to move (someone or something) from one place to another
trans=across: ferre=bear

It was surprising that Logan transferred to our department.
로건이 우리 부서로 옮겼다는 것은 놀라웠다.

transient
[trǽnziənt]

일시적인
lasting only for a short time; impermanent
trans=across: ire=go

The research team announced their discovery of transient astronomical phenomena.
그 연구팀은 순간적인 천문학적 현상에 대한 발견을 발표했다.

transitory
[trǽnsitɔ:ri]

영원하지 않은, 일시적인
not permanent
transire=go across

Tom explained that you need to distinguish transitory effects from long-run equilibria.
탐은 일시적인 결과를 장기적인 균형으로부터 구별할 필요가 있다고 설명했다.

transmit
[trænsmít]

보내다, 송달하다, 옮기다, 전염시키다
to send from one person, thing, or place to another; convey
trans=across: mittere=send

The news was transmitted to the public.
뉴스는 대중에게 전달 되었다.

transmute
[trænsmjú:t]

성질을 바꾸다, 변형하다
to change or alter in form
trans=across: mutare=change

Ryan's dissatisfaction grew bitter and transmuted into resentment.
라이언의 불만족은 점점 심해져 분노로 변했다.

transparent
[trænspé(:)ərənt]

투명한, 이해하기 쉬운, 명쾌한, 속이지 않는, 솔직한
(of a material or article) allowing light to pass through so that objects behind can be distinctly seen; easy to perceive or detect; free from guile, candid or open
trans=through: parere=appear

The consumers demanded more transparent explanations.
소비자들은 좀 더 명확한 설명을 요구했다.

transplant
[trænsplǽnt]

이식, 이주; 이식하다, 옮겨심다
to remove from one place to another
trans=across: plantare=plant

Lung transplants are generally used for people who are likely to die from lung disease.
페이식은 폐병으로 사망할 가능성이 있는 사람들을 위해 주로 사용된다.

transport
[trænspɔ́ːrt]

운송, 이송, 수송; 나르다, 옮기다, 수송하다, 추방하다
to carry from one place to another; convey
trans=across: portare=carry

The article explained how natural gas was transported.
그 기사는 천연 가스가 어떻게 수송되는지를 설명했다.

99 *umbr*

umbr 그림자 =shadow/shade
umbr은 '그림자(shadow/shade)'란 의미를 단어에 부가해 줍니다.

adumbrate
[ǽdʌmbrèit]

어렴풋이 예시하다, 희미한 모습을 그리다
to suggest, disclose, or outline partially: to intimate, indicate faintly
ad=to: umbrare=cast a shadow

The documentary movie adumbrated the idea of the next generation.
다큐멘터리 영화는 다음 세대에 대해 어렴풋이 예시해 줬다.

somber
[sɔ́mbər]

우울한, 음침한, 슬픈 듯한, 근심 어린, 침울한
dark; gloomy; melancholy; dismal
sub=under: umbra=shade

The critic said that the painter's art was of a somber character.
비평가는 그 화가의 작품은 우울한 특징을 갖고 있다고 말했다.

umbrage
[ʌ́mbridʒ]

불쾌감, 화
offense or annoyance
umbra=shade/shadow

They took umbrage at the governor's remarks concerning the immigration policy.
그들은 이민 정책에 대한 주지사의 말에 화가 났다.

100 und

und 흔들리다, 기복을 이루다 =wave
und는 '흘들리다/기복을 이루다(wave)'란 의미를 단어에 부가해 줍니다.

---

abound
[əbáund]

많이 있다, 풍부하다, 넘칠 듯하다, 충만하다
to be great in number or amount
ab=from: undare=wave/surge

Jackson's argument was unpredictable but, in fact, similar arguments abounded in the field of the social sciences.
잭슨의 주장은 예측지 못한 것이였지만 사실상 사회학 분야에는 유사한 주장이 많다.

abundance
[əbʌ́ndəns]

다수, 풍부, 충만, 부유
a great or plentiful amount
ab=from: undare=wave/surge

Surprisingly, economies with abundant natural resources tended to grow less rapidly in modern economy.
놀랍게도 현대 경제에서 풍부한 천연 자원을 갖고 있는 경제는 상대적으로 느리게 성장하는 경향이 있었다.

inundate
[ínʌndèit]

범람하다, 침수시키다, 넘치게하다
to cover with water, especially floodwaters
in=into/upon: undare=flow

The exhibition has reportedly been inundated with complaints from concerned parents.
전하는 말에 의하면 그 전시회는 걱정하는 부모들로 부터 많은 불만을 들었다.

redundant
[ridʌ́ndənt]

장황한, 여분의, 과잉의
no longer needed or useful; superfluous
re=again: unda=wave

Due to the rapid development of technology, many skills associated with the old job became redundant in the new job
기술의 급속한 발전 때문에 예전의 직업과 관련된 많은 기술들은 새로운 직업에서는 잉여의 기술이 되었다.

101 *vail / val*

vail, val 가치 =value/worth/strong/well
vail/val은 '가치(value/worth/strong/well)'란 의미를 단어에 부가해 줍니다.

---

avail
[əvéil]

도움이 되다, 유용하다
to be of use or advantage to; help
a=of: valere=value

I did not expect to get any help from Dr. Warren's seminar but some of his advice seemed to avail.
워렌 박사의 세미나에서 어떤 도움도 얻을 것이라고 기대하지 않았지만 그의 충고 중 몇몇은 도움이 될 듯 했다.

available
[əvéiləbl]

이용할 수 있는, 쓸모 있는
present and ready for use; at hand; accessible
a=of: valere=value

You can find several kinds of services available online related to Alzheimer's disease.
알츠하이머 병과 관련된 온라인 상의 여러 이용 가능한 종류의 서비스를 찾을 수 있다.

equivalent
[ikwívələnt]

동등한, 등가의, 상당하는; 동등한 것, 상당물
equal, as in value, force, or meaning
aequi=equally: valere=worth

Evan said that 10 inches of snow might be equivalent to 4 inches of rain in terms of the effects on traffic.
에반은 교통에 미치는 영향면에서 10인치의 눈은 4인치의 비와 동등하고 말했다.

evaluate
[ivǽljuèit]

평가하다, 견적하다
to ascertain or fix the value or worth of
ex=out: valere=worth

Kevin had difficulties in evaluating recent changes in education policies.
캐빈은 교육정책의 최근 변화를 평가하는데 어려움을 겪었다.

prevalent
[prévələnt]

널리 퍼진, 유행인, 효과적인
generally or widely accepted, practiced, or favored
prae=before: valere=worth

Despite the restriction, the unchecked information was already prevalent.
제한에도 불구하고 확인되지 않은 정보는 이미 널리 퍼졌다.

valediction
[vælidíkʃən]

작별, 고별, 작별인사
a speech or statement made as a farewell
vale=strong/well: dicere=say

The audience soon felt that the valediction intended to stimulate emotional upheaval.
청중은 그 고별사가 감정을 자극하려는 의도라는 것을 금방 느꼈다.

valiant
[vǽljənt]

용감한
possessing or showing courage or determination
valere=strong

Carlos's colleagues were impressed by his valiant effort against his boss.
카를로스의 동료들은 사장에게 맞서려는 그의 용감한 노력에 감동 받았다.

valid
[vǽlid]

정당한, 확실한, 유효한
well grounded; just
valere=strong

Although I spent a lot of time to get information, most of it was not valid.
정보를 얻기 위해 많은 시간을 썼음에도 불구하고 대부분의 정보는 유용하지 않았다.

valorous
[vǽlərəs]

용감한
having great courage in the face of danger, esp. in battle
valere=strong

The valorous soldier received his fourth Star.
그 용감한 군인은 그의 4번째 훈장을 받았다.

value
[vǽljuː]

가치, 진가; 평가하다, 존중하다
an amount, as of goods, services, or money, considered to be a fair and suitable equivalent for something else; a fair price or return
valere=value/strong

We can easily see that people from different cultures have different value systems.
서로 다른 문화의 사람들은 서로 다른 가치 시스템을 갖고 있다는 것을 쉽게 볼 수 있다.

V

102 ver

ver 진실 =true
ver는 '진실(true)'이란 의미를 단어에 부가해 줍니다.

---

aver
[əvə́:r]

주장하다, 단언하다, 진술하다
to affirm positively; declare
ad=to: verus=true

Consumers averred that their complaints were legitimate.
소비자들은 그들의 불만은 정당했다고 주장했다.

veracious
[vəréiʃəs]

항상 진실을 말하는, 정직한, 진실한
honest; truthful
verus=true

Leo's book gave veracious accounts for global warming.
니오의 책은 지구 온난화에 대한 진실된 설명을 했다.

verdict
[vé:rdikt]

판결, 결정, 평결
the finding of a jury in a trial
verus=true: dicere=say

We already anticipated the jury's guilty verdict.
우리는 이미 배심원의 유죄 판결을 예상했다.

verify
[vérəfài]

입증하다, 확증하다, 확인하다
to prove the truth of by presentation of evidence or testimony;
substantiate
verus=true

Cora's findings were verified by additional experiments.
코라의 연구 결과는 추가 실험에 의해 확증되었다.

verisimilar
[vèrəsimílər]

있을 법한, 사실 같은
quality of seeming to be true or real
verus=true: similis=like

Summer exemplified how verisimilar accounts were supported for the past several years.
썸머는 지난 몇 년 동안 얼마나 그럴듯한 설명들이 지지 되었는지를 예증했다.

veritable
[véritəbl]

참다운, 진실한
being in fact the thing named and not false, unreal, or imaginary
verus=true

The ad said that this hotel was the veritable boutique hotel in town.
광고는 이 호텔이 이 도시의 진정한 브띠크 호텔이라고 했다.

103 verb

verb 단어 =word
verb는 '단어(word)'란 의미를 단어에 부가해 줍니다.

---

proverb
[próvə:rb]

속담, 격언, 교훈; 속담으로 표현하다
a short, pithy saying in frequent and widespread use that expresses a basic truth or practical precept
pro=forth: verbum=word

Joss wrote her favorite proverb on the back of the book.
조스는 그녀가 좋아하는 격언을 책 뒷장에서 썼다.

verbal
[vé:rbəl]

말의, 말에 관한; 동사류
of, relating to, or associated with words
verbum=word

Cody said that, if I wanted to enforce a verbal contract, I would need to prove that it existed in the first place.
코디는 내가 만약 말로한 합의를 적용하기를 원한다면 이 합의가 처음부터 있었다는 것을 증명할 필요가 있다고 말했다.

verbalize
[və́:rbəlàiz]

말로 나타내다 , 동사화 하다, 동사로 사용하다
to express in words
verbum=word

During puberty, adolescents are often unable to verbalize their real feelings.
사춘기에 청소년들은 그들의 진정한 느낌을 말로 표현하기가 종종 불가능하다.

verbiage
[və́:rbiidʒ]

장황함
speech or writing that uses too many words or excessively technical expressions
verbum=word

The teacher's irrelevant verbiage made students confused.
선생님의 주제와 무관한 장황함은 학생들을 헷갈리게 했다.

verbose
[və:rbóus]

장황한, 수다스런
using or expressed in more words than are needed
verbum=word

The author's verbose language was obvious obstacles for readers to understand the story.
작가의 장황한 언어가 독자들이 이야기를 이해하는데 확실한 장애였다.

104 *vil*

vil 천한 =base/mean
vil은 '천한(base/mean)'이란 의미를 단어에 부가해 줍니다.

revile
[riváil]

욕하다, 욕설을 퍼붓다
to criticize in an abusive or angrily insulting manner
re=again: vil=base/mean

The review showed various opinions reviled by critics.
논평은 비평가들의 욕설을 퍼붓는 의견을 보여줬다.

vile
[vail]

몹시 나쁜, 사악한, 부도덕한, 불쾌한
extremely unpleasant, morally bad, wicked
vil=base/mean

Fiona said something vile about the performance.
피오나는 그 공연에 대해 무엇인가 몹시 나쁜 이야기를 했다.

vilify
[víləfài]

헐뜯다, 중상하다
to speak or write about in an abusively disparaging manner
vil=base/mean

Because of the recent changes by the state government, public employees are vilified.
주정부에 의한 최근의 변화 때문에 공무원들이 비난 받았다.

105 viru

viru 독 =poison
viru는 '독(poison)'이란 의미를 단어에 부가해 줍니다.

virulent
[vírjulənt]

맹독성의, 매우 해로운, 치명적인, 신랄한
poisonous, noxious, hostile
virus=poison

This review handled factors that influenced the virulent influenza.
논평은 치명적인 독감에 영향을 미친 요소들을 다뤘다.

virus
[váiərəs]

바이러스, 병원체, 악영향
any of various simple submicroscopic parasites of plants, animals, and bacteria that often cause disease and that consist essentially of a core of RNA or DNA surrounded by a protein coat
virus=poison

There are many infections due to the virus.
바이러스로 인한 많은 전염이 있다.

106 voc / vou

voc, vou 부름, 소환, 명령, 말 =call/word
voc/vou는 '부름/소환/명령/말(call/word)'이란 의미를 단어에 부가해 줍니다.

advocate
[ǽdvəkèit]

지지자, 옹호자; 지지하다, 옹호하다
to recommend or support publicly
ad=to: vocare=call

Emily was known for an advocate of immigration reform.
에밀리는 이민법 개정 지지자로 알려졌다.

avow
[əbáu]

솔직하게 말하다, 인정하다
to acknowledge openly, boldly, and unashamedly; confess
ad=to: vocare=call

Henry was one of three avowed candidates for the governor.
헨리는 공인된 세명의 주지사 후보 중 한명이다.

convoke
[kənvóuk]

소집하다
to cause to assemble in a meeting; convene
con=together: vocare=call

The council advised the leader to amend regulations and convok members.
평의회는 리더에게 규율을 수정하고 회원들을 소집할 것을 권했다.

equivocal
[ikwívəkəl]

애매한, 분명치 않은
open to more than one interpretation; ambiguous
aequus=equally: vocare=call

Although Susan was equivocal about the program at first, she became one of the strong supporters.
수잔은 처음에는 프로그램에 대해 확신이 없었음에도 불구하고 강력한 지지자 중의 한 명이 되었다.

evoke
[ivóuk]

불러일으키다, 이끌어내다
to bring or recall to the conscious mind; to elicit (a response)
e=out: vocare=call

This music evoked memories of the famous rock musician.
이 음악은 유명한 락뮤지션에 대한 기억을 불러 일으켰다.

invoke
[invóuk]

발동하다, 기원하다, 탄원하다
to reverse in position, order, or relationship
in=upon: vocare=call

Because the city invoked the amended regulation, we should follow it.
시가 수정된 규율을 실시했기 때문에 우리는 그것을 따라야 한다.

provoke
[prəvóuk]

자극하다, 화나게 하다
to stimulate or give rise to (a reaction or emotion, typically a strong or unwelcome one) in someone; to make (someone) annoyed or angry deliberately
pro=forth: vocare=call

According to the news, the violent police response provoked protesters.
뉴스에 따르면 격렬한 경찰의 대응이 항의를 하는 사람들을 자극했다.

revoke
[rivóuk]

무효로 하다, 파기하다, 취소하다; 취소
to void or annul by recalling, withdrawing, or reversing
re=back: vocare=call

Kevin claimed that the decision to revoke probation was discretionary.
케빈은 보고감찰 취소 결정이 임의적이었다고 주장했다.

vocabulary
[voukǽbjəlèri]

어휘, 단어
all the words of a language
vocare=call

Nicole's website helped users to find vocabularies of various languages.
니콜의 웹싸이트는 사용자들이 다양한 언어의 어휘를 찾는 것을 도왔다.

vocal
[vóukəl]

목소리의, 자유롭게 의견을 표현하는
expressing opinions or feelings freely or loudly
vox/voc=call/word

Alice was vocal in her iconoclastic opinions on black holes.
앨리스는 블렉홀에 대한 그녀의 인습타파적인 의견을 자유롭게 표현했다.

vocation
[voukéiʃen]

하느님의 부름, 소명, 천직
a regular occupation, especially one for which a person is
particularly suited or qualified
vocare=call

Tommy had the vocation to be a doctor since he was 13 years old.
토미는 13살 때부터 의사가 될 소명을 갖고 있었다.

vociferous
[vousífərəs]

떠들석한, 큰소리로 외치는
(esp. of a person or speech) vehement or clamorous
vocare=call

Jake has been the most vociferous opponent of genetic
engineering.
제이크는 유전공학을 가장 큰소리로 반대하는 사람이어 왔다.

vouch
[vautʃ]

(신뢰성을) 보증하다, 보장하다
confirm that someone is who they say they are or that they are of
good character
vocare=call

No matter how strongly the company vouched for the efficiency,
there was still an important missing ingredient: the security.
회사가 효율을 얼마나 강하게 보장하는 것과는 상관 없이 안전성이라는
중요한 요소가 빠져 있다.

107 volu / volv

volu, volv 회전하다 =roll, turn
volu/volv는 '회전하다(roll/turn)'란 의미를 단어에 부가해 줍니다.

---

evolve
[iválv]

차츰 전개시키다, 진화시키다, 발전하다
to produce by natural evolutionary processes; develop
e=out of: volvere=roll

After running her business for 5 years, Jane has evolved into the most successful entrepreneur.
5년 동안 사업을 운영한 후에 제인은 가장 성공적인 기업가로 발전했다.

involve
[inválv]

연류시키다, 관계하다
to contain as a part; include
in=into: volvere=roll

Since my job involved in meeting various people, I had more chances to learn about cifferent culture.
나의 직업이 다양한 사람들을 만나는 것과 관계가 있었기 때문에 나는 다른 문화에 대해 알게될 기회가 더 많았다.

revolt
[rivóult]

반항하다, 배반하다, 반감을 품다
to attempt to overthrow the authority of the state; rebel
re=back: volvere=roll

The newspaper posted images of thousands of people revolting against the state government.
신문은 주정부에 반감을 갖고 있는 수천명의 사람들이 사진들을 올렸다.

revolve
[riválv]

빙빙 돌다, 회전하다, 순환하다
to orbit a central point
re=again: volvere=roll

Ryan explained that the cost of installation of automatic revolving doors was not expensive.
라이언은 자동 회전문을 설치하는 비용은 비싸지 않다고 설명했다.

voluble
[váljəbl]

유창한, 말 많은, 수다스런
speaking or spoken incessantly and fluently
volvere=roll

We already knew that Thomas was the most voluble speaker among members.
우리는 토마스가 회원들 중에 가장 유창한 연설가였다는 것을 이미 알고 있었다.

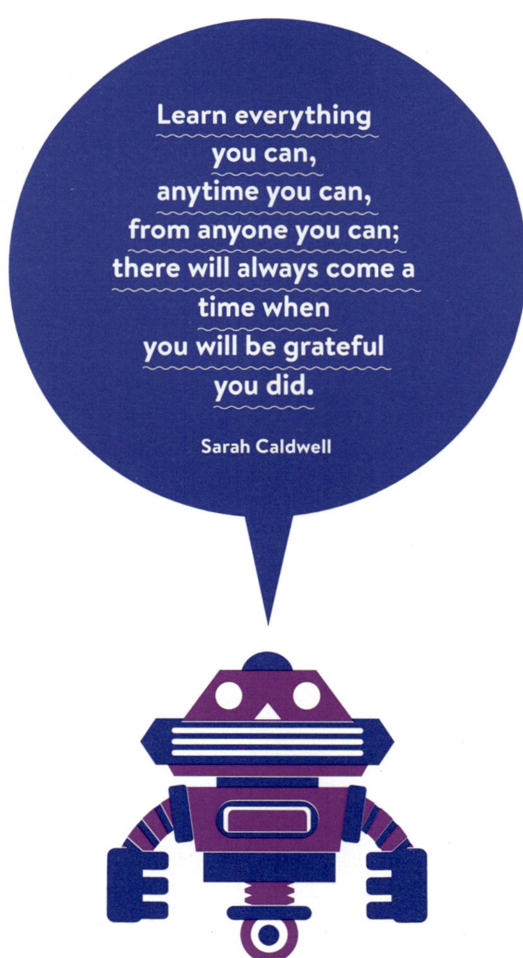

PART 2

One shot voca

abash
[əbǽʃ]
수줍게 하다, 당황하게 하다
to destroy the self-possession or self-confidence of

abbreviate
[əbǽʃ]
(단어, 문장, 글의) 길이를 줄이다
to shorten (a word, phrase, or text)

abolish
[əbáliʃ]
(법률, 제도, 관습 등을) 폐지하다, 없애다
to do away with; annul

abominate
[əbáminèit]
몹시 싫어하다, 증오하다
to detest thoroughly; abhor

abrade
[əbréid]
마모시키다
scrape or wear away by friction or erosion

abridge
[əbrídʒ]
요약하다, 축약하다
to shorten (a book, movie, speech, or other text) without losing the sense

abstract
[æbstrǽkt]
(설명이) 구체적인지 않은, 난해한, 추상적인
thought of or stated without reference to a specific instance; difficult to understand; abstruse

absurd
[əbsə́:d]
이치에 맞지 않는, 불합리한
ridiculously incongruous or unreasonable

accessible
[æksésəbl]
접근성 있는, 이용하기 쉬운, 이해하기 쉬운
able to be reached or entered; able to be easily obtained or used; easily understood

accountability
[əkàuntəbíləti]
책임, 책무
the quality or state of being accountable

accumulate
[əkjú:mjəlèit]
축적하다, 모으다
to gather or pile up; amass

acknowledge
[æknálidʒ, ək-]
인정하다, 알고 있음을 알리다
to accept or admit the existence or truth of; to recognize the fact or importance or quality of

adapt
[ədǽpt]
(필요, 목적 등에) 적응시키다, 개작하다, 각색하다
to make suitable to or fit for a specific use or situation

adept
[ədépt, ǽdept]
솜씨 좋은, 숙련된
very skilled or proficient at something

adhesive
[ədhí:siv]
점착성의; 끈적거리는, 잘 들러붙는; 접착제, 점착성이 있는 것
tending to adhere; sticky

admonish
[ædmániʃ, əd-]
경고하다, 훈계하다
to warn or reprimand someone especially in a gentle, earnest, or solicitous manner; to advise or urge earnestly

adolescent
[ædəlésnt]
성장기에 있는, 성숙하지 못한
(of a young person) in the process of developing from a child into an adult; less mature

adorn
[ədó:rn]
장식하다
to enhance the appearance of especially with beautiful objects; to decorate, embellish, bedeck

adornment
[ədó:rnmənt]
장식, 장신구
the act/something of adorning

adulate
[ǽdʒəlèit]
심하게 아부하다
to praise (someone) excessively or obsequiously

adulation
[ædʒəléiʃn]
심한 아부
excessive flattery or admiration

adulterate
[ədʌltərèit]
불순물을 섞다, (불순물을 섞어) 순도를 떨어뜨리다, 품질을 떨어뜨리다
to make impure by adding extraneous, improper, or inferior ingredients

adversary
[ǽdvərsèri]
적, 원수
one's opponent in a contest, conflict, or dispute

aerial
[eriəl]
공기의, 대기의, 공기로 된, 기체의
of, in, or caused by the air

aesthetics
[esθétiks]
미학
the branch of philosophy that deals with the nature and expression of beauty, as in the fine arts

affect
[əfékt]
영향을 미치다, 감동을 주다, 가장하다, 꾸미다
to act upon, influence; to put on a pretense of

affectation
[æfektéiʃn]
가장, 꾸밈, 허세
a show, pretense, or display

affected
[əféktid]
인위적, 허세부리는, 영향을 받은, 감동한
assumed or simulated to impress others

affinity
[əfínəti]
좋아함, 동감, 유사성
a spontaneous or natural liking or sympathy for someone or something

affix
[əfiks]
첨부하다
to secure to something; attach

afflict
[əflíkt]

괴롭히다, 고통스럽게 하다
to distress so severely, trouble, injure

affluent
[ǽfluənt]

유복한, 풍부한, 엄청나게 많은
plentiful; abundant

agitate
[ǽdʒitéit]

선동하다, (마음을) 어지럽히다, 괴롭히다, 휘젓다, 출렁이게 하다
to campaign to arouse public concern about an issue in the hope
of prompting action; to make (someone) troubled or nervous

agonize
[ǽgənáz]

몹시 괴로워하다, 몸부림치다, 번민하다
to suffer extreme pain or great anguish

agony
[ǽgəni]

큰 고통, 심한 동요
extreme physical or mental suffering

aid
[eid]

돕다, 조력하다, 촉진하다
to furnish with help, support, or relief

agreeable
[əgríːəbl]

상쾌한, 적절한, 동의하는
to one's liking; pleasing

alienate
[éiljənèit, -liə-]

멀리하다, 사귀지 않다, 소외시키다, 양도하다
to make unfriendly, hostile, or indifferent especially where
attachment formerly existed; to transfer the ownership of

align
[əláin]

제휴시키다, 연합하다, 정렬하다
to come together in alliance; place in a straight line; to put
(things) into correct or appropriate relative positions

allay
[əléi]

(두려움, 의심, 염려 등을) 가라앉히다, (고통을) 완화시키다
to diminish (fear, suspicion, or worry), relieve or alleviate (pain or
hunger)

allusive
[əlúːsiv]
암시하는, 넌지시 가리키는
containing or characterized by indirect references

altruistic
[æltruːístik]
이타적인, 이타주의적인
showing or of unselfish regard for or devotion to the welfare of others

amalgamate
[əmǽlgəmèit]
혼합시키다, 융합시키다
to combine or unite to form one organization or structure

amass
[əmǽs]
모으다, (재산 등을) 축적하다
to gather together for oneself, as for one's pleasure or profit; accumulate

amenable
[əmíːnəbl]
잘 따르는, 순종적인
open and responsive to suggestion; easily persuaded or controlled

amend
[əménd]
고치다, 개선하다; 수정하다, 개정하다
to change or modify for the better

amplify
[ǽmplifài]
확대하다, 증대하다, 증강하다
to make larger or more powerful; increase

analogous
[ənǽləgəs]
유사한
similar

anchor
[ǽŋkə]
고정시키다, 정박시키다; 닻, 고정 장치
to hold fast by or as if by an anchor

annotate
[ǽnətèit]
주석를 달다, 주해를 달다
to furnish (a literary work) with critical commentary or explanatory notes; gloss

antiquated
[ǽntikwèitid]
오래된, 고풍스런, 시대에 뒤진
old, obsolete, being out of style

aphorism
[ǽfərìzm]
경구, 금언, 격언
a pithy statement that contains a general truth

aphoristic
[æfərístik]
경구적인, 금언의
of a tersely phrased statement of a truth or opinion

apocalyptic
[əpákəlíptik(əl)]
종말론적인, 계시적인, 중요한
ultimately decisive, climactic, critical, momentous; foreboding
imminent disaster or final doom, horrible, terrible

apparel
[əpǽrəl]
의복, 복장
clothing, especially outer garments; attire

appoint
[əpɔ́int]
임명하다, 지명하다, 지정하다
to select or designate to fill an office or position

appraise
[əpréiz]
감정하다, 가치를 평가하다
to assess the value or quality of

appreciable
[əprí:ʃiəbl]
상당한, 쉽게 알아볼 수 있는
large or important enough to be noticed

appreciate
[əprí:ʃièit]
(가치를) 정당하게 평가하다, 이해하다, 감사하다, 시세를 올리다, 가격을 올리다
to recognize the quality, significance, or magnitude of

apprehend
[æprihénd]
체포하다, 이해하다, 두려워하다
seize, arrest; understand, grasp; anticipate (something) with
uneasiness or fear

apprehension
[æprihénʃn]
이해, 두려움
fearful or uneasy anticipation of the future; dread

apprehensive
[æprihénsiv]
이해가 빠른, 명석한, 걱정하는, 두려워하는
anxious or fearful about the future; uneasy

apprise
[əpràiz]
정보를 주다, 알려주다
to inform or tell (someone)

arbiter
[á:rbətər]
중재자, 결정자, 권위자
a person who settles a dispute or has ultimate authority in a matter; a person or agency whose judgment or opinion is considered authoritative

archaic
[a:rkéiik]
고대의, 고풍스러운, 구식의
very old or old-fashioned, antiquated

arouse
[əráuz]
깨우다, 유발하다, 자극하다
to awaken from or as if from sleep; to stir up

arrogant
[ǽrəgənt]
오만한, 터무니 없는, 무례한
having or revealing an exaggerated sense of one's own importance or abilities

arresting
[əréstiŋ]
주의를 끄는, 흥미를 끄는, 눈에 띄는
attracting and holding the attention; striking

articulate
[a:rtíkjulət]
똑똑히 발음된, 명확한; 똑똑하게 발음하다
having or showing the ability to speak clearly, fluently and coherently

assertive
[əsə́:rtiv]
주장이 강한, 단정적인, 공격적인
inclined to bold or confident assertion; aggressively self-assured

assess
[əsés]
평가하다, 부과하다, 매기다
to evaluate or estimate the nature, ability, or quality of

assorted
[əsɔ́:rtid]
여러 구색을 갖춘, 가지각색의, 조화된, 어울리는
consisting of various kinds

assume
[əsú:m]
가정하다, (권력, 의무 등을) 떠맡다, 가장하다
to suppose to be the case, without proof; take or begin to have
(power or responsibility) take on (a specified quality, appearance,
or extent)

assumption
[əsʌ́mpʃn]
가정, 전제, 떠맡기, 인수, 거만, 뻔뻔스러움
the act of taking to or upon oneself

astounding
[əstáundiŋ]
크게 놀라게 하는, 놀라운, 대경실색 하게 하는
bewildering

astringent
[əstríndʒənt]
수축시키는, 신랄한, (맛, 냄새 등의) 신, 떫은
sharp or severe in manner or style; (of taste or smell) sharp or bitter

asylum
[əsàiləm]
(정치범, 난민, 정신병자 등의) 보호시설, 피난처
the protection granted by a nation to someone who has left their
native country as a political refugee

asymmetrical
[èisimétrik]
비대칭의
having no balance or symmetry

attentive
[əténtiv]
주의를 기울이는, 경청하는, 배려하는, 정중한, 상냥한
assiduously attending to the comfort or wishes of others; very
polite or courteous

attenuate
[əténjuèit]
가늘게 하다, 약화시키다
to reduce in thickness; make thin; to reduce the force, effect, or
value of

attribute
[ətríbjuːt]
기인한다고 생각하다, 결과라고 생각하다, 원인이 있다고 보다
to relate to a particular cause or source; ascribe

audacious
[ɔːdéiʃəs]
대담한, 무모한
showing a willingness to take surprisingly bold risks; showing an impudent lack of respect

audible
[ɔ́ːdəbl]
(소리가) 들리는
able to be heard

augment
[ɔːgmént]
증대시키다, 증가하다
to make (something) greater by adding to it; increase

austere
[ɔːstíər]
엄격한, 금욕적인, 꾸밈없는, 소박한
severe or strict in manner, attitude, or appearance

authenticity
[ɔːθentísəti]
진짜임, 확실성, 신뢰성
the quality of being authentic; genuineness

authenticate
[ɔːθéntikèit]
(진짜임을) 입증하다
to prove or serve to prove the authenticity of

authoritarian
[ɔːθɔ́ːrətέəriən]
독재적인, 권위주의적인
of, relating to, or favoring blind submission to authority

authoritative
[əθɔ́ːrətèitiv]
권위 있는, 정식의, 당국의
having or proceeding from authority

autocratic
[ɔːtəkrǽtik]
전제의, 독재적인
of a ruler having unlimited power; of a despot

autonomous
[ɔːtáːnəməs]
자치권을 가진
not controlled by others or by outside forces; independent

autonomy
[ɔ:tánəmi]

자율성, 자치권, 자립
the quality or state of being self-governing; self-directing freedom and especially moral independence

avenge
[əvéndʒ]

복수하다
to inflict harm in return for (an injury or wrong done to oneself or another)

axiom
[ǽksiəm]

자명한 명제, 원칙, 원리, 금언
a self-evident or universally recognized truth; a maxim

axiomatic
[æksiəmǽtik(əl)]

자명한
self-evident or unquestionable

babble
[bǽbl]

재잘거리다, 옹알거리다; 분명치 않은 말, 허튼소리
to talk rapidly and continuously in a foolish, excited, or incomprehensible way

badger
[bǽdʒər]

(계속해서) 괴롭히다, 졸라대다
to harass or annoy persistently; to ask (someone) repeatedly and annoyingly for something; to pester

baffle
[bǽfl]

당황하게 하다, 어리둥절하게 하다
to bewilder or perplex totally

banal
[bənǽl]

진부한
lacking in originality, freshness, or novelty

baneful
[béinfəl]

파멸시키는, 멸망을 가져오는; 해로운, 치명적인, 독이 있는
causing death, destruction, or ruin; harmful

banish
[bǽniʃ]

추방하다
to force to leave a country or place by official decree; exile

barefaced
[bέərfèist]
뻔뻔스런, 숨김없는
shameless; undisguised

barren
[bǽrən]
열매 맺지 않는, 수확이 없는, 불임의, 메마른, 무능한
(land) too poor to produce much or any vegetation

base
[béis]
(도덕적으로) 상스러운, 천한, 비열한; 기초, 토대; 기초를 쌓다
without moral principles

bearish
[bέːəriʃ]
(시세가) 하락세인, 약세인; (경기의 전망이) 비관적인, 곰 같은, 난폭한
causing, expecting, or characterized by falling stock-market prices; pessimistic

befitting
[bifítiŋ]
안성맞춤의, 적합한
appropriate; suitable

begrudge
[bigrʌ́dʒ]
시샘하다, (주기 싫은데) 억지로 주다, 아까워하다, 꺼리다
to envy, to wish that someone did not have; to give reluctantly or resentfully

belie
[bilài]
잘못을 드러내다, 모순되다
(of an appearance) fail to give a true notion or impression of; disguise or contradict; fail to fulfill or justify (a claim or expectation)

bend
[bend]
굽히다, 구부리다, (눈, 귀, 걸음 등을) 향하다, (마음, 정력 등을) 쏟다, 기울이다
to bring (something) into a state of tension

bent
[bént]
경향, 성향, 능력; 굽은, 구부러진, (특정 방향으로) 향한
a special inclination or capacity

betray
[bitréi]
배신하다, 배반하다, 은연중에 드러내다, 폭로하다
to be disloyal to; to reveal unintentionally

better
[bétə(r)]

개선하다, 향상시키다; 더 좋은; 더 좋게; 더 좋은 것
to make better; improve

bewilder
[biwíldər]

당황하게 하다, 어리둥절하게 하다
to cause (someone) to become perplexed and confused

bewitch
[biwitʃ]

마술 걸다, 매혹시키다
to cast a spell on and gain control over (someone) by magic;
enchant and delight (someone)

bias
[báiəs]

편파적인 태도, 선입견; 선입견을 품게 하다
a particular tendency or inclination, especially one that prevents
unprejudiced consideration of a question; prejudice

biting
[bàitiŋ]

신랄한, 통렬한, 물어뜯는, 얼얼한, 자극적인
keen, smarting, nipping, sarcastic; able to grip and impress deeply

bizarre
[bizá:r]

이상한, 별난
strikingly out of the ordinary

bland
[blænd]

온화한, 상냥한
characterized by a moderate, unperturbed, or tranquil quality,
especially

blemish
[blémiʃ]

흠, 결점, 오점
a small mark or flaw that spoils the appearance of something; a
moral defect or fault

bliss
[blís]

지극한 행복, 더 없는 기쁨, 만족
complete happiness

blunder
[blʌ́ndər]

실수하다, (일을) 그르치다; 큰 실수, 큰 실책
to make a mistake through stupidity, ignorance

blunt
[blʌnt]

통명스럽고 직설적인, (칼, 연필 등이) 무딘, 무뚝뚝한
uncompromisingly forthright and direct; having a worn-down edge or point; not sharp

blur
[blə:(r)]

흐리게 하다, 더럽히다; 더러움, 얼룩, 흐릿함
to make indistinct and hazy in outline or appearance; obscure; to smear or stain; smudge

bluster
[blʌ́stəriŋ]

호통치다, 허세부리며 큰소리로 말하다, (바람, 파도 등이) 몰아치다; (파도, 바람 등이) 거칠게 몰아침, 소란함, 허세
talking in a loud, aggressive or indignant way

boast
[bóust]

자랑하다, 허풍 떨다; 자랑, 허풍
speak of or assert with excessive pride

bogus
[bóugəs]

가짜의
not genuine or true; fake

bolster
[bóulstər]

지탱하다, 지지하다, 강화하다, 받치다
to support or strengthen; to prop up

border (on)
[bó:rdər]

~에 가깝다, 접해 있다
be close to (an extreme condition)

boycott
[bóikat]

배척하다, 참가를 거부하다, 구매를 거부하다
to act together in abstaining from using, buying, or dealing with as an expression of protest or disfavor or as a means of coercion

brag
[bræg]

자랑하다, 뽐내다; 자랑, 허세
to talk boastfully

bravado
[brəvá:dou]

허세, 무모함
a bold manner or a show of boldness intended to impress or intimidate

breach
[bríːtʃ]

(법, 약속 등을) 위반하다, 어기다, (방흐벽, 제방 등에) 구멍 뚫다, 파괴하다;
위반, 불이해, 갈라진 틈, 단절, 불화
to break or fail to observe (a law, agreement, or code of conduct);
to make a gap in and break through (a wall, barrier, or defense)

breakthrough
[breikθrùː]

돌파구, (과학 등) 큰 발전
a sudden advance especially in knowledge or technique

bribe
[braib]

뇌물을 주다; 뇌물, 미끼
to give, offer, or promise a bribe to; to gain influence over or
corrupt by bribery

buffer
[bʌ́fə(r)]

(충격, 위험 등을) 막다, 덜다, (아픔을) 완화하다; 완충기
something that lessens or absorbs the shock of an impact;
to act as a buffer for or between

bullish
[búliʃ]

(시세가) 상승세의, 강세의, (경기 등의) 전망이 밝은, 황소 같은, 완고한
causing, expecting, or characterized by rising stock market prices;
optimistic or confident

bully
[búli]

약한 자를 괴롭히는 사람, 불량배; 못살게 굴다, 협박하다
a person who uses strength or power to harm or intimidate those
who are weaker

burgeon
[bə́ːrdʒən]

급성장하다, 싹트다
to begin to grow or increase rapidly; flourish

burnish
[bə́ːrniʃ]

(닦아서) 광내다; 광택, 윤
to polish (something, esp. metal) by rubbing

busybody
[bíizibàdi]

참견쟁이
a person who meddles or pries into the affairs of others

calcify
[kǽlsifài]
석회화하다, 경화시키다
to make or become inflexible and unchanging

calculated
[kǽlkjulèitid]
계산된, 계획된, 의도된
deliberate, carefully planned or intended

callous
[kǽləs]
(잔인할 정도로) 무관심한, 냉담한, 무감각한, 굳어진; 굳어지다, 무감각하게 되다
showing or having an insensitive and cruel disregard for others

camouflage
[kǽməflá:ʒ]
위장하다; 위장, 속임
mimic and hide, disguise n. the disguising especially of military
equipment or installations with paint, nets, or foliage

candid
[kǽndid]
솔직한
free from prejudice; impartial; frank

candor
[kǽndər]
솔직함
the quality of being open and honest in expression; frankness

cantankerous
[kæntǽŋkərəs]
성미 급한, 곧잘 싸우는, 심술궂은, 고약한
ill-tempered and quarrelsome; disagreeable

capability
[kèipəbíləti]
능력, 적응성, 가능성
power or ability

captivate
[kǽptəvèit]
매료시키다, 마음을 사로잡다
to attract and hold the interest and attention of; charm

carefree
[kέərfrì:]
걱정 근심이 없는
free from anxiety or responsibility

casualty
[kǽʒuəlti]
(사건, 사고 등의) 사상자, 부상자
a person killed or injured in a war or accident

catalyst
[kǽtəlist]

촉매제, 자극, 계기
a substance, usually used in small amounts relative to the reactants, that modifies and increases the rate of a reaction without being consumed in the process

catalyze
[kǽtəlàiz]

촉매작용하다, 촉진시키다
to cause or accelerate (a reaction) by acting as a catalyst

categorical
[kætəgɔ́:rik(əl)]

절대적인, 무조건의, 명확한
absolute, unqualified

cater (to)
[kéitər]

음식물을 조달하다, (요구, 필요를) 제공하다, 맞추다, 만족시키려 애쓰다
to provide with what is needed or required; try to satisfy (a need or demand)

causality
[kɔ:zǽləti]

인과관계, 인과성
the principle of or relationship between cause and effect

caustic
[kɔ́:stik]

신랄한, 부식성의
sarcastic in a scathing and bitter way

censorship
[sénsərʃip]

검열
the practice of officially examining books, movies, etc., and suppressing unacceptable parts

ceremonious
[sèrəmóuniəs]

의식의, 지나치게 격식을 갖춘
according to grand and formal usage or prescribed procedures

certitude
[sə́:rtətjù:d]

확신
absolute certainty or conviction that something is the case

challenge
[tʃǽlindʒ]

도전하다, 이의를 제기하다, 요구하다; 도전, 이의, 항의
to invite (someone) to do something that one thinks will be difficult or impossible, dare; to dispute the truth or validity of

chaos
[kéias]
무질서, 혼란 상태
a condition or place of great disorder or confusion

charitable
[tʃǽrətəbl]
자비로운, 인정이 많은
mild or tolerant in judging others; lenient

chauvinism
[ʃóuvənìzm]
맹목적인 애국심, 열렬한 성차별주의
exaggerated or aggressive patriotism; excessive or prejudiced
loyalty or support for one's own cause, group, or gender

cherish
[tʃériʃ]
소중히 여기다, 마음에 품다, 잊지 않고 있다
to protect and care for (someone) lovingly

chic
[ʃi(:)k]
멋진, 세련된, 맵시있는; 맵시있음, 고상함, 독특한 스타일
conforming to the current fashion; stylish

chuckle
[tʃʌkl]
(만족스럽게) 킬킬 웃다, 소리 없이 웃다, (어떤 상태를) 재미있어 하다;
킬킬거리는 웃음
to laugh quietly or to oneself

cipher
[sàifər]
암호
a secret or disguised way of writing

civility
[sivíləti]
공손함
formal politeness and courtesy in behavior or speech

clairvoyant
[klɛərvɔ́iənt]
천리안이 있는, 통찰력이 있는; 천리안, 통찰력이 있는 사람
having clairvoyance: able to see beyond the range of ordinary
perception

clandestine
[klændéstin]
비밀의, 은밀한
kept secret or done secretively, esp. because illicit

cleave
[klíːv]

쪼개다, 가르며 나아가다, (~ to) 지키다, 고수하다, 엉겨붙다
to split or sever; to stick fast (tc)

cliché
[kliːʃéi, kli-]

진부한 표현; 진부한
a phrase or opinion that is overused and betrays a lack of original thought

coalesce
[kòuəlés]

합쳐지다, 하나가 되다
to come together and form one mass or whole

coarse
[kɔ́ːrs]

조악한, 거친, (사람이) 저속한
rough or loose in texture or grain; (of a person or a person's speech) rude, crude, or vulgar

codify
[kádəfài]

성문화하다
to arrange (laws or rules) into a systematic code

coercion
[kouə́ːrs]

강요, 강제
practice of persuading (an unwilling person) to do something by using force or threats

cogent
[kóudʒənt]

설득력 있는, 적절한
(of an argument or case) clear, logical, and convincing

cognizance
[káːgnizəns]

알고 있음; 인식, 지식, 지각
conscious knowledge or recognition; awareness

coincidence
[kouínsidəns]

동시 발생, 우연
a remarkable concurrence of events or circumstances without apparent causal connection

coincidental
[kouínsidentl]

동시발생의, (우연히) 일치한
happening or existing at the same time

color
[kʌ́lər]
빛깔; 색칠하다, 착색하다, 윤색하다, 왜곡하다
to give a distinctive character or quality to; modify

colossal
[kəlá:sl]
거대한, 광대한, 대량의
of a size, extent, or degree that elicits awe or taxes belief;
immense

combustible
[kəmbʌ́stəbl]
가연성의, 불붙기 쉬운, 흥분하기 쉬운; 가연성 물질
able to catch fire and burn easily

commitment
[kəmítmənt]
약속, 의무, 헌신
an act of committing to a charge or trust

commodious
[kəmóudiəs]
넓은, 널찍한
roomy and comfortable, convenient

commonplace
[kámənplèis]
진부한; 진부한 문구
not unusual, ordinary; a trite saying or topic; a platitude

compatible
[kəmpǽtəbl]
양립하는, 조화를 이루는
capable of existing together in harmony

compelling
[kəmpélin]
강제적인, 주목하지 않을 수 없는, 매우 흥미로운, 매력 있는, 설득력 있는
evoking interest, attention, or admiration in a powerfully
irresistible way; not able to be refuted; inspiring conviction

complacence
[kəmpléisəns(i)]
자기만족
a feeling of uncritical satisfaction with oneself or one's
achievements

complaisant
[kəmpléisns]
정중한, 유순한, 남을 기쁘게 해주려는
willing to please others; obliging; agreeable

complementary
[kà:mpliméntəri]
보충하는, 보완하는; 보색
forming or serving as a complement; completing

compliment
[ká:mplimənt]
찬사, 칭찬하는 말, 아첨, 안부; 찬사를 던지다, 아첨하다, 경의를 표하다
an expression of praise, admiration, or congratulation;
to show fondness, regard, or respect for by giving a gift or
performing a favor

conceal
[kənsí:l]
감추다, 보이지 않게 하다
to keep from being seen, found observed, or discovered; hide

conciliate
[kənsílièit]
화해시키다, 달래다
to regain (friendship or goodwill) by pleasant behavior, to r
econcile; to stop (someone) from being angry or discontented

conciliatory
[kənsílièto:ri]
화해시키는, 달래는, 회유적인 융화적인
making or attempt to make compatible

concordant
[kankó:rdnt,kən-]
조화하는, 일치하는
in agreement, consistent

condensed
[kəndénst]
요약된, 응축된
expressed in fewer words; made concise

condescend
[kàndəsénd]
(우월함을 드러내며) 생색내다 오만하게 행동하다
to show feelings of superiority, patronize; to do something in a
haughty way, as though it is below one's dignity or level of
importance

confidential
[kànfədénʃəl]
기밀의
intended to be kept secret

confine
[kənfáin]
제한하다, 가두다
to restrain or forbid someone from leaving (a place)

congenial
[kəndʒíːnjəl]
(사람과) 마음이 통하는, 친근한, (장소 등이) 마음에 드는
pleasant because of a personality, qualities, or interests that are similar to one's own

conjunction
[kəndʒʌ́ŋkʃən]
결합, 연결, 공동, 연대
the act of joining or the condition of being joined; an instance of two or more events or things occurring at the same point in time or space

conscious
[káːnʃəs]
의식을 가지는, 자각하고 있는, 의식하고 있는
having an awareness of one's environment and one's own existence, sensations, and thoughts

consequential
[kɔnsəkwénʃəl]
결과적으로 일어나는, 필연적인, 중요한, 중대한
following as an effect, result, or conclusion; consequent; having important consequences; significant

considerable
[kənsídərəbl]
상당한, 주목할만한, 중요한
notably large in size, amount, or extent; worthy of respect, attention, etc., important; distinguished

console
[kənsóul]
위로하다, 격려하다
to comfort (someone) at a time of grief or disappointment

consonance
[kánsənəns(i)]
일치, 조화, 화음
agreement, harmony, accord; a simultaneous combination of sounds

constitute
[káːnstətùːt]
구성하다, 조성하다, 설립하다, 선임하다
to be the elements or parts of; compose

constrain
[kənstréin]
억압하다, 억제하다, (한가지 일만 하도록) 강제하다
severely restrict the scope, extent, or activity of; compel or force (someone) toward a particular course of action

contemplate
[ká:ntəmplèit]

심사 숙고하다
to consider carefully and at length; meditate on or ponder

contend
[kənténd]

싸우다, 다투다, 논쟁하다, 주장하다
to struggle in opposition; to compete; to strive in debate, dispute earnestly; to assert something as a position in an argument

content
[ká:ntent]

만족(감), 내용(물); 만족하고 있는, 불평이 없는; 만족시키다, 만족하다
contentment; satisfaction; desiring no more than what one has; satisfied; to make content or satisfied

contention
[kənténʃn]

다툼, 논쟁
the act or an instance of striving in controversy or debate

contentious
[kənténʃəs]

다투기 좋아하는, 논쟁하기 좋아하는
heated disagreement; assertion

contest
[kántest]

다투다, 논쟁하다; 다툼, 경쟁, 논쟁
to engage in competition to attain (a position of power); to engage in dispute about

contract
[ká:ntrækt]

긴장시키다, 축소하다, (병에) 걸리다, (채무, 의무 등을) 발생시키다. 초래하다; 계약(서)
to acquire or incur; to enter into or make an agreement

contrive
[kəntràiv]

고안하다, 꾸며내다
to create or bring about (an object or a situation) by deliberate use of skill and artifice

controvert
[kántrəvə́:rt]

부인하다, 반박하다
to deny the truth of (something)

conundrum
[kənʌ́ndrəm]
난제, 수수께끼
a confusing and difficult problem or question

conventional
[kənvénʃənl]
틀에 박힌, 진부한, 평범한, 전통적인, 집회의
based on or in accordance with general agreement, use, or practice, customary; conforming to established practice or accepted standards, traditional

convergence
[kənvə́:rdʒəns(i)]
합침, 집합, 집중
process or state of converging

convey
[kənvéi]
전달하다, 나르다
to take or carry from one place to another; transport

conviction
[kənvíkʃən]
확신, 신념, 유죄판결
a fixed or strong belief

corporate
[kɔ́:rpərət]
법인의; 집합적인, 단체의
formed into a corporation; incorporated

correlate
[kɔ́:rəlèit]
상관관계에 있다, 서로 연관시키다; 상호 관계에 있는 것의 한쪽
to have a mutual relationship or connection, in which one thing affects or depends on another; to establish or demonstrate as having a correlation

correspond
[kɔ́:rəspánd]
부합하다, 상응하다, 서신을 교환하다
to have a close similarity; to match or agree almost exactly; to communicate by exchanging letters

corrupt
[kərʌ́pt]
부정한, 타락한, 뇌물을 좋아하는; 매수하다, 부패시키다
marked by immorality and perversion; depraved

cosmopolitan
[kà:zməpa:litən]
전 세계에 걸친, 전 세계적인
pertinent or common to the whole world

counterpoint
[káuntərpóint]

대위법, 대조되는 것; 대치에 의해 강조하다
(the art of writing) a melody played in conjunction with another;
an argument, idea, or theme used to create a contrast with the
main element

counterproductive
[kàuntərprədʌ́ktiv]

비생산적인, 역효과의
having the opposite of the desired effect

countless
[káuntləs]

헤아릴 수 없는, 무수한
incapable of being counted; innumerable

court
[kɔːrt]

구애하다, 호의를 얻으려 하다, (재난 등을) 초래하다; 법원, 궁정, 안마당
to pay special attention to (someone) in an attempt to win their
support or favor; to risk incurring (misfortune) because of the
way one behaves

coward
[káuərd]

겁많은, 소심한, 용기가 없는, 공포에 기인하는; 겁쟁이, 비겁자
showing ignoble fear in the face of danger or pain

coy
[kɔi]

부끄러운척하는, 조신한척하는, 수줍어하는
making a pretense of shyness or modesty that is intended to be
alluring but is often regarded as irritating

cranky
[krǽŋki]

꾀까다로운, 화를 잘 내는, 마음이 비뚤어진, 심술궂은
having a bad disposition; peevish

crave
[kreiv]

갈망하다, 열망하다, 몹시 하고 싶어하다
to have an intense desire for

creep
[kríːp]

살금살금 걷다, 기다; 기기
to move slowly and carefully, esp in order to avoid being heard or
noticed

crescendo
[kriʃéndou]
점점 세어지기, 최고점; 점점 세어지는; 세어지다
gradually increasing in volume, force, or intensity

criterion
[kraitíəriən]
표준, 기준
a standard, rule, or test on which a judgment or decision can be based

crucial
[krúːʃl]
결정적인, 매우 중대한, 힘든, 어려운
extremely significant or important

crumble
[krʌ́mbl]
바스러지다, (건물, 땅 등이) 허물어지다
to break or fall apart into small fragments

cultivate
[kʌ́ltivèit]
갈다, 경작하다, 교화하다, 계발하다, (예술, 과학, 산업 등을) 장려하다, 육성하다
to improve and prepare (land), as by plowing or fertilizing, for raising crops; till; to form and refine, as by education

cumbersome
[kʌ́mbərsəm]
부담이 되는, 성가신, (가구, 장비 등이) 거추장스러운, 둔중한
difficult to handle because of weight or bulk

cunning
[kʌ́niŋ]
교활한, 교묘한; 속임수, 정직하지 않음, 교활함, 간사함
crafty, deceitful; skill in achieving one's ends by deceit; ingenuity

curative
[kjúrətiv]
병에 듣는, 병을 고치는 (힘이 있는), 치료상의; 치유력, 의약, 치료법
serving or tending to cure

curb
[kəːrb]
억제하다; 연석, 억제, 구속
to restrain or keep in check

curse
[kəːrs]
저주, 저주의 말, 주문(을 외기); 저주하다, 욕하다
an appeal or prayer for evil or misfortune to befall someone or something

cynical
[sínikəl]

냉소적인, 의심하는
scornful of the motives, virtue, or integrity of others

damp
[dæmp]

약하게 하다, 끄다; (활력, 열의 등을) 감소시키다, 꺾다, 둔화시키다; (행동을) 저지하다; (사람을) 낙담시키다; 습한, 축축한; 습기, 물기, 실망, 낙담
to restrain or check; discourage

dampen
[dǽmpən]

축축하게 하다; (활력, 열의) 꺾다
to make less strong or intense; reduce the amplitude of (a sound source)

dated
[déitid]

구식의, 오래된, 날짜가 적힌
old-fashioned, outdated

daunt
[dɔːnt]

위협하다, 겁나게 하다
to make (someone) feel intimidated or apprehensive

dauntless
[dɔ́ːntlis]

겁 없는
showing fearlessness and determination

dazzle
[dǽzl]

눈부시게 하다, (아름다움으로) 압도하다; 빛남, 눈부심
to (of a bright light) blind (a person) temporarily; to amaze or overwhelm (someone) with a particular impressive quality

deaden
[dédən]

(감각, 움직임 등을) 무디게 하다, 둔하게 하다, 말라죽게 하다
to render less intense, sensitive, or vigorous

dearth
[dəːrθ]

부족, 결핍, 기근
a lack

debilitate
[dibílətèit]

쇠약하게 만들다
to make (someone) weak and infirm

deceleration 감속
[diːsèləréiʃən] reduction of speed; slowing down

decline 쇠퇴하다, 거절하다; 내리막 경사, 감퇴
[dikláin] to become smaller, fewer, or less; decrease; to politely refuse (an invitation or offer)

decode 암호를 번역하다, 해독하다
[diːkóud] to convert from code into plain text

defame 명예를 훼손하다, 중상하다, 비방하다
[diféim] to damage the reputation, character, or good name of by slander or libel

deficiency 부족, 결점
[difíʃənsi] a lack or shortage; a failing or shortcoming

deficient 부족한
[difíʃənt] lacking an essential quality or element

definitive 명확한, 최종적인, 결론적인; (문법) 한정어
[difínətiv] precisely defined or explicit; conclusive; authoritative and complete

deleterious 해로운
[dèlitíəriəs] causing harm and damage

deliberation 심사숙고, 합의, 토의
[dilìbəréiʃən] long and careful consideration or discussion; slow and careful movement or thought

delude 속이다, 기만하다
[dilúːd] to impose a misleading belief upon (someone); to deceive, fool

demeanor
[dimíːnər]
행실, 처신, 품행
the way in which a person behaves

demography
[dimágrəfi]
인구통계학, 인구구성
the study of statistics such as births, deaths, income, or the incidence of disease, which illustrate the changing structure of human populations; the composition of a particular human population

demonstrable
[démənstrəbl]
논증할 수 있는, 증명할 수 있는, 명백한
capable of being demonstrated or proved

demystify
[diːmístəfài]
(신비함, 편견 등을) 없애다, 이해하기 쉽게 설명하다
to make (a difficult or esoteric subject) clearer and easier to understand

depict
[dipíkt]
(그림, 조각 등에 의해) 표현하다, 그리다, 묘사하다
to represent in words; describe

derivative
[dirívətiv]
유도된, 이끌어낸, 파생된; 유도물, 파생물
resulting from or employing derivation

disrepute
[dìsripjúːt]
불명예, 악평
the state of being held in low esteem by the public

designate
[dézignèit]
지정하다, 지명하다
to appoint (someone) to a specified position

despicable
[déspikəbl, dispík-]
경멸스러운, 비열한, 야비한
deserving hatred and contempt

despise
[dispàiz]
경멸하다
to feel contempt or a deep repugnance for

detain
[ditéin]
붙들다, 지체시키다, 구류하다
to hold or keep in or as if in custody

determinant
[dité:rmənənt]
결정 요인; 결정하는, 결정적인
a factor that decisively affects the nature or outcome of something

deterministic
[ditə:rmənístik]
결정론의, 결정론적인
of the philosophical doctrine that every state of affairs, including every human event, act, and decision is the inevitable consequence of antecedent states of affairs

detrimental
[dètrəméntl]
해로운, 이롭지 못한; 방해자, 방해물
causing harm and damage

devitalize
[di:váitəlàiz]
활력을 빼앗다, 약화시키다, 무기력하게 하다
to diminish or destroy the strength or vitality of

devout
[diváut]
(사람이) 경건한, 독실한, (기도 등이) 경건한 마음을 나타내는
displaying reverence or piety

dexterous
[dékstərəs]
솜씨 좋은, 능숙한, 오른손잡이의
demonstrating neat skill, esp. with the hands

didactic
[daidǽktik(əl)]
가르치기 위한, 교훈적인
intended to teach, particularly in having moral instruction as an ulterior motive

diehard
[dáihà:rd]
완강하게 저항하는; 완고한 보수주의자, 옹고집쟁이
stubbornly resisting change or clinging to a seemingly hopeless or outdated cause; a person who strongly opposes change or who continues to support something in spite of opposition

differentiate
[dìfərénʃièit]
구별하다, 식별하다
to recognize or give expression to a difference

dilate
[daitéit]
확장되다; 장황하게 말하다
to make or become wider, larger, or more open; to (dilate on) speak or write at length on (a subject)

dilatory
[dílətɔ:ri]
행동이 느린, 늑장부리는
slow to act

dilute
[dailú:t, di-]
묽게 하다, 약화시키다; 효력이 약화된, 희석된, 묽은
to make (a liquid) thinner or weaker by adding water or another solvent to it; to make (something) weaker in force, content, or value by modifying it or adding other elements to it

diplomatic
[dìpləmǽtik]
외교의, 외교적인, 수완이 있는, 능숙한, 능란한
having or showing an ability to deal with people in a sensitive and effective way

disciplinary
[dísəplinèri]
징계의, 훈련의, 단련을 위한
designed to correct or punish breaches of discipline

disciplined
[dísəplind]
규율을 따르는, 기강을 따르는, 훈련된, 단련된
marked by or possessing discipline

disclosure
[disklóuʒər]
폭로
the action of making new or secret information known

disconsolate
[diskɔ́:nsələt]
어두운, 우울한, 불행한, 절망적인
cheerless; gloomy

discordant
[diskɔ́:rdənt]
불협화음의, 조화를 이루지 못하는
(of sounds) harsh and jarring because of a lack of harmony; disagreeing or incongruous

discreet
[diskríːt]
신중한, 조심스러운
careful and circumspect in one's speech or actions in order to avoid causing offense

discriminate
[diskrímənèit]
분간하다, 식별하다, 차별하다
to make a clear distinction; distinguish

discriminating
[diskrímənèitiŋ]
식별력 있는, 안목이 있는, 차별적인
making a distinction, discerning

disgruntled
[disgrʌ́ntld]
화난, 불만족한
angry or dissatisfied

disguise
[disgáiz]
변장시키다, 위장시키다; 변장, 위장, 속임수
to modify the manner or appearance of in order to prevent recognition

disinfect
[dìsinfékt]
살균 소독하다
to clean (something) with a disinfectant in order to destroy bacteria

disingenuous
[dìsindʒénjuəs]
솔직하지 않은, 부정직한
not candid or sincere

disintegrate
[disíntəgrèit]
붕괴시키다, 분해시키다, 해체시키다
to (cause to) break up into small parts, typically as the result of impact or decay

dislocate
[dísloukèit]
(관절을) 탈구시키다, 위치를 바꾸다, 뒤죽박죽으로 만들다, 교란시키다
to disturb the normal arrangement or position of (something, typically a joint in the body)

dispatch
[dispǽtʃ]
급파하다, 파견하다
to relegate to a specific destination or send on specific business

dispensable
[dispénsəbl]
없어도 되는
capable of being dispensed with

displace
[displéis]
(위치 등을) 옮기다, 바꾸다, 강제 이주시키다, 대신하다
to move or shift from the usual place or position, especially to force to leave a homeland; dislodge

disputable
[dispjú:təbl, díspjut-]
논쟁의 여지가 있는
not established as fact, and so open to question or debate

disrupt
[disrʌ́pt]
방해하여 중단시키다, 파괴하다
to interrupt the normal course or unity of

dissemble
[disémbl]
속이다, 가장하다, 꾸미다
to conceal one's true motives, feelings, or beliefs

dissent
[disént]
의견을 달리하다, 반대하다; 의견의 차이, 불찬성
to hold or express opinions that are at variance with those previously, commonly, or officially expressed

dissolve
[dizálv]
녹이다, 용액으로 만들다, 무효화하다, 폐기하다
to cause to pass into solution; to dismiss

dissonance
[dísənəns]
불협화음, 불일치, 부조화
lack of harmony among musical notes

distend
[disténd]
부풀게 하다, 확장시키다
to cause (something) to swell by stretching it from inside

distill
[distíl]
증류하다, 거르다, 순화하다
to purify (a liquid) by vaporizing it, then condensing it by cooling the vapor, and collecting the resulting liquid

distinctive
[distíŋktiv]

특색 있는, 다른 것과 다름
serving to distinguish; characteristic

distract
[distrǽkt]

집중하지 못하게 하다, 산만하게 하다
to prevent (someone) from giving full attention to something

diversion
[daivə́:rʒn]

전환
the act or an instance of diverting or turning aside; deviation

divert
[divə́:rt]

(방향, 기분, 돈, 관심) 전환시키다, 딴 곳으로 돌리다
to turn aside from a course or direction

divine
[diváin]

신의, 신에 관한, 아주 뛰어난
superhuman

divisive
[diváisiv]

나누는, 분열하는
creating disunity or dissension

doctrinaire
[dáktrinέər]

순이론가, 공론가; 독단적인, 광신적인
one who attempts to put into effect an abstract doctrine or
theory with little or no regard for practical

doctrine
[dáktrin]

정설, 원칙, 교리, 교의
a belief or set of beliefs held and taught by a church, political
party, or other group

dodge
[dádʒ]

피하다, 발뺌하다
to avoid (someone or something) by a sudden quick movement

dogma
[dɔ́:gmə]

독단주의, 독단적 태도, 교리, 신조, 정론
a belief, principle, or doctrine or a code of beliefs, principles, or
doctrines

dogmatic
[dɔ(:)gmǽtik]

교리상의, 교리적인, 독단적인, 독선적인
relating to, characteristic of, or resulting from dogma;
characterized by an authoritative, arrogant assertion of unproved
principles

doodle
[dúːdl]

무의미한 낙서를 끄적거리다, 펀둥펀둥 시간을 보내다, 빈둥거리다; 낙서
to scribble aimlessly, especially when preoccupied; to kill time

dormant
[dɔ́ːrmənt]

활동이 없는, 동면기에 있는
temporarily inactive; having normal physical functions suspended
or slowed down for a period of time

downgrade
[dáungrèid]

(낮은 지위로) 격하시키다, 얕보다; 내리 막
to lower the status or salary of

downplay
[dáunplèi]

얕보다, 중시하지 않다
to make (something) appear less important than it really is

drab
[drǽb]

칙칙한, 재미없는, 담갈색의; 단조로움, 담갈색
characterized by dullness and monotony

drain
[dréin]

서서히 배출하다, 물기 없애다, 쭉 들이켜다; 배수 설비, 유출, 소비
to cause the water or other liquid in (something) to run out,
leaving it empty, dry, or drier

dramatize
[drǽmətàiz]

극적으로 보여주다
present in a vivid or striking way; exaggerate

drench
[dréntʃ]

흠뻑 적시다; 흠뻑 젖음
wet through and through; soak

droll
[dróul]

까부는, 우스꽝스런; 까불다
curious or unusual in a way that provokes dry amusement

drone
[dróun]
단조롭게 말하다, (벌, 비행기 등이) 윙윙거리다; 단조로운 소리, 윙윙 소리
make a continuous low humming sound

dubious
[djú:biəs]
의심하는, 의심스러운
hesitating or doubting; not to be relied

dull
[dʌl]
흐릿한, 둔탁한, 둔감한
intellectually weak or obtuse; stupid; lacking responsiveness or alertness; insensitive

duplicate
[djú:pləkit]
부본; 사본, 등본, 복사, 복제(물), 똑같이 만든 열쇠, 똑같은 것, 꼭 닮은 것; 중복된, 사본의; 사본을 만들다
identically copied from an original

dysfunctional
[disfʌ́ŋkʃənl]
기능 장애적인, 고장 난
impaired or abnormal functioning

earmark
[íərmá:rk]
(자금·물건 등을) 책정하다; 귀표, 양 등의 귀에 새겨서 소유주를 나타냄, 표시
to designate (as funds) for a specific use or owner

earnest
[ə́:rnist]
진지한, 진정인, (말, 감정 등이) 성실한, 진지한
marked by or showing deep sincerity or seriousness

earthly
[ə́:rθli]
지상의, 세속적인
of or relating to the earth or human life on the earth

earthshaking
[ə́:rθʃèikiŋ]
뿌리부터 뒤흔드는, 아주 중요한
of great consequence or importance

eavesdrop
[í:vzdráp]
몰래 엿듣다, 도청하다; 엿듣기, 도청
to listen to a conversation secretly

eclipse
[iklíps]
일식, 명성의 상실, 권위의 추락; (명예, 권위 등을) 실추시키다
the partial or complete obscuring by another; a loss of
significance, power, or prominence

economy
[ikánəmi]
간결함, 효율성, 검소함, 경제
thrifty management; frugality in the expenditure or consumption
of money: the efficient, sparing, or concise use of something

ecstatic
[ekstǽtik]
무아지경에 빠진, 법열의, 황홀한, 기뻐 날뛰는; 황홀경에 잘 빠지는 사람
marked by or expressing ecstasy; being in a state of ecstasy;
enraptured

egalitarian
[igǽlitɛ:əriən]
평등주의자; 평등주의의
affirming, promoting, or characterized by belief in equal political,
economic, social, and civil rights for all people

egocentric
[i:gouséntrik]
자기 중심적인, 자기 본위의; 자기 중심적인 사람
holding the view that the ego is the center, object, and norm of all
experience

elastic
[ilǽstik]
탄성 있는, 융통성 있는, 관대한
capable of recovering size and shape after deformation; not rigid
or constricted, adaptable

elegy
[élidʒi]
애가, 비가, 만가
a poem or song composed especially as a lament for a deceased
person

elemental
[èləméntl]
기본적인, 근본적인
primary, basic

elementary
[èləméntəri]
초보적인, 유치한, 단순한
of or relating to the most rudimentary aspects of a subject; easily
dealt with; straightforward and uncomplicated

eligible
[élidʒəbl]
선출되는 데 알맞은, 선출할 만한, 자격이 있는; 적임자
qualified or entitled to be chosen

elongate
[iló:ŋgeit]
(길이) 늘이다, 연장하다; 늘어난
to extend or grow in the length of

embark
[imbá:rk]
배에 오르다, 승선하다, 진출하다, 착수하다, 종사하다
to go aboard a vessel or aircraft, as at the start of a journey; to set out on a venture; commence

embed
[imbéd]
깊숙하게 박다, 넣다
to make something an integral part of; to surround closely; to enclose closely in

embellish
[imbéliʃ]
꾸미다, 장식하다, (이야기 등을) 꾸미다, 각색하다
to beautify by or as if by ornamentation; ornament; adorn: to enhance (a statement or narrative) with fictitious additions

embezzle
[imbézl, em-]
횡령하다, 사취하다
to steal or misappropriate (money placed in one's trust or belonging to the organization for which one works)

embody
[imbádi]
구체화하다, 구현하다, 통합하다
to make concrete and perceptible

embrace
[imbréis, em-]
포옹하다, (생각, 의견 등을) 채택하다, 알아차리다
to clasp or hold close with the arms, usually as an expression of affection

emblematic
[èmbləmǽtik]
상징적인
symbolic, representative

eminent
[éminənt]
저명한, 탁월한
towering or standing out above others; prominent

empathetic
[èmpəθétik]

공감하는
understanding of another's situation, feelings, and motives

empower
[impáuə(r)]

권리를 주다, 권한을 주다, 권리를 위임하다
to invest with power, especially legal power or official authority

enact
[inǽkt]

제정하다, (법안을) 성립시키다, (연극 등을) 상연하다
to make into law

enchant
[intʃǽnt]

매료시키다, 마술을 걸다
to fill (someone) with great delight; charm

enclosure
[inklóuʒə(r)]

(토지를) 둘러쌈, 포위, 둘러싼 상태, 에워싸인 장소, 구내, 동봉, 봉입
the act of enclosing. b. The state of being enclosed

encoded
[inkóud, en-]

암호화된
converted into coded form

encompass
[inkʌ́mpəs, en-]

둘러싸다, 포위하다, 포함하다, 성취하다
to surround and have or hold within; to include comprehensively

encumber
[inkʌ́mbər, en-]

짐 지우다, 막다, 방해하다
to restrict or burden (someone or something) in such a way that
free action or movement is difficult

encyclopedic
[insàikləpí:dik]

백과사전적인, 제반 지식에 정통한, 박식한
of, relating to, or characteristic of an encyclopedia; embracing
many subjects; comprehensive

endeavor
[indévər, en-]

노력, 시도; 노력하다, 애쓰다
earnest and industrious effort, esp. when sustained over a period
of time

endemic
[endémik]
어떤 지방 특유의, 고유의, 풍토성인
prevalent in or peculiar to a particular locality, region, or people

endorse
[indɔ́:rs, en-]
승인하다, 지지하다, 배서하다
to declare one's public approval or support of

endow
[indáu, en-]
기부하다, 주다, 부여하다
to give or bequeath an income or property to (a person or institution)

enfeeble
[infí:bl, en-]
약화시키다
to make weak or feeble

enflame
[infléim]
불태우다, 화나게 하다, 자극하다, (상황을) 악화시키다
to excite to excessive or uncontrollable action or feeling

enfranchise
[infrǽntʃaiz, en-]
투표권을 주다, 자유롭게 해주다
to give the right to vote to; free

enhance
[inhǽns]
높이다, 강화하다
heighten, increase

enlarge
[inlá:rdʒ]
크게 하다, 확대하다, 확장하다
to make larger; add to

enlighten
[inláitn]
계몽하다, 설명하다, 가르치다
to furnish knowledge to; to give spiritual insight to

ennoble
[inóubl]
높이다, 고상하게 하다
to make noble

enormous
[inɔ́:rməs]
거대한, 막대한, 극악한
marked by extraordinarily great size, number, or degree

enrage
[inréidʒ]
격노하게 하다, 성을 내다, 격노하다
to put into a rage; infuriate

entangle
[intǽŋgl, en-]
뒤엉키게 하다, 복잡하게 만들다, 말려들게 하다
to cause to become twisted together with or caught in; involve, complicate

enterprise
[éntərpràiz]
기업, 회사, 사업, 진취성, 모험심
a unit of economic organization or activity; boldness or readiness in undertaking; adventurous spirit; ingenuity

entice
[intáis, en-]
유혹하다
to attract or tempt by offering pleasure or advantage

entrammel
[intrǽməl, en-]
얽히게 하다, 구속하다, 방해하다
to involve or hold in trammels; restrain; to catch or entangle in or as in a net

entrepreneurial
[á:ŋtrəprəné:riəl]
기업가의, 모험심 있는, 진취적인
having the qualities that are needed to succeed as an entrepreneur

equilibrium
[ì:kwəlíbriəm]
평형, 균형, (마음) 평정
a state of intellectual or emotional balance

equivocation
[ikwivəkéiʃn]
애매한 언사, 말끝을 얼버무리기, 애매한 표현
the use of equivocal language; an equivocal statement or expression

erect
[irèkt]
(몸, 기둥 등이) 수직의, 곧추선; 똑바로 세우다, 곤두세우다
being in a vertical, upright position

erode
[iróud]
서서히 파괴하다, (산이) 금속을 부식하다, 침식하다
to wear (something) away by or as if by abrasion

err
[εər]
틀리다, 실수하다
to be mistaken or incorrect; make a mistake

escalate
[éskəlèit]
증대시키다, 고조되다
increase rapidly; (cause to) become more intense or serious

esteem
[istíːm, es-]
존경, 존중; 존중하다, 중히 여기다
respect and admiration, typically for a person

estimable
[éstəməbl]
존경 받을 만한
deserving of esteem; admirable

estrange
[istréindʒ, es-]
(관계를) 소원하게 하다, 벗어나게 하다
cause (someone) to be no longer close or affectionate to someone; alienate

evacuate
[ivǽkjuèit]
비우다, (위험한 지역 등에서 안전한 곳으로) 피난시키다
to empty or remove the contents of

even-handed
[íːvənhǽndid]
공정한
fair and impartial in treatment or judgment

even-tempered
[íːvəntémpərd]
(마음이) 차분한, 온화한
not easily ruffled, annoyed, or disturbed; calm

exasperate
[igzǽspərèit]
몹시 화나게 하다
to excite the anger of

excruciating
[ikskrúːʃièitiŋ]
심한 고통을 주는, 괴롭히는
intensely painful, mentally agonizing

exemplify
[igzémpləfài]
예증하다, 모범이 되다
show or illustrate by example

exemption
[igzémpʃən]
면제, 공제, 면세품
the state of being free from an obligation or liability imposed on others

exhaust
[igzɔ́:st]
지치게 하다, (연구 등) 철저히 살피다
to drain (someone) of their physical or mental resources; to tire out

exhilarate
[igzílərèit]
즐겁게 하다
to make cheerful and excited

expansive
[ikspǽnsiv]
광활한, (성격, 태도 등이) 개방적인, 너그러운, 대범한
(of a person or their manner) open, demonstrative, and communicative

expediency
[ikspí:diəns(i)]
편의, 유리, 상책, 편의주의, 방편주의, 편의적인 것, 방편
appropriateness to the purpose at hand; fitness; adherence to self-serving means

expedient
[ikspí:diənt]
편의주의적인, 신속한; 수단, 방책
(of an action) convenient and practical, although possibly improper or immoral; speedy; expeditious

expedite
[ékspədàit]
촉진시키다, 신속히 처리하다; 신속한
make (an action or process) happen sooner or be accomplished more quickly

expeditious
[èkspədíʃəs]
신속한
done with speed and efficiency

explicit
[iksplísit]
명백한, 명시적인, 솔직한
fully revealed or expressed without vagueness, implication, or ambiguity

exploit
[éksplɔit, iksplɔit]
위업, 업적; 이용하다, 착취하다
a bold or daring feat; make full use of and derive benefit from; use (a situation or person) in an unfair or selfish way

exponential
[èkspounénʃəl]
기하급수적인, 급격한, 지수의; 지수 함수
characterized by or being an extremely rapid increase

exquisite
[íkskwizit, ékskwizit]
매우 아름다운, 아주 훌륭한, (세공물 등이) 정교한; 멋쟁이, 멋부리는 사람
characterized by intricate and beautiful design or execution

extenuate
[iksténjuèit]
(죄, 과실 등을) 경감시키다, 가볍게 하다
to lessen or attempt to lessen the magnitude or seriousness of, especially by providing partial excuses; to make thin or emaciated

exterminate
[iksté:rminéit]
박멸하다, 근절하다, 멸종시키다
to get rid of by destroying completely; extirpate

extract
[ekstrǽkt]
뽑다, 빼내다, 적출하다; 추출물, 인용, 초록
to draw or pull out, using great force or effort

extraneous
[ikstréiniəs]
관련 없는, 외부로 부터의, 이질적인
irrelevant or unrelated to the subject being dealt with

extravagant
[ikstrǽvəgənt, -vi-]
사치, 낭비하는, 지나친
exceeding the limits of reason or necessity

extrinsic
[ikstrínsik, -zik]
비본질적인, 외래의, 외부의
not part of the essential nature of someone or something; coming or operating from outside

exuberant
[igzú:bərənt]
열의에 찬, 원기 왕성한, 활력적인, 풍부한
characterized by a lively energy and excitement

fabricate
[fǽbrikèit]
만들어내다, 꾸며내다, 제조하다, 조립하다
to invent or concoct (something), typically with deceitful intent;
to construct or manufacture

facet
[fǽsit]
(사물의) 한 면, 특성
any of the definable aspects that make up a subject (as of
contemplation) or an object (as of consideration); one side of
something many-sided, esp. of a cut gem

facile
[fǽsil]
피상적인, 손쉬운, 용이한, 술술 움직이는
superficial, simplistic; easily accomplished or attained

facilitate
[fəsílətèit]
용이하게 하다, 촉진하다
to make (an action or process) easy or easier, help

fad
[fǽd]
일시적인 유행, 유행물, 변덕
an intense but short-lived fashion; craze

fade
[feid]
희미해지다, 바래다, 약해지다
to lose brightness, loudness, or brilliance gradually; dim

faint
[feint]
희미한, 어렴풋한, 아련한, (생각 등이) 뚜렷하지 않은, 약한; 기절하다;
기절, 실신
lacking strength or vigor; feeble

fanatic
[fənǽtik]
광신도, 열광자; 열광적인
filled with enthusiasm and often intense uncritical devotion

fanatical
[fənǽtikəl]
광신도적인, 열광적인
possessed with or motivated by excessive, irrational zeal

fateful
[féitfəl]
운명을 결정하는, 결정적으로 중대한
itally affecting subsequent events; being of great consequence;
momentous

fatigue
[fətíːg]
피로, 피곤; 피로하게 하다
extreme tiredness, typically resulting from mental or physical exertion or illness

fatuous
[fǽtʃuəs]
어리석은, 바보 같은, 비현실적인
stupid

favor
[féivər]
편애하다, 지지하다, 유리하다; 친절한 행위, 부탁, 호의
to give unfairly preferential treatment to; work to the advantage of

favorable
[féivərəbl]
이익을 주는, (사람, 일을 위해) 유리한, 알맞은, 적합한
advantageous; helpful

feasible
[fíːzəbl]
실행 가능한, 편리한
possible to do easily or conveniently

feeble
[fíːbl]
연약한
lacking physical strength, esp. as a result of age or illness

ferocity
[fərásəti]
사나움, 광포함
fierce or violent nature

fertile
[fə́ːrtl]
비옥한, 생산력 있는
producing or bearing fruit in great quantities

fetch
[fetʃ]
가지고 오다, 데리고 오다, 불러오다
to come or go after and take or bring back

fetching
[fétʃiŋ]
매력적인
attractive

fiasco
[fiǽskou]

대실패
a thing that is a complete failure, esp. in a ludicrous or
humiliating way

fictitious
[fiktíʃəs]

거짓의, 허구의, 진짜 아닌
of, relating to, or characterized by fiction; imaginary

fidelity
[fidéləti, fai-]

충성, 정조
faithfulness to a person, cause, or belief, demonstrated by
continuing loyalty and support

figurative
[fígjurətiv]

비유적인
of or relating to representation of form or figure

filthy
[fílθi]

매우 더러운, 추잡한, 난잡한, 비열한
disgustingly dirty; obscene and offensive

finale
[finǽli, -ná:li]

공연의 마지막, 대미
the closing part, scene, or number in a public performance

fiscal
[fískəl]

재정의, 재무의, 회계의
of or relating to finance or finances

fit
[fít]

적당한, 유능한; 발작, 일시적 격발
suitable, appropriate, compatible

flamboyant
[flæmbóiənt]

눈부신, 화려한, 현란한
tending to attract attent on because of their exuberance,
confidence, and stylishness; noticeable because brightly colored,
highly patterned, or unusual in style

flatter
[flǽtər]

추켜세우다, 알랑거리다, (찬사 등으로) 기쁘게 하다
to lavish insincere praise and compliments upon (someone), esp.
to further one's own interests

flee
[flíː]

도망가다, 빠르게 지나가다, 사라지다
to run away, as from trouble or danger; to pass swiftly away, vanish

fleeting
[flíːtiŋ]

휙 지나가는, 순식간의, 덧없는
moving or passing swiftly

flicker
[flíkə(r)]

(불, 불길을) 흔들거리게 하다, (빛을) 깜박이게 하다; 흔들거리는 불빛, 희미한 불빛
to move waveringly; flutter; to burn unsteadily or fitfully

flimsy
[flímzi]

부서지기 쉬운, 약한, (주장) 설득력이 없는
comparatively light and insubstantial; easily damaged

float
[flóut]

부유하다, 뜨다; 뜨는 것, (낚시) 찌
to rest or move on or near the surface of a liquid without sinking

flock
[flaːk]

모이다, 떼 짓다, 무리를 이루다; 떼, 무리
to congregate or travel in a flock or crowd

flourish
[fláːriʃ]

번성하다
to develop rapidly and successfully

fluctuate
[flʌktʃuèit]

변동하다, 동요하다
to rise and fall irregularly in number or amount

foe
[fóu]

적, 원수, 반대자
a personal enemy, an enemy in war, an adversary

forage
[fɔːridʒ, fár-]

(식량을) 찾아 헤매다; 먹이, 사료
to wander in search of food or provisions

forbear
[fɔːrbɛ́ər]

삼가하다, 인내하다; 선조, 조상
to be tolerant or patient in the face of provocation

forbearance
[fɔːrbɛərəns]

인내심
tolerance and restraint in the face of provocation; patience

forbidding
[fərbídiŋ]

무서운, 소름 끼치는, 적개심을 가진, 위태로운, 험악한
tending or threatening to impede progress

forceful
[fɔ́ːrsfəl]

강력한
strong and assertive; vigorous and powerful

forfeit
[fɔ́ːrfit]

몰수(박탈) 당하다; 벌금, 과태, 몰수; 몰수당한, 상실한
abandon, give up

forge
[fɔːrdʒ]

대장간; 벼려서 금속제품을 만들다, 날조하다, 위조하다
counterfeit

formidable
[fɔ́ːrmidəbl]

겁먹게 하는, 위협적인, 경외감을 갖게 하는
inspiring fear or respect through being impressively large,
powerful, intense, or capable

formula
[fɔ́ːrmjələ]

인습적인 방식, 전통적인 방식, 공식; 규정대로의, 정식의
a method of doing or treating something that relies on an
established, uncontroversial model or approach

formulaic
[fɔ́ːrmjuléik]

도식적인, 공식에만 따른, 정식의
produced in accordance with a slavishly followed rule or style

forthcoming
[fɔːrθkʌ́miŋ]

다가오는, 임박한; 출현, 접근
about to happen in the near future; characterized by openness,
candidness, and forthrightness

forthright
[fɔ́ːrθràit]

기탄 없이 말하는, 입바른, (말, 평가 등이) 솔직한; 솔직히, 똑바로 앞으로
direct and without evasion; straightforward

fortify
[fɔ́:rtifài]
강화하다, 보강하다, 요새화하다
to make strong

forward
[fɔ́:rwərd]
뻔뻔한, 건방진, 앞선, 앞서 나아가 있는
presumptuous, impertinent, or bold; being in a condition of advancement; well-advanced

foster
[fɔ́:stər]
양성하다, 촉진하다, 발전시키다; 수양 자식의, 수양 부모의
to promote the growth or development of

fragile
[frǽdʒəl]
약한, 부서지기 쉬운, 덧 없는
(of a person) not strong or sturdy; delicate and vulnerable

fragmentary
[frǽgməntèri]
단편적인
weak and delicate

fragrant
[fréigrənt]
향기로운, 냄새 좋은, 방향성의
having a pleasant odor

fraudulent
[frɔ́:dʒulənt]
사기치는, 속이는
characterized by, based on, or done by fraud

freeze
[fri:z]
얼다, 동결하다, 막다; 빙결, 한파
to become clogged or jammed because of the formation of ice

frenetic
[frənétik]
광란의, 지나치게 열광적인; 광란자, 열광자
fast and energetic in a rather wild and uncontrolled way

frenzy
[frénzi]
광란, 열광, 발작; 열광시키다, 제정신을 잃게 하다
a state or period of uncontrolled excitement or wild behavior

friction
[fríkʃən]
마찰, 불화, 충돌
the action of one surface or object rubbing against another

frigid
[fríd3id]

몹시 추운, 냉담한
extremely cold

frugal
[frúːgl]

검소한, 절약하는
practicing or marked by economy, as in the expenditure of money or the use of material resources

fruitful
[frúːtfəl]

많이 만들어 내는, 다작인, 효과적인, 이익이 되는
producing results; profitable

frugal
[frúːgl]

검소한, 절약하는
practicing or marked by economy, as in the expenditure of money or the use of material resources

fugitive
[fjúːdʒətiv]

도망자; 도망치는, 덧없는, 금방 사라지는
quick to disappear; fleeting

fundamental
[fʌndəméntəl]

기본이 되는, 토대를 이루는, 중요한; 근본, 원칙
forming or serving as an essential component of a system or structure; central

fuse
[fjuːz]

융합 시키다, 혼연일체가 되게 하다; 퓨즈, 도화선
to become mixed or united by or as if by melting together

fussy
[fʌsi]

지나치게 꼼꼼한, 안달복달하는
(of a person) fastidious about one's needs or requirements; hard to please; showing excessive or anxious concern about detail

futile
[fjúːtl, -tail]

쓸모 없는, 무익한
incapable of producing any useful result; pointlessness

futility
[fjuːtíləti]

쓸모 없음, 무익함
the quality of having no useful result; uselessness

gainful
[géinfl]
이득이 되는, 유리한
providing a gain; profitable

galvanize
[gǽlvənàiz]
전기자극을 주다, 자극하다
to stimulate or shock with an electric current; to arouse to awareness or action; spur

gambit
[gǽmbit]
우세를 확보하는 수, 선수
an opening in chess in which a minor piece, or pieces, usually a pawn, is offered in exchange for a favorable position

garnish
[gá:rniʃ]
장식하다; 고명, 곁들임, 장식
to decorate or embellish

garrulous
[gǽrələs, -rju-]
지나치게 수다스러운, 장황한
excessively talkative, esp. on trivial matters

gauge
[geidʒ]
치수, 계측기; 양 등을 측정하다, 재다, 평가하다
to measure precisely

generic
[dʒənérik]
일반적인, 포괄적인
characteristic of a whole group or class; general; not specific

genial
[dʒí:njəl, -niəl]
친절하고 쾌활한, 상냥한, 온난한
friendly and cheerful

genuine
[dʒénjuin]
진짜의, 순혈의, 순종의
sincerely and honestly felt or experienced; actual, true

glacial
[gléiʃəl]
매우 추운, 매우 느린, (태도, 눈빛 등이) 매우 차가운, 빙하의
extremely cold; extremely slow (like the movement of a glacier); lacking warmth and friendliness

glamorize
[glǽməràiz]
매혹적으로 하다, 매력을 더하다
to make glamorous

glance
[glǽns]
흘긋 보기; 흘긋 보다, 번득이다
(take) a brief or hurried look

glaring
[glέərin]
눈부시게 빛나는, (색이) 지나치게 야한, 눈에 띄는, 뻔한
shining intensely and blindingly; tastelessly showy or bright, garish; conspicuous, obvious

glare
[gler]
눈부시게 빛나다, 노려보다; 번쩍이는 빛, 노려보기
to shine intensely and blindingly

glaze
[gleiz]
유약을 바르다, (음식에) 글레이즈를 바르다, (닦거나 문질러서) 광택을 내다; 표면의 윤기, 광택제
to give a smooth, lustrous surface to

glee
[glí:]
큰 기쁨, 환희
great delight

glide
[glàid]
미끄러지듯 움직이다; 미끄러지는 듯한 동작, 활주
move in a smooth, effortless manner

glimmer
[glímər]
희미하게 빛나다, 어렴풋이 보이다; 깜박기는 빛, 암시, 소량
shine faintly with a wavering light

gloomy
[glú:mi]
어두운, 어두컴컴한, 어둡게 그늘진, 우울한, 침울한, 음침한
depressing

glorify
[glɔ́:rifai]
찬미하다, 영광을 찬송하다, 숭상하다
to give glory, honor, or high praise to; exalt

glut
[glʌt]
과도, 과다; 실컷 먹이다, 채우다, 싫증나게 하다
an excessively abundant supply of something

glutton
[glʌ́tən]
식신, 식탐이 과한 사람, 열중하는 사람
a person who eats or consumes immoderate amounts of food
and drink

gourmand
[guərmá:nd]
미식가, 대식가
a person who enjoys eating and often eats too much

grant
[grænt]
주다, 수여하다, 동의하다; 수여, 교부, 허가
to bestow; confer; to transfer (property) by a deed

gratuitous
[grətjú:ətəs]
무료의, 필요 없는, 근거 없는
free of charge; unnecessary; without cause

grave
[gréiv]
무덤, 죽음; 엄숙한, 진지한; 조각하다, 새기다
giving cause for alarm; serious

gravity
[grǽvəti]
중력, 무게, 엄숙함, 진지함
grave consequence; seriousness or importance

graze
[greiz]
(가축이) 풀을 뜯어먹다
to feed on (herbage) in a field or on pastureland

greedy
[grí:di]
탐욕스러운, 욕심 많은
excessively desirous of acquiring or possessing, especially wishing
to possess more than what one needs or deserves

grievous
[grí:vəs]
심각한, 중대한, 슬픈
(of something bad) very severe or serious

grill
[gríl]
석쇠, 구운 요리; 석쇠에 굽다, 엄중히 심문하다, 취조하다
to subject (someone) to intense questioning or interrogation

grin
[grin]
(이를 드러내고) 밝게 생긋 웃다, 방긋 웃다; 밝은 웃음
to draw back the lips and bare the teeth, as in mirth or good
humor

grip
[grip]
단단히 잡음, 파악, 통제; 단단히 잡다, 감동시키다
a tight hold; a firm grasp

gripping
[grípiŋ]
주의를 끄는, 흥미로운, 재미있는
holding the attention or interest intensely; fascinating; enthralling

grotesque
[groutésk]
기괴한, 그로테스크한; 기괴한 것, 그로테스크한 것
characterized by ludicrcus or incongruous distortion, as of
appearance or manner

grouch
[gràutʃ]
불평꾼, 짜증 잘 내는 사람; 시무룩해지다, 투덜거리다
a habitually grumpy person; a habitually complaining or irritable
person

groundless
[gráundlis]
근거 없는
not based on any good reason

growl
[gràul]
으르렁 거리다, 투덜거리다
(of an animal, esp. a dog) to make a low guttural sound of hostility
in the throat

grudge
[grʌdʒ]
원한, 유감; 주기 싫어하다, 질투하다
a persistent feeling of ill will or resentment resulting from a past
insult or injury

guarded
[gáːrdid]
조심하는, 신중한
cautious; careful; prudent

gull
[gʌl]

속이다; 갈매기
to fool or deceive (someone)

gullible
[gʌ́ləbl]

잘 속는
easily persuaded to believe something; credulous

gust
[gʌst]

(갑자기) 휙 부는 바람, 돌풍, (감정의) 격발, 폭발; 급격하게 바람이 불다,
분출하다
a brief, strong rush of wind

habitable
[hǽbitəbl]

살 수 있는, 살기에 알맞은
suitable to live in or on; inhabitable

hack
[hæk]

마구 자르다, 난도질하다, 깊게 베다, (땅, 흙을 괭이, 곡괭이 등으로) 파다, 갈다;
잘린자국, 마구 자르기
to cut or chop with repeated and irregular blows

hallmark
[hɔ́ːlmáːrk]

특질, 특징, 순도 검증 각인; 순도 검증 각인을 찍다, 품질을 보증하다
any distinguishing feature or characteristic

hallucinate
[həlúːsənèit]

환각을 일으키게 하다
to undergo perception of visual, auditory, tactile, olfactory, or
gustatory experiences without an external stimulus and
with a compelling sense of their reality

halt
[hɔːlt]

멎다, 정지하다, 휴지하다, 그치다, 중지되다; 중지, 정지
to cause to stop; arrest

hamper
[hǽmpər]

막다, 방해하다; 방해가 되는 것, 속박
to hinder or impede the movement or progress

hanker
[hǽŋkər]

항상 연연해 하다, 못내 그리워하다, 갈망하다
to have a strong, often restless desire

harass
[həræs, hǽrəs]
괴롭히다
to annoy persistently

harbinger
[háːrbindʒər]
예언자, 전조; 선구자가 되다, 예고하다
a person or thing that announces or signals the approach of another; a forerunner of something

harbor
[háːrbər]
피난처를 제공하다, 숨겨주다, 마음에 품다; 항구, 은신처
to give shelter or refuge to

hardy
[háːrdi]
강건한, 용감한; 튼튼한 사람
robust; capable of enduring difficult conditions

hasten
[héisn]
서두르다
to be quick to do something

haven
[héivən]
항구, 피난처; 피난 시키다
a harbor or anchorage; a port; a place of refuge or rest; a sanctuary

heart-rending
[háːrtrèndiŋ]
마음을 찢어지게 하는, 매우 슬픈
(of a story or event) causing great sadness or distress

heated
[híːtid]
화난, 격렬한, 열렬한
angry; vehement; impassioned

heckle
[hékl]
괴롭히다, 야유를 퍼붓다
to harass and try to disconcert or interrupt with questions, challenges, or gibes; badger

hectic
[héktik]
매우 흥분한, (시기 등이) 법석을 떠는
characterized by intense activity, confusion, or haste

hedonism
[híːdənìzm]
쾌락주의, 향락주의
the pursuit of pleasure; sensual self-indulgence

hedonistic
[hìːdənístik]
쾌작주의의
of pursuit of or devotion to pleasure, especially to the pleasures of the senses

heed
[híːd]
주의를 기울이다; 주의, 조심
to pay attention to; take notice of

helter-skelter
[héltərskéltər]
허둥지둥, 엉터리로; 혼돈, 당황; 허둥거리는, 엉터리인
in disorderly haste or confusedly hurried, precipitate; marked by a lack of order or plan; haphazard

herald
[hérəld]
알리다, 고지하다; 전령, 통보관
to be a sign that something is going to happen

heroic
[hiróuik]
영웅적인, 용감한
having the characteristics of a hero or heroine; very brave

heterodox
[hétərədáks]
이단, 이설, 이교의
not conforming with accepted or orthodox standards or beliefs

heyday
[héidèi]
전성기
the period of a person's or thing's greatest success, popularity, or vigor

hilarious
[hilɛ́ːəriəs]
유쾌한, 즐거운
characterized by or causing great merriment

hinder
[híndə(r)]
지연시키다, 방해하다
to interfere with action or progress

hiss
[hís]

'쉬' 소리를 내다, 비난하다
to make a sharp sibilant sound as of the letter 's', to express (a negative view or reaction) by uttering a sharp, sibilant sound

hoard
[hɔːrd]

보관하다, (몰래) 저장하다; 저장, 저축, 축적
to amass (money or valued objects) and hide or store away; to accumulate a supply of (something) in a time of scarcity

hoarse
[hɔːrs]

(목소리가) 거친, 쉰 소리가 나는
(of a person's voice) sounding rough and harsh, typically as the result of a sore throat or of shouting

hoax
[houks]

짓궂은 속임수; 속이다
a humorous or malicious deception; to deceive with a hoax

hollow
[hɔ́lou]

텅빈, 내용 없는; 구멍, 속이 텅 빔; 속이 비게 하다
having a hole or empty space inside; without significance

homage
[hámidʒ]

존경
special honor or respect shown publicly

homogeneous
[hòumədʒíːniəs]

동종의, 균질의, 비슷한
of the same kind, alike; consisting of parts all of the same kind

hospitality
[hàspitǽləti]

후대, 환대, 이해, 수용
cordial and generous reception of or disposition toward guests

hue
[hjúː]

색깔, 색조, 경향, 특색
a color or shade

humdrum
[hʌ́mdrʌm]

단조로운, 재미없는; 단조로움, 지루함, 평범함
dull, dreary, boring, tedious, monotonous, prosaic

humiliate
[hju:mílièit]
굴욕스럽게 하다
to reduce to a lower position in one's own eyes or others' eyes

humility
[hju:míləti]
겸손함
a modest or low view of one's own importance; humbleness

hunch
[hʌntʃ]
예감, 직감, 느낌
a strong intuitive feeling concerning especially a future event or result

husky
[hʌ́ski]
(소리가) 거친, 건장한
hoarse or rough in quality: strongly built, robust, burly

hybrid
[hàibrid]
잡종의, 혼혈의; 잡종, 혼혈아, 합성물
of mixed character; composed of mixed parts

hygiene
[hàidʒi:n]
위생
conditions or practices conducive to maintaining health and preventing disease, esp. through cleanliness

hyperbole
[haipé:rbəli]
과장된 말, 과장법
exaggerated statements or claims not meant to be taken literally

hyperbolic
[hàipərbá:lik]
과장된, 과장법을 쓴
of, relating to, or employing hyperbole

hypnotize
[hípnətàiz]
최면술을 걸다, 매료하다, 무력하게 하다
to fascinate by or as if by hypnosis

hypothesis
[haipáθisis]
가설, 전제, 추측
a tentative explanation that accounts for a set of facts and can be tested by further investigation; a theory

hypothetical
[hàipəθétikl]

가설의
theoretical, speculative conjectured, conjectural

idealize
[aidí:əláiz]

이상화하다, 이상적인 것으로서 다루다
to regard as ideal

idiocy
[ídiəsi]

우둔함, 백치, 천치
stupidity, folly, foolishness, foolhardiness, ignorance

idiosyncrasy
[ìdiəsíŋkrəsi, -sín-]

특유의 성질
a distinctive or peculiar feature or characteristic of a
individual, place or thing

idiosyncratic
[ìdiousiŋkrǽtik,
 ìdiousinkrǽtik]

개인에게 특유한 성질을 지닌
of a structural or behavioral characteristic peculiar to an
individual or a group

idolatrous
[aidálətrəs]

우상숭배의, 맹신하는
of or having to do with idolatry

ignite
[ignáit]

불을 붙이다, 작열시키다, (마음을) 불타오르게 하다
to set fire to

illiteracy
[ilítərəsi]

무학, 문맹, 무교양
state of being uncultured or poorly educated; lacking the ability
to read and write

illuminate
[ilú:mənèit]

조명하다, 계몽하다, 알게하다
to supply or brighten with light; to enlighten, as with knowledge

illustrate
[íləstrèit]

(그림, 챠트, 예를 이용해서) 설명하다
explain or make (something) clear by using examples, charts,
pictures, etc

imminent
[ímənənt]

임박한
about to happen; impending

immune
[imjú:n]

면역의, 면제된; 면역자
not susceptible or responsive; not responsible: exempt

impair
[impέər]

약화시키다, 손상시키다
to weaken or damage (esp. a human faculty or function)

impassionate
[impǽʃənət]

열정적인
filled with passion, impassioned, perfervid

impeachable
[impí:tʃəbəl]

탄핵 받을 만한, 비난 받을 만한
making one subject to impeachment, as misconduct in office;
liable to be impeached

impede
[impí:d]

방해하다, 훼방 놓다
to delay or prevent (someone or something) by obstructing
them; hinder

impediment
[impédəmənt]

장애물
hindrance, obstruction, obstacle, barrier, bar

impending
[impéndiŋ]

임박한
about to happen; imminent

impertinent
[impέ:rtnənt]

주제넘은, 뻔뻔스러운, 버릇없는, 무례한, 건방진, 불손한
exceeding the limits of propriety or good manners; improperly
forward or bold

implicate
[ímplikèit]

(범죄 등에) 연루시키다, 암시하다
to imply as a necessary circumstance, or as something to be
inferred or understood

implicit
[implísit]
암시된, 암묵적인
implied though not plairly expressed

impose
[impóuz]
부과하다, 지우다, 강제하다
to put or set by or as if by authority

impromptu
[imprámptjuː]
즉흥적인, 즉석에서; 즉흥연주
done without being planned, organized, or rehearsed; a short piece of instrumental music, esp. a solo, that is reminiscent of an improvisation

improvise
[ímprəvàiz]
즉흥적으로 하다
to compose, recite, play or sing extemporaneously

impulsive
[impʌ́lsiv]
충동적인
inclined to act on impulse rather than thought

inanimate
[inǽnəmət]
살아 있지 않은, 생명이 없는
not alive, esp. not in the manner of animals and humans; showing no sign of life; lifeless

inaugurate
[inɔ́ːgjurèit]
시작하다, 취임시키다
to begin or introduce (a system, policy, or period); to admit (someone) formally to public office

incense
[ínsens]
향기를 풍기다, 몹시 화나게 하다; 향, 존경, 경의
to perfume with incense, make very angry

incentive
[inséntiv]
격려, 자극; 자극적인, 격려적인
motivation, motive, reason, stimulus, stimulant, spur, impetus

incidental
[ìnsədéntl]
우연적인, 부수적인
happening in connection with or resulting from something more important; casual or fortuitous

inclement
[inklémənt]
(날씨가) 혹독한, 궂은
(of the weather) unpleasantly cold or wet

incoherent
[ìnkouhíərənt, -hér-]
(말, 글) 조리가 없는, 통일성 없는
(of spoken or written language) expressed in an incomprehensible or confusing way; inconsistent, illogical

incompetent
[inká:mpitənt]
무능한, 무자격의, 서투른
not qualified in legal terms

incomprehensible
[ìnkà:mprihénsəbl]
이해할 수 없는, 불가해한
difficult or impossible to understand or comprehend; unintelligible

inconclusive
[ìnkənklú:siv]
결정적이지 않은
not leading to a firm conclusion; not ending doubt or dispute

incongruous
[inkáŋgruəs]
조화롭지 않은, 일치하지 않는
inappropriate, unsuitable, unsuited; wrong, strange

inconsistent
[ìnkənsístənt]
일치하지 않는, 일관성 없는, 모순적인
not compatible or in keeping with; not staying the same throughout; having self-contradictory elements

incumbent
[inkʌ́mbənt]
현직의, 의무로서 지워지는, 책무인
holding an indicated position, role, office, etc., currently

indenture
[indéntʃər]
고용을 계약서로써 정하다, 기한부 도제로 받아들이다; 계약서, 증서, 도제살이 계약서
a contract by which a person, as an apprentice, is bound to service

indifferent
[indífərənt]
무관심한, 개의치 않는, 무감각한, 냉담한, 편견을 갖지 않은; 무관심한 행위, 중립적인 사람
characterized by a lack of partiality; unbiased

indistinguishable
[indistíŋgwiʃəbl]
구별 안 되는
not clearly recognizable or uncerstandable

indulge
[indʌ́ldʒ]
탐닉하다, 관대히 대하다
allow oneself to enjoy the pleasure of; allow (someone) to enjoy a desired pleasure

indulgence
[indʌ́ldʒəns]
탐닉, 욕망의 만족
the act or an instance of indulging; gratification

indulgent
[indʌ́ldʒənt]
관대한, 너그럽게 봐주는, 응석 받아주는, 무른
showing, characterized by, or given to indulgence; lenient

inedible
[inédəbl]
먹을 수 없는, 못 먹는, 식용에 적합하지 않은
unfit to be eaten; not edible

inert
[iné:rt]
움직이지 않는, 활력 없는, 불활성의
lacking the ability or strength to move, lacking vigor

inestimable
[inéstəməbl]
측량할 수 없는, 헤아릴 수 없을 만큼 가치 있는
impossible to estimate or compute

inevitable
[inévətəbl]
피할 수 없는, 불가피한; 피할 수 없는 것
certain to happen; unavoidable

infatuate
[infǽtʃuèit]
얼빠지게 하다, 멍하게 하다, (놀이, 생각 등으로) 열중하게 하다
to inspire with unreasoning love or attachment

infirm
[infə́:rm]

약한, (마음 등이) 불확실한
not physically or mentally strong, esp. through age or illness; irresolute

inflame
[infléim]

불타게 하다, 자극하다
to excite to excessive or uncontrollable action or feeling

inform
[infɔ́:rm]

특징이 되다, 정보를 주다, 알리다
to give character or essence to; to give or impart knowledge of a fact or circumstance to

inhibit
[inhíbit]

억제하다, 억누르다, 방해하다, 저지하다
to prohibit; forbid

inimical
[inímikəl]

해로운, 적대적인
tending to obstruct or harm; unfriendly, hostile

inquisitive
[inkwízətiv]

호기심 많은, 질문이 많은; 조사하기 좋아하는 사람
curious, interested, intrigued

inscrutable
[inskrú:təbl]

불가사의한, 난해한
impossible to understand or interpret

insensate
[insénseit,-sət]

감정 없는, 무정한, 잔혹한
lacking sensation or awareness; inanimate

insensible
[insénsəbl]

감각을 잃은, 지각을 잃은, 인사 불성의
lacking meaning; unintelligible

insert
[insə́:rt]

삽입하다, 끼워 넣다, 끼우다; 삽입물, 끼워넣는 페이지
to put or set into, between, or among

insight
[ínsàit]

직관력, 식견, 통찰, 간파
the capacity to gain an accurate and deep intuitive understanding of a person or thing

instable
[instéibl]

불안정한
not stable; unstable

institute
[ínstitù:t]

(제도, 습관 등을) 마련하다, 제정하다, 개시하다; 학회, 협회, 원리, 원칙, (이공계의) 대학
to establish, organize, and set in operation

insubstantial
[ìnsəbstǽnʃəl]

허약한, 튼튼하지 않은, 실질적이지 못한
flimsy, frail; not substantial or real; lacking substance

insufferable
[insʌ́frəbl]

견딜 수 없는, 참을 수 없는
difficult or impossible to endure; intolerable

integral
[íntigrəl, intég-]

불가결한, 필수의, 완전한; 전체, 총체
necessary to make a whole complete; essential or fundamental

integrate
[íntəgrèit]

통합하다, 완성하다; 완전한, 각 부분이 갖추어진
combine (one thing) with another so that they become a whole

integrity
[intégrəti]

정직, 청렴, 흠 없는 상태, 보전
steadfast adherence to a strict moral or ethical code; the quality or condition of being whole or undivided

intensify
[inténsəfài]

심화시키다, 강화시키다
to become or make more intense; to strengthen

interdisciplinary
[ìntərdísəplənèri]

다른 학문 분야 사이에 제휴하는; 많은 학문 분야에 관련이 있는
combining or involving two or more academic disciplines or fields of study

interim
[íntərəm]
중간의, 임시의; 짬, 잠시, 잠정 협정
in or for the intervening period; provisional or temporary

intervene
[intərvíːn]
화해시키다, 개입하다, 간섭하다
to occur, fall, or come between points of time or events

intimate
[íntəmèit]
넌지시 알려주다, 암시하다; 친밀감 있는, 일신상의; 절친한 친구
to make known subtly and indirectly; to hint

intriguing
[intríːgiŋ]
호기심을 자아내는, 재미를 자아내는, 매력적인, 음모를 꾸미는
arousing the curiosity or interest of; fascinating

intrinsic
[intrínsik(əl), -zik(əl)]
본질적인
belonging naturally; essential

introspective
[intrəspéktiv]
내성의, 내성적인
being contemplation of one's own thoughts, feelings, and sensations; self-examination

introverted
[intrəvə́ːrt]
내성적인
to turn inward or in upon itself

intrusive
[intrúːsiv]
참견하는, 강요하는
characterized by intrusion; projecting inward

intuitive
[intúːitiv]
직관적으로 인식하는, 직관력 있는
of, relating to, or arising from intuition

invalidate
[invǽlədèit]
무효로 하다
to weaken or destroy the cogency of

inventory
[ínvəntɔ̀:ri]
재고목록, 품목 일람, 재고조사; 목록을 만들다, 재고 조사를 하다
a complete list of items such as property or goods in stock

inviolate
[invàiələt, -lèit]
신성한, 더럽혀지지 않은
free or safe from injury or violation

invulnerable
[invʌ́lnərəbl]
무적의, 확고한
immune to or proof against attack; impregnable

irregular
[irégjulər]
불규칙한, 흐트러진; 불규칙적인 것, 불규칙적인 사람
uneven, unusual, strange, inconsistent

irritate
[ìrətéit]
짜증나게 하다, 안달나게 하다, 초조하게 만들다, 화나게 하다
to rouse to impatience or anger; annoy

jaded
[dʒéidid]
지친, 지긋지긋한, 싫증난
tired, bored, or lacking enthusiasm, typically after having had too
much of something

jargon
[dʒá:rgən]
전문어, 허튼 소리; 전문어를 쓰다, 은어를 쓰다, 횡설수설하다
the technical terminology or characteristic idiom of a special
activity or group

jot
[dʒa:t]
간결하게 적다, 간단히 메모하다; 극소량
to write down briefly or hastily

jubilant
[dʒú:bələnt]
환희에 가득 찬, 매우 기뻐하는
exultingly joyful, expressing joy

keen
[kí:n]
열렬한, 예리한, 날카로운
eagerness or enthusiastic; intellectually alert: acute, shrewdly
astute

kindle
[kíndl]
불타게 하다, 부채질하다, 충동질하다
to cause to glow; light up

kinetic
[kinétik]
운동의, 운동에 의해 생기는, 움직임을 특징으로 하는, 동적인
of, relating to, or produced by motion

knotty
[náti]
매듭으로 가득한, 풀기 어려운
full of knots; so full of difficulties and complications as to be likely
to defy solution

lackluster
[lǽklʌstər]
빛(광택)이 없는, 활기 없는; 빛이 없음, 활기가 없음
(of the hair or the eyes) not shining; dull; lacking in vitality, force
or conviction

lament
[ləmént]
한탄하다, 슬퍼하다, 애통해하다; 슬픔, 한탄, 애가, 만가
to mourn (a person's loss or death); to express one's deep grief
about; express regret or disappointment over something
considered unsatisfactory, unreasonable, or unfair

lapse
[lǽps]
(일시적인) 쇠퇴, 잘못, 과실, (시간의) 경과, 기간; 사소한 잘못을 저지르다,
쇠퇴하다, 빠지다, 들어가다, 시간이 경과하다
a temporary failure of concentration, memory, or judgment, a
weak or careless decline from previously high standards; an
interval or passage of time

larval
[lá:rvəl]
유충의, 유생의 모양을 한
of the newly hatched, wingless, often wormlike form of many
insects before metamorphosis

latent
[léitnt]
잠재성의
(of a quality or state) existing but not yet developed or manifest;
hidden; concealed

latitude
[lǽtətjùːd]
위도, (행동, 사항, 견해 등의) 자유, 허용 정도
scope for freedom of action or thought

lavish
[lǽviʃ]
사치스런, 아낌없는; 아낌없이 주다, 낭비하다
sumptuously rich, elaborate, or luxurious; very generous or extravagant

leaden
[lédn]
둔한, 느릿한, 활기 없는, 무거운; 둔하게 하다, 활기없게 하다
dull, heavy, or slow, sluggish; lacking spirit or animation

leaning
[líːniŋ]
기호, 편애, 기울기, 경사
a tendency or partiality of a particular kind

learned
[lə́ːrnid]
유식한
(of a person) having much knowledge acquired by study

legendary
[lédʒəndèri]
전설적인, 매우 유명한; 전설집
remarkable enough to be famous; very well known

lethal
[líːθl]
치명적인, 죽음을 초래하는, 치사의
capable of causing death

liberality
[lìbərǽləti]
후함, 관대함
the quality of being open to new ideas and free from prejudice; the quality of giving or spending freely

limber
[límbər]
유연한, 민첩한; 유연하게 하다
bending or flexing readily; pliable

limp
[límp]
절뚝거리다, 느리게 나아가다; 절뚝거리기
to walk with difficulty, typically because of a damaged or stiff leg or foot

linger
[líŋgər]
(아쉬운 듯이) 남아 있다, (떠나지 않고) 꾸물거리다, 서성대다
to be slow in parting or in quitting something

loath
[lóuθ, lóuð]
내켜 하지 않는
unwilling to do something contrary to one's ways of thinking

loathe
[louð]
몹시 싫어하다, 싫어하다
to dislike (someone or something) greatly; abhor

lofty
[lɔ́:fti]
숭고한, 아주 높은
of imposing height; of a noble or exalted nature

longevity
[landʒévəti]
장수, 오래 지속됨
long life, long duration of service

loyal
[landʒévəti]
충성스러운, 충직한, 충절을 다하는
steadfast in allegiance to one's homeland, government, or sovereign

lull
[lʌl]
일시적 잠잠함, 소강상태; 달래다, 어르다, 재우다
a temporary interval of quiet or lack of activity; to calm or send to sleep, typically with soothing sounds or movements; to allay (a person's doubts, fears, or suspicions), typically by deception

luminous
[lú:mənəs]
빛나는, 반짝이는, 총명한
emitting or reflecting usually steady, suffused, or glowing light

luxurious
[lʌgʒúəriəs]
사치스런, 호사스런
giving self-indulgent or sensuous pleasure; extremely comfortable, elegant, or enjoyable, esp. in a way that involves great expense

majestic
[mədʒéstik(əl)]
위엄한, 당당한, 장엄한
having or showing impressive beauty or dignity

maniac
[méiniæk]
광적으로 열중하는 사람; 광란의, 미친
a person exhibiting extreme symptoms of wild behavior, esp. when violent and dangerous

marginal
[máːrdʒinl]
사소한, 중요하지 않은, 가장자리의
of secondary or minor importance; not central

martial
[máːrʃəl]
호전적인, 용감한
experienced in or inclined to war; warlike

mask
[mæsk]
가면, 속임수; 숨기다, 가리다
a covering worn as a disguise, or to amuse or terrify other people; conceal (something) from view; disguise or hide

masterful
[mæstərfəl]
명인 솜씨의, 대가의, 훌륭한
performed or performing very skillfully

masticate
[mǽstəkèit]
씹다
to chew

matchless
[mǽtʃlis]
적수가 없는, 대단한
unable to be equaled; incomparable

matriculation
[mətrìkjuléiʃən]
입학, 입학허가
enrollment at a college or university; admission to a college or university

matter-of-fact
[mǽtərəvfǽkt]
현실적인, 실질적인, 평범한
unemotional and practical; adhering to the unembellished facts, straightforward

meager
[míːgər]
부족한, 빈약한
scanty, scarce, deficient in quantity, fullness, or extent

measly
[míːzli]
(양이) 아주 조금인, 홍역에 걸린
contemptibly small or few

measured
[méʒərd]
정확히 측정한, 신중한
marked by due proportion; deliberate, calculated

meddle
[médl]
참견하다
to interfere in or busy oneself unduly with something that is not one's concern

meet
[míːt]
적절한; 만나다, 교류하다, 채우다, 만족시키다
suitable; fit; proper

melodious
[məlóudiəs]
듣기 좋은
having a pleasant tune; tuneful

mend
[ménd]
고치다, 수선하다
to repair

mendacious
[mendéiʃəs]
거짓말하는
not telling the truth; lying

mendacity
[mendǽsəti]
부정직한 일, 거짓말하는 버릇
a lie; a falsehood

mentor
[méntɔːr, -tər]
조언자, 지도자, 지지자
an experienced and trusted adviser

mercenary
[mə́ːrsəneri]
보수가 목적인, 돈만 바라는; 용병, 돈만 바라고 일하는 사람
motivated solely by a desire for monetary or material gain

merge
[mə́ːrdʒ]
합병하다, 변하게 하다
to blend or come together without abrupt change

merited
[méritid]
(상, 벌, 주목 등을) 받을 자격이 있는, 당연한
deserving, worthy of (something, esp. reward, punishment or attention)

mesmerize
[mézməràiz]
최면술을 걸다, 매료하다
to spellbind; enthrall

metaphoric[al]
[mètəfɔːrik(əl)]
은유의, 은유적인
using or of metaphor

metaphysical
[mètəfízikəl]
형이상학적인, 극히 추상적인 난해한
based on abstract (typically, excessively abstract) reasoning

metaphysics
[mètəfíziks]
순수 철학, (넓은 뜻의) 형이상학, 심리학, 탁상 공론, 추상론
the branch of philosophy that examines the nature of reality, including the relationship between mind and matter, substance and attribute, fact and value

milestone
[máilstòun]
이정표, 기념비적인(획기적인) 사건, 일
landmark, a significant point in cevelopment

mind
[maind]
꺼리다, 복종하다, 조심하다, 신경쓰다; 머리. 정신, (지성의 소유자로서의) 인간, 사람, 사고방식, 의견, 생각
to be reluctant to do something (often used in polite requests); to be obedient to

mindful
[máindfəl]
인식하는, 알고 있는, 신경쓰는
conscious or aware of something

mingle
[míŋgl]
섞이다, 혼합되다
to mix or bring together in combination, usually without loss of individual characteristics

miscellaneous
[mìsəléiniəs]
갖가지 잡다한; 잡동사니의
(of items or people gathered or considered together) of various types or from different sources

miserly
[máizərli]
구두쇠의, 인색한
marked by grasping meanness and penuriousness

misogynist
[misádʒənist]
여자를 싫어하는 사람
one who hates women

moderate
[mádərət]
적절하게 하다, 완화시키다; 온건한, 절도를 지키는; 온건한 사람
to lessen the violence, severity, or extremeness of

mold
[móuld]
주조하다, 만들다; 주형, 거푸집, 모양, 원형
to give a shape to (a malleable substance)

momentous
[mouméntəs]
중요한, 중대한
of utmost importance; of outstanding significance or consequence

momentum
[mouméntəm]
힘, 기세, 여세, 운동량
the quantity of motion of a moving body, measured as a product of its mass and velocity

monopolize
[mənápəlàiz]
독점하다
get or keep exclusively to oneself

monotony
[mənátəni]
단조로움, 변화가 없음, 한결같음, 변화가 없는 것
uniformity or lack of variation in pitch, intonation, or inflection

moralistic
[mɔ́rəlístik]
도덕적인
characterized by or expressive of a narrow moral attitude

moratorium
[mɔːrətóːriəm]

(지불, 집행) 유예 , 일시 정지
a temporary prohibition of an activity

morose
[məróus]

시무룩하고 언짢은
sullen and ill-tempered

motley
[mátli]

잡동사니의, 잡색의; 잡색, 얼룩덜룩함, 잡동사니
incongruously varied in appearance or character; disparate

mottle
[mátl]

점, 얼룩; 얼룩을 묻히다
mark with spots or smears of color

mournful
[mɔ́ːrnfl]

구슬픈, 슬픔에 잠긴
feeling or expressing sorrow or grief; sorrowful

murky
[mə́ːrki]

어둑어둑한, 안개가 자욱한, 므호한, 애개한
dark, dim or gloomy; heavy with smoke, mist, fog; lacking clarity

mutability
[mjúːtəbl]

변화성
state of being liable to change

mute
[mjúːt]

소리 없는, 말 못하는; 소리를 약하게 하다
characterized by an absence of sound; quiet

naïve
[naːíːv]

순진한, 경험이 없는; 순진한 사람, 경험이 없는 사람
showing a lack of experience, wisdom, or judgment; (person) natural and unaffected, innocent

nebulous
[nébjuləs]

흐린, 구름 같은, 뚜렷하지 않은
in the form of a cloud or haze; hazy; unclear, vague

negligent
[néglidʒənt]

태만한, 적절한 주의를 기울이지 못하는
failing to take proper care in doing something

negligible
[néglidʒəbl]
하찮은, 무시해도 좋은
so small or unimportant as to be not worth considering; insignificant

negotiate
[nigóuʃièit]
교섭하다, 협의하다, 협상하다
to confer with another or others in order to come to terms or reach an agreement

nestle
[nésl]
(보금자리 안의 새처럼) 기분 좋게 드러눕다
to settle snugly and comfortably

neutralize
[njú:trəlàiz]
중립으로 하다, 무효로 하다, 상쇄하다
to make neutral

nibble
[níbl]
조금씩 물어뜯다, 잠식하다; (음식 등의) 한 입, 헐뜯기
to take small bites out of

noncommittal
[nánkəmítl]
분명한 의견을 표명하지 않은, 애매한, 확실하지 않은
not expressing or revealing commitment to a definite opinion or course of action

nonconformity
[nánkənfɔ:rməti]
(표준, 전통, 규칙, 법률 등) 따르지 않음, 불순응, 불일치
refusal or failure to conform to accepted standards, conventions, rules, or laws, unconventionality; lack of agreement

nondescript
[nándiskrípt]
뚜렷한 특징이 없는; 특징 없는 것
lacking distinctive or interesting features or characteristics

notoriety
[nòutəràiəti]
(악명으로) 유명함
state of being famous or well known, typically for some bad quality or deed

nourish
[nə́:riʃ]
영양분을 주다, (음식, 영양물을 주어로 하여) 키우다
to provide with food or other substances necessary for life and growth; feed

noxious
[nákʃəs]
해로운, 불쾌한
harmful, poisonous, or very unpleasant

nuance
[njú:a:ns]
미묘한 차이, 음영
a subtle difference in or shade of meaning, expression, or sound

nuisance
[njú:sns]
불쾌한 것, 귀찮은 것, 성가신 것
a person, thing, or circumstance causing inconvenience or annoyance

numb
[nʌm]
마비된; 마비시키다
deprived of the power to feel or move normally; benumbed; to make or become numb

numberless
[nʌ́mbərlis]
셀 수 없이 많은
too many to be counted; innumerable

nurture
[nə́:rtʃər]
양육하다, 돌보다; 양육, 양성 교육, 자양물, 음식물
to care for and encourage the growth or development of

obligatory
[əbligətɔ́:ri]
의무를 지우는, 의무적인, 강제적인, 필수의
morally or legally constraining; binding

oblige
[əbláidʒ]
의무 지우다, 강제하다
to constrain by physical, legal, social, or moral means

oblivion
[əblíviən]
망각
the fact or condition of forgetting or having forgotten

oblivious
[əblíviəs]
알아채지 못한, 염두에 없는, 망각한
not aware of or not concerned about what is happening around one

obnoxious
[əbná:kʃəs]
아주 싫은, 불쾌한, 욕지기 나는, 추악한
very objectionable; odious

obscure
[əbskjúər]
불명료하게 하다; 불명료한, 유명하지 않은
to make unclear and difficult to understand; uncertain, not clearly expressed; not prominent or famous

observable
[əbzə́:rvəbl]
관찰할 수 있는, 남의 눈을 끄는, 식별할 수 있는, 주목할 만한
possible to observe

observant
[əbzə́:rvənt]
지각이 예민한, 기민한
quick to notice things

obsolete
[ábsəli:t]
구식의, 못쓰게 된; 시대에 뒤떨어지게 하다
no longer in use, no longer current

obstinacy
[ábstənəsi]
완고함, 고집셈, 집요한 끈기
the state or quality of being stubborn or refractory

obstinate
[ábstənət]
완고한, 완강한
stubbornly refusing to change one's opinion or chosen course of action, despite attempts to persuade one to do so

obtain
[ətéin]
획득하다, 손에 넣다, 널리 행해지다, 유행하다, 성립하다
to be established, accepted, or customary

obtuse
[əbtjú:s]
둔한, 이해가 매우 느린, 뭉퉁한, 둔한
annoyingly slow to understand; not sharp, pointed, or acute in form; blunt

occult
[əkʌ́lt, akʌ́lt]

숨겨진, 눈에 보이지 않는, 난해한; 신비, 초자연적인 것
beyond the range of ordinary knowledge or experience; mysterious

offbeat
[ɔ́(:)fbíːt]

색다른, 자유스러운
unconventional; unusua

offend
[əfénd]

불쾌하게 하다
to cause dislike, anger, or vexation

offset
[ɔ́ːfsèt]

상쇄하다, 벌충하다; 보상, 상쇄하는 것
balance, compensate

onset
[á:nsèt, ɔ́ːn-]

시작
the beginning of something, esp. something unpleasant

opaque
[oupéik]

불투명한; 불투명한 것; 불투명하게 만들다
not able to be seen through; not transparent

opportune
[àpərtjúːn]

(시기, 시간 등이) 적절한
(of a time) well-chosen or particularly favorable or appropriate, done or occurring at a favorable or useful time; well-timed

opportunist
[àpərtjúːnist]

기회주의자
one who takes advantage of any opportunity to achieve an end, often with no regard for principles or consequences

opportunistic
[àpərtjuːnístik]

기회주의적인
taking advantage of opportunities as they arise

opulent
[ápjulənt]

부유한, 풍성한
ostentatiously rich and luxurious or lavish

orthodox
[ɔ́:rθədàks]
정설, 정교의; 정통파의 사랑
conforming to established doctrine orthodoxy

outcome
[áutkʌm]
결과
something that follows as a result or consequence

outdated
[áutdéitid]
구식의
no longer current

outmoded
[àutmóudid]
구식의
old-fashioned, unfashionable; obsolete

outspoken
[àutspóukən]
솔직한
direct and open in speech or expression

overpower
[òuvərpáuər]
압도하다
to overcome by superior force

overriding
[òuvərráidiŋ]
가장 중요한, 최우선의
chief, principal

overrule
[òuvərrú:l]
(결정 등을) 뒤엎다, 파기하다, 거부하다
to prevail over

overshadow
[òuvərʃǽdou]
그늘지게 하다, 희미하게 하다
to cast a shadow over; to exceed in importance

pacify
[pǽsəfài]
달래다, 진정시키다
to quell the anger, agitation, or excitement of

painstaking
[péinstèikiŋ]
애쓰는, 수고를 아끼지 않는, 면밀한, 철저한; 애씀, 고심, 근면
done with or employing great care and thoroughness

paradigm
[pǽrədàim]

전형, 모범
example, pattern

paradoxically
[pærədáksikəli]

역설적으로
of the nature of a paradox; not being the normal or usual kind

paragon
[pǽrəgən]

완벽한 예가 되는 사람이나 사물, 모범, 전형; 비교하다, 필적하다
a person or thing regarded as a perfect example of
a particular quality

parallel
[pǽrəlèl]

평행, 유사; 평행시키다; 평행인
extending in the same direction, everywhere equidistant, and not
meeting

paralyze
[pǽrəlàiz]

마비시키다
to cause (a person or part of the body) to become partly or
wholly incapable of movement

paranoid
[pǽrənɔid]

편집증의, 지나치게 의심하는
unreasonably or obsessively anxious, suspicious, or mistrustful

parasite
[pǽrəsàit]

기생 식물(동물)
a person who exploits the hospitality of the rich and earns
welcome by flattery

parch
[pa:rtʃ]

바짝 말리다, 갈증을 느끼게 하다
to make thirsty

parody
[pǽrədi]

패러디, 익살스런 변곡, 풍자적인 것의 흉내, 서투른 모방; 풍자적으로 모방하다,
희화하다
a literary or artistic work that imitates the characteristic style of
an author or a work for comic effect or ridicule

passionate
[pǽʃənət]
열정적인
showing or caused by strong feelings or a strong belief

pastoral
[pǽstərəl]
전원적인, 양치기인
associated with country life; (of a work of art) portraying or evoking country life, typically in a romanticized or idealized form

patronize
[pǽtrənàiz]
후원하다, 우월하게 행동하다, 생색내다
to give encouragement and financial support to (a person, esp. an artist, or a cause); to treat in a condescending manner

paucity
[pɔ́:səti]
소량, 결핍, 부족
the presence of something only in small or insufficient quantities or amounts; scarcity

peculiar
[pikjú:liə(r)]
특유한, 독특한, 특징적인; 개인의 특유한 것
unusual or eccentric; odd; distinct from all others; belonging distinctively or primarily to one person, group, or kind; special or unique

pedantry
[pédəntri]
학자라고 뽐내기, 박식한 체하기, 규칙 세부에 얽매이기
pedantic attention to detail or rules; an instance of pedantic behavior

pedestrian
[pədéstriən]
평범한, 진부한; 보행자
lacking inspiration or excitement; dull

peerless
[píərlis, pǽrədi]
적수가 없는, 비길 데 없는
matchless, incomparable

penetrate
[pénətrèit]
관통하다, 꿰뚫다, (사실, 진리 등을) 간파하다, 통찰하다, 이해하다
to succeed in forcing a way into or through (a thing); to succeed in understanding or gaining insight into (something complex or mysterious)

penetrating
[pénitrèitiŋ]
관통하는, 통찰력 있는
able or seeming to penetrate

pensive
[pénsiv]
멍하니 생각에 잠긴, 수심에 잠긴
deeply, often wistfully or dreamily thoughtful

perceive
[pərsí:v]
인식하다, 이해하다
to become aware or conscious of (something); to come to realize or understand

perceptual
[pərséptʃuəl]
지각의
aware of something through the senses

percipient
[pərsípiənt]
지각하는, 감지하는, 통찰력 있는; 지각하는 사람, 천리안
having the power of perceiving, especially perceiving keenly and readily

perforate
[pə́:rfərèit]
구멍뚫다
to pierce, punch, or bore a hole or holes in; to penetrate; to pierce or stamp with rows of ho es, as those between postage stamps, to allow easy separation

permeable
[pə́:rmiəbl]
투기성이 있는, 삼투될 수 있는
that can be permeated or penetrated, especially by liquids or gases

perpetrate
[pə́:rpətrèit]
(범죄, 과실, 실책 등을) 범하다, 저지르다
to be responsible for; to commit

persevere
[pə:rsəvíər]
인내하다, 견디다
to persist in or remain constant to a purpose, idea, or task in the face of obstacles or discouragement

persistent
[pərsístənt]
집요한, 고집부리는, 지속하는
firm or obstinate continuance in a course of action in spite of difficulty or opposition; the continued or prolonged existence of something

personify
[pərsánəfài]
의인화하다, 구체화하다
to conceive of or represent as a person or as having human qualities or powers

persuasive
[pərswéisiv]
설득력 있는; 설득하는 것, 자극, 동기
tending to persuade

pertain
[pərtéin]
부속하다, 관계있다, 어울리다
to belong as a part, member, accessory, or product

pertinent
[pə́:rtənənt]
관련된, 적절한
relevant or applicable to a particular matter; apposite

perturb
[pərtə́:rb]
마음을 동요시키다
to make (someone) anxious or unsettled

pervade
[pərvéid]
퍼지다, 온통가득하다
to spread through and be perceived in every part of; to be present and apparent throughout

pervasive
[pərvéisiv]
널리 퍼져있는
spreading widely throughout an area or a group of people

pester
[péstər]
괴롭히다, 조르다
to trouble or annoy (someone) with frequent or persistent requests or interruptions

petition
[pətíʃn]
탄원하다, 청원하다; 탄원서, 진술서
to address a petition to; to ask for by petition; request formally

petty
[péti]

사소한, 하찮은
of little importance; trivial

phantom
[fǽntəm]

유령, 환영; 환영의, 유령의
a ghost

phenomenal
[finámənl]

경이로운, 대단한
very remarkable; extraordinary

philanthropist
[filǽnθrəpist]

박애주의자, 자선활동
person of love of humankind in general

philanthropy
[filǽnθrəpi]

박애주의
active effort to promote human welfare; an act or gift done or made for humanitarian purposes

pine
[pain]

그리워하다, 갈망하다, 초췌해지다, 수척해지다; 소나무
to feel a lingering, often nostalgic desire; to wither or waste away from longing or grief

pious
[páiəs]

깊은, 독실한, 신실한, 경건한
having or exhibiting religious reverence; earnestly compliant in the observance of religion; devout

pirate
[páiərət]

해적, 해적선, 저작권 침해자; 해적질하다, 저작권을 침해하다
to make use of or reproduce others' work without authorization

pitfall
[pítfɔːl]

함정, 숨겨진 위험
a hidden or unsuspected danger or difficulty

pivotal
[pívətəl]

중추적인, 극히 중요한
being of vital or central importance; crucial

plagiarism
[pléidʒərìzm]
표절
the practice of taking someone else's work or ideas and passing
them off as one's own

plague
[pléig]
괴롭히다, 전염병에 걸리게 하다; 전염병, 재앙, 불운
to cause continual trouble or distress to

plainspoken
[plainspóukən]
솔직한
frank; straightforward; blunt

plastic
[plǽstik]
플라스틱의, 비닐의; 모양이 마음대로 되는, 소조할 수 있는, 가소성의;
플라스틱 제품
capable of being shaped or formed

plead
[plí:d]
간청하다, 탄원하다
to argue for or against a claim; to entreat or appeal earnestly

plot
[plát]
음모, (극, 이야기 등의) 구성, 플롯; 음모를 짜다
a plan made in secret by a group of people to do something illegal
or harmful; the main events of a play, novel, movie, or similar
work; interrelated sequence

plummet
[plʌ́mit]
수직으로 떨어지다, 급락, 폭락하다
to fall or drop straight down at high speed

polarity
[poulǽrəti]
양극성, 정반대
the state of having two opposite or contradictory tendencies,
opinions, or aspects

polarize
[póuləràiz]
양극화하다, 분열시키다, (빛을) 편광시키다
to divide or cause to divide into two sharply contrasting groups or
sets of opinions or beliefs

polemical
[pallémikəl]

논쟁적인
of, relating to, or involving strongly critical, controversial, or disputatious writing or speech

politic
[pálətik]

현명한, 분별력 있는, 정치상의
characterized by shrewdness in managing, contriving, or dealing; shrewdly tactful

ponder
[pándər]

심사숙고하다
to weigh in the mind with thoroughness and care

ponderable
[pándərəbl]

숙고할 만한, 무게를 잴 수 있는
considerable enough to be weighed or assessed; appreciable

ponderous
[pándərəs]

무거운, 육중한, 지루한
slow and clumsy because of great weight; dull, laborious, excessively solemn

pragmatic
[prægmǽtik]

실용적인
relating to matters of fact or practical affairs often to the exclusion of intellectual or artistic matters

prate
[préit]

재잘재잘 말하다
to talk idly, at length, or to little purpose; to chatter

prattle
[prǽtl]

재잘재잘 말하다
to talk or chatter idly or meaninglessly; babble or prate

precedent
[prisíːdnt,
 présədənt]

선례, 전례; 선행하는, 먼저의
an earlier event or action that is regarded as an example or guide to be considered in subsequent similar circumstances
precede

preconception 편견, 선입견, 예상, 예측
[prìːkənsépʃən]
a preconceived idea

predecessor 전임자
[prédəsèsər]
someone or something that precedes another in time, especially
in holding an office or position.

predestine 숙명을 지우다, 운명 짓다
[pridéstin]
to fix upon, decide, or decree in advance; foreordain

preeminence 가장 뛰어남, 탁월함
[priémənəns]
state of surpassing all others, state of being very distinguished in
some way

preeminent 우위의, 상위의, 현저한, 돋보이는, 탁월한, 출중한
[priːémənent]
superior to or notable above all others; outstanding

premeditate 미리 계획, 생각하다
[priːmédətèit]
to think about and revolve in the mind beforehand

preoccupation 몰두, 열중, 선입견, 편견
[priːakjupéiʃən]
the state or condition of being preoccupied or engrossed with
something

prerequisite 필요조건; 사전에 필요한
[priːrékwəzit]
something that is necessary to an end or to the carrying out of a
function

preservative 방부제, 예방약; 보존하는, 방부의
[prizéːrvətiv]
something used to preserve, especially a chemical added to foods
to inhibit spoilage

prestigious 훌륭한, 일류의
[prestídʒəs]
inspiring respect and admiration; having high status

presume
[prizú:m]
추정하다, 참견하다, 우쭐대다
to suppose to be true without proof

presumptuous
[prizʌ́mptʃuəs]
건방진, 뻔뻔스러운
overstepping due bounds

pretentious
[priténʃəs]
허세부리는, 과시하는
attempting to impress by affecting greater importance, talent, culture, etc., than is actually possessed

prevailing
[privéiliŋ]
널리 퍼져있는, 유행하는, 유력한
to gain ascendancy through strength or superiority

prime
[práim]
주요한, 탁월한, 최고의, 최초의; 전성기, 한창때
first in rank, authority, or significance

primeval
[praimí:vəl]
원시시대의
of or resembling the earliest ages in the history of the world

principal
[prínsəpəl]
주요한, 주된, 중요한; 장, 교장, 주연배우
first, highest, or foremost in importance, rank, worth, or degree; chief

principle
[prínsəpl]
원리, 원칙, 공리, (자연 현상, 기계 등의) 원리, 법칙
a basic truth, law, or assumption

pristine
[prísti:n]
원래 그대로의, 오염되지 않은, 깨끗한
in its original condition; unspoiled

privilege
[prívəlidʒ]
특권; 특권을 주다
a right or immunity granted as a peculiar benefit, advantage, or favor

probity
[próubəti]

정직, 청렴
the quality of having strong moral principles; honesty and decency

procrastinate
[proukrǽstənèit]

미루다, 지연하다, 늑장부리다
to delay or postpone action; to put off doing something

prodigious
[prədídʒəs]

거대한, 유별난, 비상한
extraordinary in bulk, quantity, or degree

prodigy
[prádədʒi]

신동, 천재, 불가사의한 것, 경이로움
a highly talented child or youth; an extraordinary, marvelous, or unusual accomplishment, deed, or event

proficient
[prəfíʃənt]

능숙한, 유능한; 숙달자, 명인
competent or skilled in doing or using something

profound
[prəfàund]

심오한, (사람이) 큰 지식과 통찰력이 있는
extremely deep; (of a person or statement) having or showing great knowledge or insight

profundity
[prəfʌ́ndəti]

심오함, 깊음, 심연
intellectual depth

prohibitive
[prouhíbitiv]

(가격) 지나치게 비싼, 금지하는, 제한하는
(of a price or charge) excessively high; difficult or impossible to pay (esp. of a law or rule) forbidding or restricting something

proliferate
[prəlífərèit]

증식하다, 만연하다, 풍부하게 만들어내다
to increase or spread at a rapid rate

prolific
[prəlífik]

다산의, 비옥한, 다작의, 풍부한
(of a plant, animal, or person) producing much fruit or foliage or many offspring

prolong
[prəlɔ́:ŋ]

연장하다, 연기하다, 늘리다
to lengthen in duration; protract

prominence
[prámənəns(i)]

명성, 중요함
the state of being important or famous

proofread
[pùːfríːd]

교정하다
to read (printer's proofs or other written or printed material) and
mark any errors

prosaic
[prouzéiik]

진부한, 산문형식의
commonplace; unromantic; having the style or diction of prose;
lacking poetic beauty

prosecution
[prásikjúːʃən]

기소, 수행
the initiation and conducting of legal proceedings or court action
against someone in respect of a criminal charge

prosperous
[práːspərəs]

번영하는, 성공하고 있는, 순조로운, 형편 좋은, 행운인
having success; flourishing

protract
[proutrǽkt]

(기간을) 연장하다, (몸을 앞으로) 쭉 뻗다
to prolong; to extend a part of the body, to extend forward

provision
[prəvíʒən]

(법) 조항, (장래) 준비, (pl.) 식량, 공급; 식량을 공급하다
a condition or requirement in a egal document; the action of
providing or supplying something for use; supplies of food, drink,
or equipment, esp. for a journey

provisional
[prəvíʒənəl]

임시의, 잠정적인, 일시적인, 조건부의
provided or serving only for the time being; temporary

proxy
[prá:ksi]

대리, 대리권, (주주 총회 등의) 대리 위임장, 대리인, 대용품
a person authorized to act for another; an agent or a substitute; the authority to act for

pry
[prài]

사적인 문제를 지나치게 캐묻다
to inquire too closely into a person's private affairs

pseudonym
[súːdənìm]

(작가) 필명
a fictitious name, esp. one used by an author

qualified
[kwáləfàid]

자격있는, 제한적인, 조건부의
officially recognized as being trained to perform a particular job; competent or knowledgeable to do something; capable; not complete or absolute; limited

qualify
[kwáləfài]

제한하다, 한정하다, 자격을 주다
to modify, limit, or restrict, as by giving exceptions

quarrelsome
[kwɔ́ːrəlsəm]

말다툼하기 좋아하는, 성급한, 토론을 좋아하는
given to quarreling; contentious

quotidian
[kwoutídiən]

일상적인, 매일매일의, 평범한; 매일 일어나는 일
of or occurring every day; daily ordinary or everyday, esp. when mundane

racy
[réisi]

활발한, 활기 있는, 시원시원한, 짜릿한, 통렬한, 통쾌한, (이야기가) 아슬아슬한, 선정적인
strong and sharp in flavor or odor; piquant or pungent; ribald

radical
[rǽdikəl]

근본적인, 급진적인; 급진주의자
(esp. of change or action) relating to or affecting the fundamental nature of something; far-reaching or thorough; advocating thorough or complete political or social reform

ramification
[ræməfəkéiʃən]
(사건의) 결과, 추이, 세분화, 분파
a consequence of an action or event, esp. when complex or unwelcome

ramify
[ræməfài]
가지 모양으로 퍼지게 하다, 분기 시키다
to have complicating consequences or outgrowths

rampant
[ræmpənt]
(나쁜 것 등이) 만연하는, 횡행하는, (사람, 행동 등이) 사나운, 미쳐 날뛰는
(esp. of something unwelcome or unpleasant) flourishing or spreading unchecked; (cf a person or activity) violent or unrestrained in action or performance

rarity
[réərəti]
희귀함; 희귀하고 진귀한 것
the state or quality of being rare

rash
[ræʃ]
무모한, 서두르는, 성급한
marked by or proceeding from undue haste or lack of deliberation or caution

ratify
[rætifài]
승인하다, 인가하다, 비준하다
to approve and give formal sanction to; confirm

rational
[ræʃnəl]
합리적인, 도리에 맞는; 합리적인 것
having or exercising the ability to reason

rationale
[ræʃənæl]
이론적 근거, 논리적 근거, 정당화
an explanation of controling principles of opinion, belief, practice, or phenomena

rationalization
[ræʃənəlizéiʃən]
합리화
the cognitive process of making something seem consistent with or based on reason

realized
[ríːəlàiz]

현실화된
in concrete and practical existence

rebellious
[ribéljəs]

반항적인, 거부하는, 반체제의, 순종치 않는, 반대하는
resisting treatment or control; unruly

recede
[risíːd]

물러나다, 감소하다
to move back or away; to grow less or smaller

recess
[risés, ríːses]

쉬는 시간, 휴식기간, 활동의 임시적 중단; 휴교하다, 휴업하다
a temporary cessation of the customary activities of an
engagement, occupation, or pursuit

recession
[riséʃən]

경기침체기, 쇠퇴
a period of temporary economic decline, withdrawal

reciprocity
[rèsəprásəti]

호혜주의, 상호이익
the quality or state of being reciprocal: mutual dependence,
action, or influence

reconcile
[rékənsàil]

화해시키다, 조화롭게 하다, 중재하다
to restore friendly relations between; to cause to coexist in
harmony; make or show to be compatible

rectitude
[réktətjùːd]

(행동) 정의로움, 옳음, 정직
morally correct behavior or thinking; righteousness

recuperative
[rikjúːpərèitiv]

(건강) 회복시켜주는
having the effect of restoring health or strength

recurrent
[riké:rənt]

재현되는, 주기적으로 일어나는, 순환하는
returning or happening time after time

redeem
[ridíːm]

되찾다, 상환하다, 회복하다
to free from what distresses or harms; to extricate from or help
to overcome something detrimental

redundancy
[ridʌ́ndənsi]

과잉, 여분, (특히 말의) 쓸데없는 반복, 장황함, 다언
a superfluity; an excess; unnecessary repetition

refrain
[rifréin]

삼가하다, 억제하다
to keep oneself from doing, feeling, or indulging in something and
especially from following a passing impulse

refute
[rifjúːt]

논박하다
to prove (a statement or theory) to be wrong or false; disprove

rehabilitate
[riːəbílitèit]

사회로 복귀시키다, 건강 상태로 회복시키다, 갱생시키다
to restore to good health or useful life, as through therapy and
education

reinforce
[riːinfɔ́ːrs]

강화시키다, 활력을 되착게 하다
to give more force or effectiveness to; strengthen

rejuvenate
[ridʒúːvənèit]

다시 젊게 하다, 활력을 되찾게 하다
to make young or youthful again

rekindle
[riːkíndl]

다시 불 붙이다, 다시 불러 일으키다
to relight (a fire); to revive (something that has been lost)

relegate
[réləgèit]

강등시키다, 쫓아 보내다, 위임하다
to consign or dismiss to an inferior rank or position

relentless
[riléntlis]

엄격한, 가혹한, 무자비한
oppressively constant; incessant; harsh, inflexible

relinquish
[rilíŋkwiʃ]
포기하다, 양보하다, 양도하다
voluntarily cease to keep or claim; give up

relish
[réliʃ]
즐기다, 음미하다, 좋아하다; 맛, 풍미, 즐기며 음미하기
to enjoy the flavor of

reluctant
[rilʌ́ktənt]
내키지 않는
unwilling and hesitant; disinclined

remedy
[rémədi]
치료, 교정(법); 치료하다, 교정하다
something that corrects or counteracts

reminisce
[rèmənís]
회상하다, 이야기하다
to indulge in enjoyable recollection of past events

remorse
[rimɔ́:rs]
양심의 가책, 후회
deep regret or guilt for a wrong committed

remorseful
[rimɔ́:rsfəl]
깊이 뉘우치고 있는, 양심의 가책에 고민한
marked by or filled with remorse

remorseless
[rimɔ́:rsləs]
가혹한, 무자비한
having no pity or compassion; merciless

rend
[rénd]
(잡아) 찢다
to tear (something) into two or more pieces

replicate
[réplikèit]
복사하다, 접혀 겹쳐지다; 접어 겹친
to duplicate

repulsive
[ripʌ́lsiv]
불쾌감을 주는, 역겨운
arousing intense distaste or disgust

requisite
[rékwəzit]
필요한, 필수적인; 필수품, 필수 조건
made necessary by particular circumstances or regulations

rescission
[risíʒən]
철회, 취소
the revocation, cancellation, or repeal of a law, order, or agreement

resentful
[rizéntfəl]
분개한, 화를 잘 내는
feeling or expressing bitterness or indignation at having been treated unfairly

resentment
[rizéntmənt]
분개, 화
a feeling of indignant displeasure or persistent ill will

reserve
[rizə́:rv]
보유, 제한, 유보적 태도, 의심; 저장해 두다, 예약하다, 유보하다
a lack of warmth or openness in manner or expression; qualification or doubt attached to some statement or claim; to hold in reserve; to retain or hold over to a future time or place

residency
[rézidənsi]
거주, 체재, 주재
residence

resilience
[rizíljəns(i)]
탄력, 회복력
ability to recoil or spring back into shape after bending, stretching, or being compressed

resilient
[riziliənt]
되로 튀는, 탄력이 있는
marked by the ability to recover readily, as from misfortune

resolute
[rézəlù:t]
마음이 확고한
admirably purposeful, determined, and unwavering

resolve
[rizálv]
결심하다, 분해하다, 해결하다; 결심, 결의
to decide firmly on a course of action

resonant
[rézənənt]
낭랑하게 울리는, 공명하는
deep, clear, and continuing to sound or ring

respire
[rispáiə(r)]
호흡하다, 숨쉬다
to breathe in and out; inhale and exhale

responsive
[rispá:nsiv]
응답하는, 민감한, 공명하기 쉬운, 반응을 보이는
answering or replying; responding

restless
[réstləs]
가만히 있지 않는, 침착하지 못한, 불안한, 편안히 못 자는
marked by a lack of quiet, repose, or rest

restore
[ristó:(r)]
원상태로 되돌리다, 회복시키다, 복귀시키다
to bring back into existence or use; reestablish

restrain
[ristréin]
제한하다, 억제하다, 구금하다
to prevent (someone or something) from doing something; to keep under control or within limits

resume
[rizú:m]
재개하다, 회복하다
to return to or begin again

resurge
[risə́:rdʒ]
다시 나타나다, 소생하다
to rise again from

resurrect
[rèzərékt]
되살리다, 부활시키다
to bring to view, attention, or use again

retain
[ritéin]
보유하다, 유지하다
hold, keep

retaliate
[ritǽlièit]

(같은 수단으로) 보복하다, 복수하다, 앙갚음하다
make an attack or assault in return for a similar attack; repay (an injury or insult) in kind

retard
[ritá:rd]

(성장, 진보 등을) 더디게 하다, 늦추다, 저지하다, 방해하다; 지연, 지체, 지능 발달이 늦은 사람
to cause to move or proceed slowly; delay or impede

retouch
[ri:tʌ́tʃ]

손질하다, 수정하다; 수정
to add new details or touches to for correction or improvement

retract
[ritrǽkt]

취소하다, 철회하다, 물러서게 하다
to draw or pull (something) back or back in; to withdraw (a statement or accusation) as untrue or unjustified

retreat
[ritrí:t]

후퇴하다, 철수하다, 철회하다, 물러서다; 철수, 후퇴
(of an army) to withdraw from enemy forces as a result of their superior power or after a defeat; to change one's decisions, plans, or attitude, as a result of criticism from others

retrieve
[ritrí:v]

되찾다, 회수하다; 회복, 되찾기
to get (something) back; regain possession of

retrospective
[rètrəspéktiv]

추억에 잠기는, 회고적인, 되돌아 보는, 뒤를 향하는; 회고, 전시회
looking back on, contemplating, or directed to the past

revise
[riváiz]

개정하다, 수정하다; 개정판, 수정
to reconsider and change or modify

revisionist
[rivíʒənist]

수정주의자
one who advocates the revision of an accepted, usually long-standing view, theory, or doctrine, especially a revision of historical events and movements

revive
[riváiv]
(남을) 되살아나게 하다, (생명, 의식 등을) 소생 시키다, 기운 나게 하다, 활기차게 하다
to bring back to life or consciousness; resuscitate

rhetoric
[rétərik]
수사법, 수사학, 미사 여구의 사용, 과장된 말
the art or study of using language effectively and persuasively

riddle
[rídl]
수수께끼, 난제; 수수께끼를 내다
a puzzling problem; conundrum, enigma

righteous
[ráitʃəs]
도덕적인, 바른, 정의로운
morally right or justifiable

rigid
[rídʒid]
휘지 않는, 융통성 없는, 엄격한
unable to bend or be forced out of shape; not flexible

rigor
[rígər]
정확함, 엄격함, 고생
severity, austerity, exactness

riot
[ráiət]
폭동, 소동, 큰 혼란; 폭동에 참가하다
a wild or turbulent disturbance created by a large number of people

rip
[ríp]
거칠게 찢다, 갈기갈기 찢다; 터진 곳, 상처
to cut, tear apart, or tear away roughly or energetically

ripen
[ráipən]
익다, 숙성하다, 익히다, 숙성시키다
to become or make ripe

rubric
[rú:brik]
주서, 항목, 표제, 규정
a class or category

rue
[rúː]
뉘우치다, 후회하다, 유감으로 여기다; 비탄, 후회
to regret bitterly (something one has done or allowed to happen)

rueful
[rúːfl]
가엾은, 안쓰러운, 애처로운, 슬퍼 보이는, 침울한
causing, feeling, or expressing sorrow or regret

ruminant
[rúːminənt]
반추하는, 생각에 잠긴
meditative; contemplat ve

ruminate
[rúːmənèit]
반추해보다, 깊이 생각해 보다
to think deeply about scmething

ruminative
[rúːmineitiv]
반추하는, 생각에 잠긴
of the act of pondering; of med tation

rural
[rúːərəl]
(좋은 뜻에서의) 전원의, 시골 풍의, 촌락의, 지방 생활의, 시골 사람의, 시골에 사는
of, relating to, or characteristic of the country

rustic
[rʌ́stik]
전원적인, 시골의
having a simplicity and charm that is considered typical of the countryside

sabbatical
[səbǽtikl]
안식일에 어울리는, 휴식의, 안식의, 유급 휴가의; 유급 휴가, 안식일
relating to a sabbatical year

sabotage
[sǽbətàːʒ]
고의적으로 방해하다, 파괴하다; 사보타주, 방해 행위
to destroy, damage, or obstruct (something) deliberately , esp. for political or military advantage

saga
[sáːgə]
무용담, 영웅이야기
a long story of heroic achievement, esp. a medieval prose narrative

sarcasm
[sáːrkæzm]
비꼼, 빈정거림, 풍자
the use of irony to mock or convey contempt

sarcastic
[saːrkǽstik]
비꼬는
given to using sarcasm

sartorial
[saːrtɔ́ːriəl]
재단사의, 의복의
of or relating to a tailor or tailored clothes

satire
[sǽtaiər]
풍자
a literary work holding up human vices and follies to ridicule or scorn

satirical
[sətirikəl]
풍자의, 풍자적인, 비꼬는
of, relating to, or characterized by satire

satirize
[sǽtəraiz]
풍자하다, 풍자로 공격하다, 비꼬다, 비아냥거리다
to ridicule or attack by means of satire

savory
[séivəri]
맛 좋은, 기분 좋은, 안락한
(of food) belonging to the category that is salty or spicy rather than sweet; morally wholesome or acceptable

savvy
[sǽvi]
지식이 있는, 잘 아는; 이해력, 재치, 수완; 알다, 이해하다
well informed and perceptive; shrewd

scant
[skænt]
적은, 불충분한; (공급, 수량 등을) 줄이다
barely sufficient or adequate; to provide grudgingly or in insufficient amounts

scanty
[skǽnti]
적은, 불충분한
small or insufficient in quantity or amount

scathing
[skéiðiŋ]

상처 내는, 신랄한
bitterly severe

scheme
[skí:m]

음모, 모의; 음모를 꾸미다
a secret or underhanded plan; a plot; to make plans, esp. in a devious way or with intent to do something illegal or wrong

schematic
[ski:mǽtik]

개요의, 도식의, 도식적인
of, relating to, or in the form of a scheme or diagram

scrutinize
[skrú:tənàiz]

면밀히 살피다
to examine or inspect closely and thoroughly

scrutiny
[skrú:təni]

면밀한 조사
a close, careful examination or study

seasoned
[sí:zn]

경험 있는, 능숙한, (목재 등이) 잘 건조된, 맛을 곁들인
accustomed to particular conditions; experienced

secrete
[sikrí:t]

분비하다, 숨기다, 감추다
to give off, exude, release

secure
[səkjúər]

안전한, 위험이 없는, 안심한, 확고한; 안전하게 하다, 확보하다
free from danger or attack

seemly
[sí:mli]

예절을 지키는, (행동 등이) 적절한
conforming to accepted notions of propriety or good taste; decorous

semantics
[simǽntiks]

의미론, 의미 체계
the branch of linguistics and logic concerned with meaning

sensate
[sénseit]
오감으로 지각할 수 있는
perceived by a sense or the senses

sensible
[sénsəbl]
분별있는, 현명한, ~을 알 수 있는
perceptible by the senses or by the mind

sequence
[síːkwəns]
순서, 연속, 결과, 후속하여 일어나는 일
order of succession, consequence, result

sequent
[síːkwənt]
추후의, 나중의, 잇따라 일어나는, 필연적인; 연속, 결과
following in a sequence or as a logical conclusion, later

sequential
[sikwénʃəl]
순차적인
forming or following in a logical order or sequence

serendipity
[sèrəndípəti]
운수 좋은 뜻밖의 발견(물)
the occurrence and development of events by chance in a happy or beneficial way

serene
[səríːn]
고요한, 평온한
calm, peaceful, and untroubled; tranquil

shabby
[ʃǽbi]
누더기를 걸친, 초라한, 황폐한
showing signs of wear and tear; threadbare or worn-out

shadow
[ʃǽdou]
미행하다, 그늘지게 하다, 너지시 비치다; 그림자, 그늘, 전조
to follow and observe (someone) closely and typically secretly

shadowy
[ʃǽdoui]
그림자 드리워진, 희미한, 애매한
full of shadows; dim; lacking clarity or distinctness

sham
[ʃǽm]
가짜의, 모조의; 모조품, 가짜; 위조하다, 가장하다
bogus; false; a thing that is not what it is purported to be;
pretense

shrewd
[ʃrúːd]
현명한, 명민한, 교활한
having or showing sharp powers of judgment; astute

shrug (off)
[ʃrʌg]
(무관심, 의문, 불쾌의 표시 등으로) 양 어깨를 으쓱하다; 어깨를 으쓱하기
to raise (one's shoulders) slightly and momentarily to express
doubt, ignorance, or indifference

simulation
[sìmjuléiʃən]
모조품, 가짜; ~인체하기
sham object; counterfeit

singular
[síŋgjulər]
별난, 특이한, 탁월한
unusual or distinctive manner or behavior

sip
[sip]
홀짝홀짝 조금씩 마시다
to drink in small quantities

skeptic
[sképtikəl]
회의적인; 회의론자, 의심 많은 사람
relating to, characteristic of, or marked by skepticism

sketchy
[skétʃi]
대략적인
not thorough or detailed

skirt
[skə́ːrt]
가장자리에 있다, 회피하다; 스커트, 가장자리
to go around or past the edge of; to attempt to ignore, avoid
dealing with

slick
[slik]
매끈매끈하고 윤기 나는, 매끄러운, 반들반들한, 교활한; 매끈매끈한 곳;
매끈매끈하게 하다
smooth, glossy, and slippery

slight
[slait]
사소한, 대수롭지 않은; 무시하다, 경시하다; 경시, 경멸
small in degree; inconsiderable; insult (someone) by treating or speaking of them without proper respect or attention

sloppy
[slá:pi]
부주의한, 겉날리는, 질척질척한
marked by a lack of care or precision; slipshod

sly
[slai]
교활한, 간사한, 음흉한
having or showing a cunning and deceitful nature

smash
[smæʃ]
박살내다, 파괴하다, 격렬하게 충돌하다; 분쇄함, 강타, 파괴
to break (something) into pieces suddenly, noisily, and violently; to shatter; to strike or collide suddenly, noisily, and violently

smirk
[smə́:rk]
(자기만족 또는 비웃 듯이) 히죽웃다
smile in an irritatingly smug, conceited, or silly way

smudge
[smʌdʒ]
더러워지다, 얼룩지다; 더러움, 얼룩
to smear something as with dirt, soot, or ink

smug
[smʌg]
자기 만족하는, 우쭐한, 자부심 넘치는
highly self-satisfied: complacent

smuggle
[smʌgl]
밀수하다
to move (goods) illegally into or out of a country

sneak
[sni:k]
살금살금 걷다, 몰래 돌아다니다; 은밀한, 몰래 하는
to go or move in a quiet, stealthy way

snug
[snʌg]
아늑한, 편안한, 따뜻하고 기분 좋은; 아늑하게 해주다
comfortably sheltered; cozy

soak
[sóuk]
흠뻑 적시다; 담그기
make or allow (something) to become thoroughly wet by immersing it in liquid

sober
[sóubə(r)]
술 취하지 않은, 술 마시지 않은; 침착해지다, 술이 깨다
not affected by alcohol; not drunk; serious, sensible, and solemn

sobriety
[səbráiəti]
근엄, 엄숙, 금주
the state of being sober

soggy
[sági]
함빡 젖은, 기운이 없는, 맥 빠진
saturated or sodden with moisture; soaked: soggy clothes; lacking spirit; dull

soothing
[súːðiŋ]
진정시키는
gently calming

sound
[saund]
건전한, 건강한, 손상되지 않은, 완전한; 소리; 소리를 내다
free from defect, decay, or damage; in good condition

sparse
[spáːrs]
희박한, 드문드문 있는
of few and scattered elements

Spartan
[spáːrtn]
엄격한, 간소한, 사치부리지 않는
showing the indifference to comfort or luxury traditionally associated with ancient Sparta

spectrum
[spéktrəm]
빛의 분산, 스펙트럼, 범위
the distribution of energy emitted by a radiant source, as by an incandescent body, arranged in order of wavelengths

speculation
[spèkjuléiʃən]
사색, 성찰, 고찰, 견해, 추론
the forming of a theory or conjecture without firm evidence

spoil
[spɔil]
망쳐놓다, 손상하다, 결딴내다, 못 쓰게 만들다, 썩이다
to impair the value or quality of

spontaneous
[spantéiniəs]
사전계획 없이 행해진, 자발적으로 움직이는
performed or occurring as a result of a sudden inner impulse or inclination and without premeditation or external stimulus

sprawling
[sprɔ́:liŋ]
(도시, 가로 등) 불규칙하게 넓어지는
spreading out in different directions

squander
[skwándər]
탕진하다, 낭비하다; 낭비
to waste (something, esp. money or time) in a reckless and foolish manner

squat
[skwa:t]
땅딸막한, 웅크린, 웅크리고 앉은; 웅크리다; 웅크리기
short and thick; low and broad

stabilize
[stéibəlàiz]
안정시키다, 변동하지 않게 되다
to make stable or steadfast

stagnant
[stǽgnənt]
(물이) 흐르지 않고 고여있는
having no current or flow and often having an unpleasant smell as a consequence

stain
[stéin]
얼룩; 더럽히다
a colored patch or dirty mark that is difficult to remove; mark (something) with colored patches or dirty marks that are not easily removed

stalk
[stɔ:k]
몰래 다가가다, 살그머니 접근하다, 몰래 추적하다; 몰래 추적하기
to pursue by tracking stealthily

stammer
[stǽmə(r)]
말을 더듬다; 말더듬이
to speak with involuntary pauses or repetitions

stark
[stáːrk]
장식없는, 간소한, 뚜렷한, 분명한, 완전한, 강한, 굳센
simple, bluntly plain, naked; sharply clear; complete, sheer; strong and powerful

starry-eyed
[stáːriàid]
순진하게 열정적이고 이상적인, 비현실적인, 이상적인
naively enthusiastic or idealistic; failing to recognize the practical realities of a situation

startle
[stáːrtl]
흠칫하다, 소스라치다, 깜짝 놀라다; 놀람
to alarm, frighten, or surprise suddenly

static
[stǽtik]
정지된, 움직이지 않는
having no motion

steadfast
[stédfæst]
확고한, 부동의, 변치 않는, 고정된, 견실한
fixed or unchanging; steady

steep
[stíːp]
가파른; 경사가 급한 장소; 흠뻑 적시다
extremely or excessively high

sterile
[stérəl]
균이 없는, 살균한, 불임의, 새끼를 낳지 못하는, 메마른, 불모의, 열매를 맺지 못하는, 결실이 없는, 무익한
not producing or incapable of producing offspring

sterilize
[stérəlàiz]
살균하다, 소독하다, (토지, 토양을) 메마르게 하다, 불모화하다
to make free from live bacteria or other microorganisms

stiff
[stif]
굳은, 딱딱한, 휘지 않는; 딱딱하게, 경직되어
difficult to bend; rigid

still
[stíl]
움직임, 소리가 없는
not moving or making a sound

stingy
[stíndʒi]
인색한, 구두쇠의
giving or spending reluctantly

stir
[stə:(r)]
휘젓다, 뒤섞다, 각성시키다, 불러일으키다, 북돋우다; 휘젓기, 동요
to alter the placement of slightly; disarrange; to cause to move briskly or vigorously; bestir

Stoic
[stóuik]
고통을 참고 내색하지 않는, 감정을 드러내지 않는, 스토아 학파의
enduring pain and hardship without showing one's feelings or complaining

straightforward
[strèitfɔ́:rwərd]
솔직한, 애매함 없는
precise, candid, undeviating

streamline
[strí:mlàin]
(일, 과정 등을) 능률적으로 하다, 간소화하다, 유선형으로 하다; 유선형
to design or construct with a streamline; to make simpler or more efficient

stringent
[stríndʒənt]
엄격한, 엄한
rigorous, tight

strive
[stráiv]
노력하다, 애쓰다
to devote serious effort or energy

stumble
[stʌ́mbl]
채어 비틀거리다, 망설이다, 더듬거리다; 비틀거림, 실수
to miss one's step in walking or running; trip and almost fall

stun
[stʌ́n]
깜짝 놀라게 하다, 실신케 하다; 놀라게 하는것, 기절시키기
to knock unconscious or into a dazed or semiconscious state; to astonish or shock (someone) so that they are temporarily unable to react

stupefy
[stú:pifài]
감각을 (술, 마약으로) 마비시키다, (감동으로) 망연하게 하다, 대경 실색케 하다
to dull the senses or faculties of

subdue
[səbdúː]

정복하다, (사람, 적을) 압도하다, 제압하다, 진압하다
to quiet or bring under control by physical force or persuasion; make tractable

submerge
[səbmə́ːrdʒ]

물에 푹 빠뜨리다, 잠수시키다
to cause to be under water

subsidiary
[səbsídièri]

보조적인, 보충하는; 보조물, 부속자
furnishing aid or support, of secondary importance

subsidize
[sʌ́bsədàiz]

보조금을 지급하며 돕다
to support (an organization or activity) financially

substantial
[səbstǽnʃəl]

상당히 크고 중요한, 튼튼한, 실제적인, 현실적인; 실질적인 것
of considerable importance, size, or worth; strongly built or made; real and tangible rather than imaginary

substantiate
[səbstǽnʃièit]

입증하다, 구체화하다
to establish by proof or competent evidence

subtle
[sʌ́tl]

미묘한, 분석이나 설명이 힘든 복잡한
so delicate or precise as to be difficult to analyze or describe, delicately complex

suffocate
[sʌ́fəkèit]

호흡이 곤란하게 하다, 숨차게 하다, 불쾌하게 하다
to impair the respiration of; asphyxiate

suppress
[səprés]

억제하다, 참다, 억누르다
to put an end to forcibly; subdue

summon
[sʌ́mən]

호출하다, 소환하다, (특히 법원으로) 출두를 명하다
to call together; convene

supreme
[səprémosi]
최고의, 최상의
(of authority or an office, or someone holding it) superior to all others; strongest, most important, or most powerful

surge
[sə́:rdʒ]
쇄도, 밀려옴; 물결치게 하다, 끓어오르게 하다
a sudden powerful forward or upward movement, esp. by a crowd or by a natural force such as the waves or tide

surrender
[səréndər]
포기하다, 양보하다; 항복, 양도, 포기
to give up or hand over (a person, right, or possession), typically on compulsion or demand

surrogate
[sə́:rəgèit]
대리인, 대행자; 대리를 시키다, 대용하다
a substitute, esp. a person deputizing for another in a specific role or office

susceptible
[səséptəbl]
~하기 쉬운
impressionable, responsive, liable

suspend
[səspénd]
매달다, 막다, 연기시키다
to hang, dangle; to prevent; to defer, delay

sustain
[səstéin]
유지하다, 지탱하다, 떠받치다, 격려하다
to continue, keep; to support or strengthen physically or mentally

symmetry
[símətri]
대칭, 균형
balanced proportions

synergy
[sínərdʒi]
공동 작용, 협동, (근육 등의) 협력 작용, (약물의) 상승 작용
the interaction of two or more agents or forces so that their combined effect is greater than the sum of their individual effects

synopsis
[sinápsis]
요약, 개요
a brief summary or general survey of something

synoptic
[sináptik]

요약의

affording a general view of a whole

synthesis
[sínθisis]

종합, 통합, 합성

the combining of separate elements or substances to form a coherent whole

synthesize
[sínθəsàiz]

합성하다, 종합하다

to combine (a number of things) into a coherent whole

tacky
[tǽki]

촌스런, 저속한, 끈끈한

showing poor taste and quality, shabby, seedy, dowdy; (of glue, paint, or other substances) retaining a slightly sticky feel; not fully dry

tainted
[téintid]

더렵혀진

contaminated or polluted

tangible
[tǽndʒəbl]

만질 수 있는, 현실적인, 구체적인

perceptible by touch; clear and definite; real

tardy
[tá:rdi]

느린, 더딘, 마지못해 하는; 지각하기

occurring, arriving, acting, or done after the scheduled, expected, or usual time; late

tarnish
[tá:rniʃ]

광택을 잃다, 더럽히다; 흐림, 변색, 오점

to lose or cause to lose luster, esp. as a result of exposure to air or moisture

tasty
[téisti]

재미있는, 흥미를 끄는, 맛있는

having or showing good taste; tasteful

tear
[tɛər]
찢다, 분리하다, 화급하게 움직이다, 돌진하다; 찢기, 갈라진 틈
to separate, rend, lacerate, divide; to move with heedless speed; to rush headlong

tease
[ti:z]
놀리다, 괴롭히다, 노리개로 삼다; 괴롭히기
to annoy or pester; vex

technical
[téknikəl]
기술적인, 전문적인
(esp. of a book or article) requiring special knowledge to be understood

tedious
[tí:diəs]
지루한, 재미없는
too long, slow, or dull; tiresome or monotonous

tenacious
[tənéiʃəs]
꽉 쥐고 놓지 않는, 몹시 집착하는, 끈질긴, 고집센
tending to keep a firm hold of something; determined

tenacity
[tənǽsəti]
고집, 인내, 끈기, 집착
state of being tenacious

tentative
[téntətiv]
임시적인, 주저하는; 가설, 시도
not certain or fixed; provisional

tenuous
[ténjuəs]
가느다란, 희박한, (논거가) 박약한
having little substance or strength

terrify
[térəfài]
매우 두렵게 하다, 위협하다
to cause to feel extreme fear

testimonial
[tèstəmóuniəl]
추천서, 감사, 찬양의 표현; 증명이 되는, 감사를 나타내는
a written affirmation of another's character or worth: a personal recommendation

therapeutic
[θèrəpjú:tik]
치료의, 치료의 힘이 있는
having or exhibiting healing powers

thoroughgoing
[θə́:rougòuiŋ]
철저한
involving or attending to every detail or aspect of something

thrift
[θríft]
검소함
the quality of using money and other resources carefully and not wastefully

thrive
[θráiv]
번성하다, 무성하게 자라다
(of a child, animal, or plant) grow or develop well or vigorously

tilt
[tílt]
기울다, 기울게 하다; 기울기, 경사
(cause) to slope, as by raising one end; incline

timeless
[táimlis]
영원한, 무한한
independent of time; eternal

tiresome
[táiərsəm]
지루하게 하는, 짜증나게 하는
causing one to feel bored or annoyed

tolerant
[tálərənt]
자신과 다른 의견이나 행동양식을 인정해 주는, 관대한, 인내해 주는
showing willingness to allow the existence of opinions or behavior that one does not necessarily agree with

tongue-tied
[tʌ́ŋtàid]
(당황하여) 말문이 막힌
too shy or embarrassed to speak

torrential
[tərénʃəl]
급류 같이 빠른, 급류 같이 세찬, (비가) 억수로 쏟아지는, 격렬한, 압도적인
flowing or surging abundantly; wild

totalitarianism
[toutǽlətέəriən]
전체주의
of or relating to a system of government that is centralized and dictatorial and requires complete subservience to the state

touchy
[tʌ́tʃi]
민감하게 구는, 화를 잘 내는
(of a person) oversensitive and irritable

trail
[treil]
(흔적을) 따라가다; 오솔길, 발자국
to follow (a person or animal), typically by using marks, signs, or scent left behind

tranquility
[trænkwíləti]
고요함, 평온함
the quality or state of being tranquil; serenity; composure

transition
[trænzíʃən]
변화, 전이
the process or a period of changing from one state or condition to another

treasure
[tréʒər]
소중히 여기다, 간직하다; 보물, 재산, 귀중품
to value highly, keep carefully (a valuable or valued item)

trepidation
[trèpədéiʃən]
두려움, 당황, 혼란
a feeling of fear or agitation about something that may happen

trespass
[tréspæs]
(종교 또는 도덕적인) 죄, 위반, 부정, 불법 침해, 불법 침입; 죄를 범하다, 침해하다, 침입하다
violation of moral or social ethics; an unlawful act committed on the person, property, or rights of another; to commit an offense or a sin, to transgress or err; to make an unwarranted or uninvited incursion

tribute
[tríbjuːt]
감사, 존경, 찬양의 표시
an act, statement, or gift that is intended to show gratitude, respect, or admiration

trivial
[tríviəl]

사소한
of little value or importance

turbulent
[tə́:rbjulənt]

무질서하고 혼란스러운, 동요한, 험한
characterized by conflict, disorder, or confusion; not controlled or calm

turmoil
[tə́:rmɔil]

소란, 혼란, 불안, 동요
a state of great disturbance, confusion, or uncertainty

tyranny
[tírəni]

폭정, 전제정치
cruel and oppressive government or rule

ubiquitous
[ju:bíkwətəs]

어디에나 있는, 도처에 있는
present, appearing, or found everywhere

unabashed
[ʌnəbǽʃt]

부끄러워하지 않는, 겁먹지 않는, 당황하지 않는, 침착한
unashamed, shameless

unaffected
[ʌnəféktid]

꾸밈 없는, 가장 없는, 허세부리지 않는
free from affectation; genuine

unassailable
[ʌnəséiləbl]

(폭풍우, 세력, 활기 등이) 줄어들지 않는, 약해지지 않는, 공격할 수 없는, 논쟁의 여지가 없는
undiminished

unassuming
[ʌnəsú:miŋ]

겸손한, 주제넘지 않는, 삼가는
not pretentious or arrogant; modest

unavailing
[ʌnəvéiliŋ]

효과 없는, 소용없는
achieving little or nothing; ineffective; useless, futile

uncanny
[ʌnkǽni]
신비로운, 이상한, 예리한
strange or mysterious, esp. in an unsettling way

undercut
[ʌndərkʌ́t]
약화시키다, 밑을 잘라내다
to diminish or destroy the province or effectiveness of; undermine

underestimate
[ʌndəréstəmèit]
과소평가하다
to estimate as being less than the actual

undermine
[ʌndərmàin]
약화시키다
to damage or weaken (someone or something), esp. gradually or insidiously

underplay
[ʌndərpléi]
하찮게 보이게 하다
to raise or support by something laid under

understated
[ʌndərstéitid]
과소평가된
avoiding obvious emphasis

undeserved
[ʌndizə́:rvd]
가치 없는, 정당성 없는, 부당한
unmerited

unexceptionable
[ʌniksépʃənəbl]
반대의 여지가 없는
beyond any reasonable objection; irreproachable

ungovernable
[ʌngʌ́vərnəbl]
통제나 지배가 불가능한
impossible to control or govern

unorthodox
[ʌnɔ́:rθədɑ:ks]
정통이 아닌, 이단의
breaking with convention or tradition; not orthodox

unprecedented
[ʌnprésədèntid]
전례 없는
never done or known before, novel, unexampled

unruly
[ʌnrúːli]
규칙을 따르지 않는, 제어하기 어려운
disorderly and disruptive and not amenable to discipline or control

unseemly
[ʌnsíːmli]
(행동 등이) 적절하지 않은, 브적당하거
(of behavior or actions) not prcper or appropriate

unspoken
[ʌnspóukən]
무언의, 암묵적인
not expressed in speech; tacit

unsubstantiated
[ʌnsəbstǽnʃieitid]
입증되지 않은, 증거가 없는, 근거가 없는
not supported with proof or evidence; not verified

untainted
[ʌntéintid]
더럽혀지지 않은
not tarnished, contaminated, o⁻ polluted

unveil
[ʌnvéil]
덮개를 걷다, 공개하다
show or announce publicly for the first time

unwarranted
[ʌnwɔ́ːrəntid]
정당성 없는, 보증없는
indefensible, insupportable, un_ustifiable, unwarrantable, baseless

uphold
[ʌphóuld]
수호하다, 지지하다
to give support to

uptight
[ʌptáit]
긴장한; 초조한, 신경질인, 딱딱한, 격식 차린, 보수적인
tense; nervous

urbane
[əːrbéin]
세련된, 예의 바른, 도시풍의
(of a person, esp. a man) suave courteous, and refined in manner

urge
[ə:rdʒ]
강력히 밀고 나아가다, 강력히 추진하다, 강제하다, 열심히 권하다, 촉구하다;
사람을 몰아대기, 자극, 추진력
force or drive forward or onward; impel

utter
[ʌtər]
완전한, 절대적인; 말하다
complete, absolute; to make (a sound) with one's voice

vaccinate
[vǽksənèit]
예방 접종하다
to treat with a vaccine to produce immunity against a disease;
inoculate

vacuous
[vǽkjuəs]
생각이 없는, 어리석은
having or showing a lack of thought or intelligence; mindless

vacuum
[vǽkjuəm]
진공상태; 빈, 공허한, 무의미한
absence of matter; a space empty of matter; a state of
emptiness; a void a. of, relating to, or used to create a vacuum

vagabond
[vǽgəbànd]
방랑하는; 방랑자
moving from place to place without a fixed home; wandering; one
leading a vagabond life; vagrant

vagary
[vəgɛ́əri, véigəri]
변덕, 엉뚱한 짓
an unexpected and inexplicable change in a situation or in
someone's behavior

vagrant
[véigrənt]
방랑자, 부랑자; 방랑하는, (생각 등이) 변덕스런, 불안정한
a person without a settled home or regular work who wanders
from place to place and lives by begging; moving or occurring
unpredictably; inconstant

vague
[veig]
분명치 않은, 막연한, 모호한
not clearly expressed; inexplicit

vain
[véin]

헛된; 허영심 강한
producing no result; useless; excessively proud

vainglorious
[vèinglɔ́ːriəs]

허영심 강한
having inordinate pride in oneself or one's achievements; showing excessive vanity

vanity
[vǽnəti]

허영심, 무가치
something that is vain, empty, or valueless

vaporous
[véipərəs]

증기의, 실질적이 않은, 공허한, 가벼운, 신뢰할 수 없는, 자주 변하는
relating to or resembling vapor; nsubstantial, vague, or ethereal; extravagantly fanciful; high-flown

varnish
[váːrniʃ]

니스칠하다, 광내다; 바니스, 니스를 칠한 표면, 광택
to cover with varnish (a paint containing a solvent and an oxidizing or evaporating binder, used to coat a surface with a hard, glossy, transparent film); resin dissolved in a liquid for applying on wood, metal, or other materials to form a hard, clear, shiny surface when dry

velocity
[vəlásəti]

속도
the speed of something in a given direction

venture
[véntʃər]

감히 ~하다, 모험적으로 해보다; 모험, 투기
to undertake the risks and dangers of

versatile
[vɛ́ːrsətl]

다재 다능한, 다용도의
variable, having many uses or applications

veto
[víːtou]

거부권, 금지, 거부; 거부하다, 금지하다
an authoritative prohibition or rejection of a proposed or intended act

viable
[váiəbl]
실행 가능한; 생존할 수 있는
capable of working successfully; feasible; (of a plant, animal, or cell) capable of surviving or living successfully

vicious
[víʃəs]
부도덕한, 악의적인
having the nature of vice

victimize
[víktimàiz]
(남에게) 손해를 주다, 고통을 주다; (남을) 피해자로 만들다
to subject to swindle or fraud

vigilant
[vídʒələnt]
경계하는, 방심하지 않는
keeping careful watch for possible danger or difficulties

vigorous
[vígərəs]
원기 왕성한, 활력적인
full of physical or mental strength or active force

vital
[váitl]
매우 중요한, 활기 넘치는, 생명의
absolutely necessary or important; essential; full of energy; lively

void
[vɔid]
법적 효력이 없는, 빈, 공허한
not valid or legally binding

volatile
[válətail]
휘발성의, 변덕스러운, 변하기 쉬운
evaporating readily at normal temperatures and pressures

voluminous
[vəlú:mənəs]
부피가 큰, 방대한, 헐거운, 권수가 많은, 저작이 많은
having great volume, fullness, size, or number

vulgar
[vʌ́lgər]
저속한
lacking sophistication or good taste; unrefined

vulnerable
[vʌ́lnərəbl]
연약한, 상처받기 쉬운, 공격받기 쉬운
capable of being physically or emotionally wounded

wander
[wándər]

(정처 없이) 헤매다, 배회하다; 어슬렁 거리기, 산책
to walk or move in a leisurely, casual, or aimless way; to move slowly away from a fixed point or place

warrant
[wɔ́:rənt, wár-]

정당화하다, 허가하다; 허가, 인가, 담보, 증명서
to authorize, guarantee

wary
[wɛ́əri]

조심하는, 주의하는
feeling or showing caution about possible dangers or problems

watchful
[wátʃfəl]

경계를 서는, 조심하는, 주의 깊은
watching or observing someone or something closely; alert and vigilant

waver
[véivər]

흔들리다, 머뭇거리다; 흔들림, 동요
to move unsteadily back and forth

weary
[wíːri]

피곤한, 지친, 울적한; 싫증이 나다
physically or mentally fatigued; expressive of or prompted by fatigue

weighty
[wéiti]

무거운, 중요한, 중대한, 영향력 있는, 유력한
having considerable weight; heavy

weld
[weld]

용접하다, 접합하다, 결합하다, (하나로) 합치다, 통일하다; 용접
to bring into close association or union

whet
[hwét]

날카롭게 하다, 자극하다; 갈기, 벼리기, 자극물
to sharpen the blade of; to excite or stimulate (someone's desire, interest, or appetite)

whimsical
[hwímzikəl]

변덕스런, 예측 불허의
acting or behaving in a capricious manner

whimsy
[wímzi]
변덕, 기묘한 생각
an odd or fanciful idea; a whim

willful
[wílfəl]
고집불통의, 고의적인
stubborn, intentional

willowy
[wíloui]
(사람이) 키 크고 날씬한, 유연한, 버드나무 같은
resembling a willow; pliant; gracefully tall and slender

wiretap
[wáiətæp]
전화 도청하다
to connect a listening device to a telephone line to secretly monitor a conversation

wit
[wít]
재치, 지혜가 있는 사람
mental sharpness and inventiveness, keen intelligence; a person who has wit

withdrawn
[wiðdrɔ́:n]
사교적이지 않은
socially detached and unresponsive

withhold
[wiθhóuld]
보류하다, 주지 않다, 억제하다
to hold back from action

withstand
[wiθstǽnd]
저항하다, 버티다
to stand up against

worldly
[wə́:rldli]
세속적인, 경험 많고 세상을 잘 아는
of or concerned with material values or ordinary life rather than a spiritual existence; experienced, sophisticated

yearn
[jə́:rn]
갈망하다, 동경하다, 그리워하다, 사모하다
to have a strong, often melancholy desire

yield
[ji:ld]

포기하다, 내주다, 양도하다, 주다, 산출하다, 낳다
to give up, as in defeat; surrender or submit

yielding
[jí:ldiŋ]

유순한, 순종적인, 고분고분한
(of a person) complying with the requests or desires of others

zealot
[zélət]

광신도, 열광자
overenthusiastic person

zealous
[zéləs]

열심인, 열렬한, 열광적인
ardent, fervent

zest
[zést]

기분좋은 맛, 자극, 흥미, 관심; 풍미를 더해주다
piquancy, exciting quality, gusto

zone
[zoun]

지구로 나누다, 구분하다, 구획하다; 지역, 지구
to divide into zones

How to study English?

영어강사를 십여 년 하면서 제일 많이 받는 질문은 "어떻게 영어공부를 해야 하나요?"입니다.
저의 대답은 늘 "영어랑 친해지세요~"였죠.

한번은 제 주치의가 교환교수로 미국에 가게 되셨는데, 제가 영어 강사이니 "영어공부를 어떻게 해야
하나요?"라고 물으시더군요. 제가 그 분께 드린 말씀은 "병원과 관련된 '미드'를 많이 보세요"였습니다.
그 분은 현직 의사이시니 당연히 전문 의학 용어들은 영어로 이미 알고 계실테죠. 그러면 어떻게 회화를
늘려야 할까요? 익숙한 상황에서 내가 이미 알고 있는 어휘들이 어떻게 사용되는지를 확인하고 거기서
하나 하나 생활영어를 습득해 나가는 것이죠. 물론 처음에는 제자리 걸음을 한다는 느낌도 들 수
있겠지만, 내가 알고 있는 단어가 배우들의 대사로 내게 이해 될 때의 기분은~ 경험해 보지 않으면
그 재미를 모르실 거예요. 장기적으로 봤을 때, 쉽지 않은 영어공부를 꾸준히 할 수 있는 방법은 공부를
"재미"있게 하는 방법이고, 그럴 때 우리가 손쉽게 이용할 수 있는 방법이 미드나 영화죠.

영어 공부법(How to study English)을 이해하기 위해서 먼저 생각해 봐야 할 것이 바로 what is
English?입니다. 물론 English가 언어(language)인 것은 모두 알고 있죠. 그럼 여기서 말하는 what
is English?에 대한 대답은, English는 단순한 의사소통의 수단인 language로써의 English 뿐만
아니라 culture를 담고 있다는 것이죠. 다시 말해서 언어를 이해하기 위해서는 문화를 이해해야 한다는
것입니다. 사과가 apple이고 강아지가 puppy인 것은 암기를 해야 하는 부분이겠죠. 하지만
Big Apple이 '큰 사과'가 아닌 '뉴욕'을 칭하는 것이란 걸 이해해야 English를 안다고 할 수 있겠죠.

그래서 제일 먼저 기본적인 어휘를 암기하시고, 그것이 끝나면 곧바로 마구마구 영어와 친해져서 그
문화를 이해하는 것이 영어 공부의 최선의 방법입니다. 물론 단기적으로 영어시험 점수를 따야 하는
상황이라면 얘기는 달라지겠지만, 일반적인 언어 English를 공부하는 방법은 이 방법이 최선이죠.

One Shot Voca는 여러분이 어떤 분야의 English가 필요하시던지 기본적인 어휘를 암기하는데
지침서가 되어 줄 것입니다. 그 기본 위에, 내가 알고 있는 어휘들이 일상 회화에서 어떻게 활용되는지를
보고, 듣고, 그리고 따라 하면서, 다음 번에는 내가 직접 회화에서 한 번 써보고 이메일에도 써보고
영어는 그렇게 익혀나가는 것입니다.

물론 첫단계 -단어암기- 가 만만치 않죠. 제일 단순한 듯 하지만, 제일 지루할 수도 있는 단계인데요,
이것만 넘어서면 영어를 재미있게 공부하는 단계에 한 걸음 성큼 다가갈 수 있습니다.

그 첫 단계 One Shot Voca와 함께 시작해 보세요!

PART 3

One shot voca

abeyance
[əbéiəns]
(일시적) 중지, 중단
temporary inactivity

abreast of
[əbrést]
~와 나란히 하는, 뒤떨어지지 않는, (최신 정보 등) 알고 있는
up to a particular standard or level especially of knowledge of recent developments

abscission
[æbsiʒən]
절단, 절제, 갑작스러운 중단
the act of cutting off

abscond
[æbskánd]
종적을 감추다, 몰래 도주하다, 실종하다
to leave quickly and secretly and hide oneself, often to avoid arrest or prosecution

abstruse
[æbstrú:s]
난해한, 심오한
difficult to understand; obscure

abysmal
[əbízməl]
심연의, 매우 깊은, 끔찍한, 매우 나쁜
having immense or fathomless extension downward, backward, or inward; extremely bad; appalling

acclaim
[əkléim]
칭송하다, 환호를 보내다, 갈채를 보내다
to praise enthusiastically and publicly

accolade
[ǽkəlèid]
영예, 영광, 찬양, 기사 작위 수여
an award or privilege granted as a special honor or as an acknowledgment of merit

accrue
[əkrú:]
(증가, 첨가에 의해서) 생기다
to accumulate or be added periodically

achromatic
[ǽkrəmǽtik]
무색의
designating color perceived to have zero saturation and therefore no hue, such as neutral grays, white, or black

acquiesce
[ӕkwiés]

(마지못해) 순응하다, 따르다
to accept something reluctantly but without protest

adjourn
[ədʒə́:rn]

(토의, 회의 등을) 연기하다, 후회시키다
to suspend until a later stated time

adrift
[ədríft]

표류하는, 떠내려가는, 불안정한, 방황하는
floating without being either moored or steered

adroit
[ədróit]

솜씨좋은, 능숙한
clever or skillful in using the hands or mind

affront
[əfrʌ́nt]

(면전에서) 모욕; 모욕하다
open insult; to insult openly

aggrandize
[əgrǽndaiz]

(권력, 힘, 지위, 재산, 명성 등) 증대시키다
to increase the power, status, or wealth of; to enhance the
reputation of (someone) beyond what is justified by the facts

aggrieved
[əgrí:vd]

(부당한 대우에) 분개한, 억울해 하는
feeling resentment at having been unfairly treated

agile
[ǽdʒəl]

(행동 등이) 민첩하고 유연한, 빠른, 머리회전이 빠른
able to move quickly and easily

alacrity
[əlǽkrət]

민활, 기민, 선뜻함
cheerful willingness; eagerness; speed or quickness; celerity

alloy
[ǽlɔi, əlɔi]

합금하다, 불순하게 하다; 합금 혼합
to combine (metals) to form an alloy, to debase by the addition of
an inferior element

aloof
[əlúːf]
쌀쌀맞은, 무관심한, 초연한
not friendly or forthcoming; cool and distant, remote in manner

ambrosial
[æmbróuʒəl]
아주 맛있는, 향기로운
suggestive of ambrosia; fragrant or delicious

ameliorate
[əmíːljərèit, -liər-]
개선하다, 개량하다
to make (something bad or unsatisfactory) better

amenity
[əménəti, əmíːn-]
편의시설, 쾌적함, 예의
a desirable or useful feature or facility of a building or place; the pleasantness of a place or a person

amiable
[éimiəbl]
상냥한, 남에게 호감을 주는, 친절한, 우호적인
friendly and agreeable in disposition; good-natured and likable

amicable
[ǽmikəbl]
우호적인, 평화적인
characterized by or exhibiting friendliness or goodwill; friendly

amity
[ǽməti]
우호, 우정, 친목
a friendly relationship

amorphous
[əmɔ́ːrfəs]
(형태, 정의가) 불명확한
without a clearly defined shape or form

analgesic
[ænəldʒíːsik]
통증을 없애주는; 진통제
(a drug) acting to relieve pain; an analgesic drug

ancillary
[ǽnsəlèri]
부속의, 보조의; 협력자, 하인, 부속물
subordinate, auxiliary

antic
[ǽntik]
익살스런, 장난끼 있는; 익살, 장난; 장난치다
ludicrously odd; fantastic

apotheosis
[əpàθióusis]
신격화; 신성시, 이상화, 숭배
exaltation to divine rark or stature; deification

appease
[əpíːz]
(요구를 들어주어 적대감 등을) 달래다, 진정시키다
to pacify or placate (someone) by acceding to their demands; to relieve or satisfy (a demand or a feeling)

apposite
[ǽpəzit]
적절한, 딱 들어맞는
strikingly appropriate and relevant

approbation
[æprəbéiʃən]
(공식적) 승인, 칭찬
an expression of warm approval; praise; official approval

appropriate
[əpróuprièit]
(무단으로) 쓰다, 전용하다, (비용) 책정하다, 지출을 승인하다; 적절한, 타당한
to take or make use of without authority or right; to set apart for or assign to a particular purpose or use

apropos
[æprəpóu]
적절한, 알맞은, 시기 적절한
being both relevant and opportune

arbitrary
[áːrbətrèri]
임의의, 제멋대로의, 독재적인
based on random choice or personal whim, rather than any reason or system

arboreal
[aːrbɔ́ːriəl]
나무의
relating to or resembling a tree

arcane
[aːrkéin]
불가사의한, 신비한
understood by few; mysterious or secret

archetype
[áːrkitàip]
원형, 전형
the original or ideal pattern or model,

ardent
[á:rdənt]
열정적인
characterized by warmth of feeling typically expressed in eager zealous support or activity

arduous
[á:rdʒuəs]
몹시 힘든, 견디기 어려운, 벅찬
demanding great effort or labor; difficult

arid
[ǽrid]
매우 건조한, 불모의, 재미없는, 무미 건조한
very dry

artless
[á:rtlis]
꾸밈없는, 솔직한, 자연스러운, 솜씨 없는, 기교 없는
without guile or deception; without effort or pretentiousness; natural and simple; without art, knowledge, skill or finesse

ascendency
[əséndənsi]
영향력, 우세함
superiority or decisive advantage; domination

ascendant
[əséndənt]
상승하는, 올라가는, (힘, 영향력) 우세해지는; 우세, 우위
rising in power or influence

ascent
[əsént]
상승, 올라감
the act or process of rising or going upward

ascertain
[æsərtéin]
확인하다, 명백히 하다
to find out or learn with certainty

ascetic
[əsétik]
금욕적인; 금욕적인 사람
practicing strict self-denial as a measure of personal and especially spiritual discipline; such a person

askew
[əskjú:]
비스듬히, 기울어져, 구부러져, 비뚤어지게; 비스듬한, 비뚤어진
to one side; awry

asperity
[əspérəti]

(말, 태도 등이) 신랄함, 거침, 무뚝뚝함
harshness of tone or manner

aspersion
[əspə́:rʃən, -ʒən]

비방
an attack on the reputation or integrity of someone or something

aspire
[əspáiə(r)]

(특히 위대한 것이나 가치 있는 것을) 갈망하다
to have a great ambition or ultimate goal; desire strongly

assay
[əséi]

조사하다, 분석하다, 시험해 보다
to evaluate; assess

assert
[əsə́:rt]

단언하다, 확언하다, 단호하게 주장하다
to state or declare confidently and positively and often forcefully or aggressively

assertion
[əsə́:rʃn]

단호한 주장
the act of asserting

assimilate
[əsíməlèit]

(지식, 정보 등을) 흡수하다, 소화하다, 동화시키다
to take in (information, ideas, or culture) and understand fully

astute
[əstjú:t, æs-]

명민한, 기민한, 영리한, 약삭빠른
having or showing shrewdness and perspicacity

asunder
[əsʌ́ndə(r)]

(하나로 된 것이) 조각조각으로, 산산이, 따로 따로 떨어져
into separate parts or pieces

attune
[ətjú:n]

조화를 이루다, 조율하다, 적응하다
to make harmonious

augur
[ɔ́ːgər]
전조가 되다, 예언하다
(of an event or circumstance) to portend a good or bad outcome

augury
[ɔ́ːgjər]
예언, 징조, 전조
the art, ability, or practice of auguring; divination

august
[ɔːgʌ́st]
위엄 있는, 장엄한, 당당한, 거룩한, 존엄한, 신분이 높은
inspiring awe or admiration; majestic

auspice
[ɔ́ːspis]
보호, 원조, 전조, 길조
protection or support; a sign indicative of future prospects;
an omen

avarice
[ǽvəris]
탐욕
extreme greed for wealth or material gain

aversion
[əvə́ːrʒən, -ʃən]
혐오감
a strong dislike or disinclination

avert
[əvə́ːrt]
막다, 피하다, (시선을) 돌리다
to prevent or ward off (an undesirable occurrence); turn away
(one's eyes or thoughts)

avid
[ǽvid]
열심인, 열정적인, 탐욕적인
marked by interest and enthusiasm; having an ardent desire or
unbounded craving; greedy

awry
[ərái]
휘어진, 비틀어진, 잘못된, 빗나가는
in a turned or twisted position or direction, askew

baleful
[béilfəl]
해로운, 악의가 있는, 파멸을 가져오는, 불길한
portending evil; ominous

balk
[bɔːk]

주저하다, 방해하다, 막다, 좌절시키다; 방해물, 좌절
to stop short and refuse to proceed; to check or stop by an obstacle, thwart or hinder

balky
[bɔ́ːki]

고집이 센, 말을 안 듣는
reluctant; uncooperative

balm
[báːm]

향유, (피부, 마음 등의) 진정제
a fragrant ointment or preparation used to heal or soothe the skin; something that has a comforting, soothing, or restorative effect

bamboozle
[bæmbúːzl]

(남을) 속이다, 속여먹다
to take in by elaborate methods of deceit; hoodwink

barter
[báːrtə(r)]

물물 교환을 하다, 교역하다
to trade goods or services without the exchange of money

bauble
[bɔ́ːbl]

싸구려, 시시한 것
a small, showy trinket or decoration; something of no importance

beatific
[bìːətífik]

행복이 넘치는
blissfully happy

bedizen
[bidáizən]

꾸미다, 치장하다
to ornament or dress in a showy or gaudy manner

befuddled
[bifə́rd]

혼란스러워하는
confused, unable to think clearly

beguile
[bigàil]

매혹시키다, 속이다, 기만하다
to charm or enchant; to mislead, deceive

belabor
[biléibər]
(논쟁, 일 등을) 오래도록 하다, 계속하다, 길게 늘어놓다
to discuss repeatedly or at length; harp on

beleaguer
[bilí:gər]
괴롭히다, 포위 공격하다
to trouble, harass; to besiege

bemoan
[bimóun]
슬퍼하다, 비탄하다
to mourn over, lament

beneficence
[bənéfəsəns]
선행, 자비
the state or quality of being kind, charitable, or beneficial

benighted
[bináitid]
선악을 분간 못하는, 무지한, 미개의
overtaken by night or darkness; being in a state of moral or
intellectual darkness; unenlightened

benumbed
[binʌmd]
무감각해진
deprived of physical or emotional feeling

bequeath
[bikwí:ð, -kwí:θ]
유증하다, 증여하다, 남기다
to leave (a personal estate or one's body) to a person or other
beneficiary by a will

bequest
[bikwést]
유증으로 남긴 재산, 유언으로 재산 남기기
the act of giving, leaving by will, or passing on to another

berate
[biréit]
호되게 꾸짖다
to scold or criticize (someone) angrily

besmirch
[bismə́:rtʃ]
더럽히다, (명성을) 훼손하다
to make dirty; to damage the reputation of (someone or
something) in the opinion of others

bewail
[biwéil]

통곡하다, 통탄하다
cry or wail loudly about (something); express great regret, disappointment, or bitterness over (something) by complaining about it to others

bifurcate
[báifərkeit]

두 갈래로 가르다, 분기하다
to cause to divide into two branches or parts

bigot
[bígət]

편협한 사람 (나와 생각, 종교, 사상 등이 다른 사람을 배척하는 사람)
a person who is obstinately convinced of the superiority or correctness of one's own opinions and prejudiced against those who hold different

blackmail
[blǽkmèil]

갈취한 금품, 공갈, 협박; 공갈 협박하다
something of value extorted in this manner; to extort or coerce or demand money by threats especially of public exposure or criminal prosecution

blandish
[blǽŋkit]

감언으로 설득하다
to coax (someone) with kind words or flattery

blare
[blέər]

(소리가) 울려 퍼지다, 요란하게 울리다, 떠들어대다; 요란한 소리
to sound loudly and harshly; to cause (something) to sound loudly and harshly

blaspheme
[blǽsfí:m]

모독하다, 욕하다, 중상하다
to execrate

blatant
[bléitənt]

뻔한, 명백한, 떠들 석한, 뻔뻔스런
done openly and unashamedly, completely lacking in subtlety, very obvious

blazon
[bléizn]

(방패에) 문장을 그리다, 과시하다, 자랑하다, 공표하다, 장식하다; 방패형의 문장 바탕, 자랑, 과시
to display prominently or vividly

blight
[bláit]

말라죽게 하다, 해를 가하다, 파괴하다, 망치다; 마름병, 손상의 원인
to infect (plant) with blight; to spoil, harm, or destroy

blithe
[bláið, bláiθ]

명랑한, 쾌활한, 경솔한
showing a casual and cheerful indifference considered to be callous or improper; happy

blurt
[blə:rt]

(말을) 불쑥 내뱉다, 무심코 말하다; 불쑥 말하기
to say (something) suddenly and without careful consideration

boisterous
[bóistərəs]

시끄러운, 야단법석하는
rowdy, noisily turbulent

bombast
[bá:mbæst]

허풍, 과장
grandiloquent, pompous speech or writing

bombastic
[bambǽstik]

허풍떠는, 허세부리는
using high-sounding language with little meaning to impress people

boorish
[búər]

무례한, 촌스런
rude, unmannerly or insensitive

bootless
[bú:tlis]

소용없는, 쓸모 없는
(of a task or undertaking) ineffectual; useless

brackish
[brǽkiʃ]

짭짤한, 맛없는, 불쾌한
having a somewhat salty taste, especially from containing a mixture of seawater and fresh water; distasteful; unpalatable

brandish
[brǽndiʃ]

과시하다
to display ostentatiously

brash
[bræʃ]

(사람, 행위 등이) 성급한, 경솔한, 무모한, (사람, 말씨 등이) 버릇없는, 무례한, 노골적인
lacking in sensitivity or tact

brassy
[bræsi]

뻔뻔스러운, 철면피의, 저속한, 겉치레의, 야한, 가식적인
brazen; insolent; cheap and showy; flashy

brazen
[bréizn]

뻔뻔한, 철면피의
bold and without shame

brevity
[brévəti]

간결함
concise and exact use of words in writing or speech

brisk
[brisk]

팔팔한, 활발한, 기운찬, 기세 좋은; 활기띠게 하다
marked by speed, liveliness, and vigor; energetic

broach
[bróutʃ]

(민감한 이야기를) 꺼내다, 발의하다; 브로치
to raise (a sensitive or difficult subject) for discussion

bromide
[bróumaid]

진부하고 상투적인 말
a trite and unoriginal idea or remark, typically intended to soothe or placate

brook
[brúk]

참다, (반대의견을) 용납하다
to tolerate or allow (something, typically dissent or opposition)

bucolic
[bju:kálik]

전원적인, 양치기의, 목양자의; 전원시 , 목가
of the countryside; of shepherds

bumptious
[bʌmpʃəs]

거만한, 오만한, 자기주장이 지나치게 강한
self-assertive or proud to an irritating degree

bungle
[bʌŋgl]
어설픈 짓 하다, 실수하다; 서투른 솜씨, 실수
to carry out (a task) clumsily or incompetently, leading to failure or an unsatisfactory outcome

buoyant
[bɔiənt, búːjənt]
부력이 있는, 기운찬, 명랑한
able to stay afloat or rise to the top of a liquid or gas; cheerful and optimistic

buttress
[bʌtris]
지탱하다, 지지하다; 부벽, 지지자, 후원
to support a wall, to support, justify, strengthen

cacophony
[kækɔ́fəni]
귀에 거슬리는 음, 불협화음; 소음
jarring, discordant sound; dissonance

cagey
[kéidʒi]
터놓지 않는, 조심하는
reluctant to give information owing to caution or suspicion

cajole
[kədʒóul]
감언으로 꼬셔서 ~하게하다
to persuade with flattery or gentle urging especially in the face of reluctance

calamitous
[kəlǽmitəs]
재앙을 가져오는, 불행한, 비참한
causing or involving calamity; disastrous

calamity
[kəlǽməti]
재앙, 재난
an event causing great and often sudden damage or distress; disastrous

calibrate
[kǽləbrèit]
(총의) 구경을 재다, (온도계, 자 등) 눈금을 정하다, 조정하다
to standardize (as a measuring instrument) by determining the deviation from a standard so as to ascertain the proper correction factors

callow
[kǽlou]
미성숙한, 경험이 없는
inexperienced and immature

calumniate
[kəlʌ́mnièit]
중상하다, 비방하다
to make maliciously or knowingly false statements about

calumny
[kǽləmni]
중상, 비방
the making of false and defamatory statements in order to damage someone's reputation; slander

camaraderie
[ka:mərá:dəri]
우정, 동지애
mutual trust and friendship among people who spend a lot of time together

canvass
[kǽnvəs]
(선거구) 유세하다, 여론조사하다, 면밀히 살피다, 간청하다, 부탁하다; 조사, 호별 방문
to seek orders or votes; to examine in detail

capitulate
[kəpítʃulèit]
항복하다
to surrender, cease to resist

caprice
[kəprí:s]
변덕, 예측 할 수 없는 변화
a sudden and unaccountable change of mood or behavior

capricious
[kəpríʃəs]
변덕스런
characterized by or subject to whim; impulsive and unpredictable

captious
[kǽpʃəs]
트집잡는, 심술 사나운
(of a person) tending to find fault or raise petty objections

cardinal
[ká:rdinəl]
으뜸인, 가장 중요한, 기본적인
of foremost importance; paramount

castigate
[kǽstəgèit]
징계하다, 비난하다
to reprimand (someone) severely

catholic
[kǽθəlik]
(취향이) 폭넓은, 보편적인
including a wide variety of things; all-embracing

cavil
[kǽvəl]
트집잡다, 덮어 놓고 이의를 제기하다; 쓸데없는 이의, 트집잡기
to make petty or unnecessary objections

cavort
[kəvɔ́:rt]
흥청거리다, 뛰놀다
to apply oneself enthusiastically to sexual or disreputable pursuits; to leap or dance about in a lively manner

cement
[simént]
접합되다, 교착하다; 접합제, 시멘트
to bind with or as if with cement; to become cemented

censorious
[sensɔ́:riəs]
매우 비난적인
critical, marked by or given to censure

censure
[sénʃər]
비난하다; 심판 비난, 책망
to express severe disapproval of (someone or something), typically in a formal statement

chagrin
[ʃǽgrɪn]
원통함, 분함; 원통하게 여기게 하다
a keen feeling of mental unease, as of annoyance or embarrassment, caused by failure, disappointment, or a disconcerting event; to cause to feel chagrin; mortify or discomfit

champion
[tʃǽmpiən]
옹호하다, 지지하다; 챔피언, 옹호자
to support the cause of; defend; to support, uphold

chary
[tʃɛ́əri]
조심하는, 신중한
cautious, wary; cautious about the amount one gives or reveals

chasten
[tʃéisn]
훈육하다, (마음을) 정화시키다, 겸손하게 하다, 억제하다
to correct by punishment or suffering, discipline; to cause to be more humble or restrained, subdue

chastise
[tʃæstáiz]
체벌하다, 몹시 비난하다
to punish; to rebuke or reprimand severely

chicanery
[ʃikéinəri, tʃi-]
얼버무리기, 핑계, 발뺌
use of trickery to achieve a political, financial, or legal purpose

chide
[tʃàid]
꾸짖다
scold or rebuke

chivalrous
[ʃívəlrəs]
기사도적인, 용감한, 예의 바른
(of a man or his behavior) courteous and gallant, esp. toward women

choleric
[kálərik, kəlér-]
담즙질의, 화를 잘 내는
easily moved to often unreasonable or excessive anger, hot-tempered; angry, irate

churlish
[tʃə́ːrliʃ]
무례한, 막됨, 인색한, 농부의
rude, boorish

clan
[klǽn]
씨족, (일반적으로) 문중, 일족, 한 집안
a division of a tribe tracing descent from a common ancestor

clemency
[klémənsi]
자비, 관대함
mercy; lenience

coagulate
[kouǽgjulèit]
(혈액 등) 응고하다
(of a fluid, esp. blood) change to a solid or semisolid state

coax
[kouks]
(남을 ~하도록) 부추기다, 구슬려 빼앗다
to persuade or try to persuade by pleading or flattery; cajole

coddle
[kάdl]
관대하게 대하다, 너그럽게 대하다, 버릇없이 기르다
to treat in an indulgent or overprotective way

comely
[kʌ́mli]
어여쁜, 아름다운, 걸맞는, 훌륭한
pleasing and wholesome in appearance; attractive; suitable; seemly

compendious
[kəmpéndiəs]
요점을 잘 잡은, 간결한
containing or presenting the essential facts of something in a comprehensive but concise way

compliance
[kəmpláiəns]
순응
the act of complying with a wish, request, or demand; acquiescence

compliant
[kəmpláiənt]
순응하는
inclined to agree with others or obey rules, esp. to an excessive degree; acquiescent

composure
[kəmpóuʒər]
평상심
the state or feeling of being calm and in control of oneself

comradeship
[kάmrædʃip]
동료애, 우정
friendship

concession
[kənseʃn]
시인, 패배인정, 양보
the act of conceding

concomitant
[kənkά:mitənt]
공존하는, 동시에 일어나는, 부수하는; 공존성, 부수성
occurring or existing concurrently; attendant

condemn
[kəndém]

비난하다, 책망하다, 유죄를 입증하다
to express strong disapproval of

confer
[kənfə́:r]

부여하다, 수여하다
to grant or bestow (a title, degree, benefit, or right)

configuration
[kənfìgjuréiʃən]

형상, 외형, 배열
an arrangement of elements in a particular form, figure, or combination

congeal
[kəndʒí:l]

응결시키다, 응고시키다
to solidify or coagulate, esp. by cooling

congenital
[kəndʒénətl]

타고난, 선천적인
inherent, innate

congruence
[káŋgruəns]

적합, 일치, 합동
agreement or harmony, state of coinciding exactly when superimposed

congruent
[ká:ŋgruənt]

들어맞는, 적합한, 부합하는, 조화된
corresponding; congruous

congruity
[kəngrú:əti]

적합, 일치, 합동
the quality or fact of being congruent

conjure
[kándʒər]

간청하다, (기억, 생각 등을) 불러내다, 마술부리다, 마법을 걸다
to implore (someone) to do something; to call to mind; make something appear by magic

connive
[kənàiv]

공모하다 , 묵인하다
to conspire to do something considered immoral, illegal, or harmful

connoisseur
[kànəsə́:r]
전문가, 권위자, 감정가
an expert in art or matters of taste

consign
[kənsáin]
위임하다, 위탁하다
to give, transfer, or deliver into the hands or control of another

consummate
[kánsəmèit]
(기술, 실력 등이) 완전한, 완벽한; 완료하다, 달성하다
showing a high degree of skill and flair; complete or perfect

contempt
[kəntémpt]
경멸, 멸시
the feeling that a person or a thing is beneath consideration, worthless, or deserving scorn

contravene
[kántrəví:n]
위반하다, 모순되다, 반박하다
to violate the prohibition or order of (a law, treaty, or code of conduct); to conflict with (a right, principle, etc.)

contrite
[kəntràit, kántrait]
뉘우치는
feeling or expressing remorse or penitence; affected by guilt

contrition
[kəntríʃən]
뉘우침, 회개
sincere remorse for wrongdoing; repentance

contumacious
[kántjuméiʃəs]
고집이 센, 반항적인, 응하지 않는
stubbornly or willfully disobedient to authority

convene
[kənví:n]
소집하다
to assemble or cause to assemble for a common purpose

copious
[kóupiəs]
풍부한, 많은
abundant in supply or quantity

cornucopia
[kɔ:rnjukóupiə]
풍요의 뿔, 풍요의 상징, 풍부, 풍작
an abundant supply of good things of a specified kind

corporeal
[kɔ:rpó:riəl]
육신의, 물질적인, 유형의, 실체적인
bodily; consisting of material objects; tangible

corrigible
[kɔ́(:)ridʒəbl]
고칠 수 있는, 교정 가능한,
capable of being corrected, reformed, or improved

corroborate
[kəráborèit]
확증하다
to strengthen or support with other evidence; make more certain

cosset
[kásit]
응석을 받아주다, 귀여워하다
to care for and protect in an overindulgent way

countenance
[káuntənəns]
찬성하다, 지지하다, 용인하다 참다; 겉모양, 안색, 얼굴, 냉점, 침착, 찬성, 격력
to tolerate, support, approve

covert
[kóuvərt, kʌv-]
숨겨진, 비밀의 ; 덮개, 은폐물, 위장, 은신처
not openly acknowledged or displayed

covetous
[kʌ́vitəs]
탐내는, 갈망하는
having or showing a great desire to possess something, typically
something belonging to someone else

cower
[káuər]
두려워 움츠리다
to crouch down in fear

cozen
[kʌ́zən]
속여 빼앗다, 환심을 사서 자기 것으로 만들다, 속이다
to mislead by means of a petty trick or fraud; deceive

craven
[kréivən]
비겁한; 비겁한 사람
characterized by abject fear; cowardly

craving
[kréiviŋ]
갈망, 열망; 갈망하는
a powerful desire for something

crest
[krést]
닭 벼슬, (산, 파도 등의) 최정상; 깃장식을 달다, 꼭대기에 이르다
a comb on the head of a bird or other animal; the top of
something, esp. a mountain or hill; the curling foamy top of a wave

crestfallen
[kréstfɔːlən]
풀 죽은
dejected

crotchety
[krátʃəti]
화 잘 내는, 까다로운, 변덕스런
irritable

culminate
[kʌlmənèit]
정점에 달하다, ~로 끝나다
to reach a climax or point of highest development

cursory
[kə́rsəri]
겉핥기의, 엉성한, 황급한, 몹시 서두르는, 피상적인
performed with haste and scant attention to detail

curt
[kə́rt]
(말이) 퉁명스럽게 짧은, 무뚝뚝한
rudely brief

curtail
[kərtéil]
단축하다, 줄이다, (비용을) 절감하다
to reduce in extent or quantity; to impose a restriction on

dabble
[dǽbl]
(물을) 튀기다, 재미 삼아 ~ 하다
to immerse (one's hands or feet) partially in water and move them
around gently; to take part in an activity in a casual or
superficial way

dabbler
[dǽblər]
재미로 하는 사람, 장난 삼아 하는 사람
one who engages in an activity superficially or without
serious intent

dash
[dǽʃ]

박살내다, 끼얹다, 돌진하다
to rush, scurry; spirit, verve, energy, vigor

dawdle
[dɔ́:dl]

시간 낭비하다, 허비하다, 꾸물거리다, 늑장부리다; 시간 낭비
one who spends time idly or moves lackadaisically

dearth
[dəːrθ]

부족, 결핍
a scarce supply; a lack

debacle
[dibá:kl]

파괴, 전복, 붕괴, 와해, 큰 재해, 대실패
a sudden, disastrous collapse, downfall, or defeat

debauchery
[dibɔ́:tʃəri]

방탕함
excessive indulgence in sensual pleasures

debunk
[dibʌ́:ŋk]

(허구임을) 드러내다
to expose the falseness or hollowness of (a myth, idea, or belief)

decimate
[désəmèit]

많은 사람을 죽이다, 파괴하다
to kill, destroy, or remove a large percentage or part of; to destroy in large numbers

decipher
[disàifər]

(암호, 수수께끼 등을) 풀다, 해독하다; 해독, 판독
to convert (a text written in code, or a coded signal) into normal language

decorum
[dikɔ́:rəm]

단정함, 예의 바름, 적절함
behavior in keeping with good taste and propriety

decorous
[dékərəs]

단정한, 예의 바른
in keeping with good taste and propriety; polite and restrained

decrepit
[dikrépit]
나이 들어 쇠약해진
elderly and infirm; worn out or ruined because of age or neglect

decrepitude
[dikrépitju:d]
노쇠 (상태), 늙어빠짐, 노망, 망령
the quality or condition of being weakened, worn out, impaired, or broken down by old age, illness, or hard use

defeasible
[difí:zəbl]
무효화할 수 있는, 파기할 수 있는
open to revision, valid objection, forfeiture, or annulment

defer
[difə́:r]
존경하다, 뜻을 따라주다, 연기하다
to submit humbly to (a person or a person's wishes or qualities); to postpone

deferential
[dèfərénʃəl]
공손한
showing deference; respectful

deferrable
[difə́:rəbl]
미룰 수 있는
able to postpone

deflate
[difléit]
수축시키다, 풀 죽게 하다
to collapse by releasing contained air or gas; to cause (someone) to suddenly lose confidence or feel less important

defraud
[difrɔ́:d]
(남을) 속여 (물품을) 빼앗다, 사취하다
to take something from by fraud; swindle

deft
[déft]
솜씨 좋은, 민첩한
neatly skillful and quick in one's movements

defuse
[di:fjú:z]
(긴장 등을) 완화시키다
to reduce the danger or tension in (a difficult situation)

defiant
[difáiənt]
도전적인, 반항적인, 시비조의, 대담한, 오만한
marked by defiance; boldly resisting

defy
[difái]
(공공연하게) 저항하다, 도전하다, 불복종하다; 도전, 공공연한, 반항, 무시
to resist openly or refuse to obey

deification
[dìːəfikéiʃən]
신격화
act of making a god of, glorifying as supreme worth

delineate
[dilínièit]
정확하게 묘사하다
to describe or portray (something) precisely

delve
[delv]
(문제, 자료, 정보 등을) 깊이 파고들다, 철저히 조사하다, 깊이 탐구하다
to search deeply and laboriously

demurrable
[dimə́ːrəbl]
이의를 주장할 수 있는
worthy of objecting

demurral
[dimə́ːrəl]
반대하기, 주저하기
the act or an instance of demurring or hesitating

demure
[dimjúər]
얌전한, 조신한
(of a woman or her behavior) reserved, modest, and shy

denigration
[denigreiʃn]
중상, 비방
the making of false and defamatory statements in order to
damage someone's reputation

denounce
[dináuns]
공공연히 비난하다, (조약) 폐기를 선언하다
to declare publicly to be wrong or evil; to give formal
announcement of the ending of (a treaty)

denunciate
[dinʌ́nsièit]
공공연히 비난하다, 탄핵하다
to denounce, condemn or censure

denude
[dinjú:d]
박탈하다, 발가벗기다
to strip (something) of its covering, possessions, or assets;
make bare

deplore
[diplɔ́:r]
비난하다, 개탄하다
to feel or express strong disapproval of (something)

depraved
[dipréivd]
타락한, 부패한
morally corrupt; perverted

depravity
[diprǽvəti]
타락, 부패, 사악
moral corruption

depredate
[dépridèit]
강탈하다, 약탈하다
to ransack; plunder

deride
[diràid]
조롱하다
to express contempt for; to ridicule

derogate
[dérəgèit]
비하하다, 격하시키다
to disparage

desecrate
[désikrèit]
신성 모독하다
to treat (a sacred place or thing) with violent disrespect; violate

desiccate
[désikèit]
건조시키다
to remove the moisture from (something, esp. food), typically in
order to preserve it

despondent
[dispándənt]

낙심한, 풀 죽은
in low spirits from loss of hope or courage; dejected

destitute
[déstitu:t]

가난한, 빈곤한
utterly lacking; devoid

desuetude
[déswitjù:d]

폐지, 쇠퇴함
a state of disuse or inactivity

desultory
[désəltɔ:ri]

계획 없는, 목적 없는, 성의 없는
lacking a plan, purpose, or enthusiasm

deteriorate
[ditíəriərèit]

악화시키다, 손상시키다
to make inferior in quality or value; become progressively worse

detract
[ditrǽkt]

(가치가) 떨어지다, (주의를) 딴 데로 들리다, 깎아내리다 비방하다
to undergo reduction in value, importance, or quality;
become reduced, as in effect

devastate
[dévəstèit]

황폐시키다, 유린하다
to lay waste; destroy

devious
[dí:viəs]

부정한, 사악한, 돌아가는, 우회하는
showing a skillful use of underhanded tactics to achieve goals;
secret and dishonest; longer and less direct than the most
straightforward way

diaphanous
[daiǽfənəs]

(천이) 얇은, 비치는
(esp. of fabric) light, delicate, and translucent; insubstantial, vague

diatribe
[dáiətràib]

통렬한 비난, 혹평
a forceful and bitter verbal attack against someone or something

dichotomy
[daikátəmi]

이분법
division into two usually contradictory parts or opinions

diffident
[dífədənt]

자신 없는, 기가 죽은, 수줍어하는
modest or shy because of a lack of self-confidence

diffuse
[difjú:z]

퍼뜨리다, 확산시키다; 산만한, 장황한, 확산한, 흩어진
to spread or cause to spread over a wide area or among a large
number of people

digress
[digrés, dai-]

(주제, 본론에서) 벗어나다, 탈선하다
to leave the main subject temporarily in speech or writing

dilettante
[dílitá:nt, dìlitá:nt]

아마추어 (예술가); 아마추어의
a person who cultivates an area of interest, such as the
arts, without real commitment or knowledge

dingy
[díndʒi]

칙칙한, 지저분한
darkened with smoke and grime; dirty or discolored, gloomy
and drab

dire
[dáiər]

끔직한, 불길한, 절박한
(of a situation or event) extremely serious or urgent;
(of a warning or threat) presaging disaster

dirge
[də́:rdʒ]

만가, 비가
a lament for the dead, esp. one forming part of a funeral rite;
a mournful song, piece of music, or poem

disabuse
[dìsəbjú:z]

(그릇된 생각 등을) 바로잡아 주다,
(오해) 풀어주다 to free from a falsehood or misconception

disaffect
[dìsəfékt]

정떨어지게 하다, 불만을 품게 하다
alienate or diminish the affection of; to make unfriendly or less friendly; fill with discontent and unfriendliness; disorder

disaggregate
[disǽgrigèit]

분해하다
to divide into constituent parts

disarming
[disá:rmiŋ]

적개심을 없애주는, 달래는
removing hostility, suspicion, etc., as by being charming

disarray
[disəréi]

어지르다, 혼란 시키다
a state of disorder; confusion

disclaim
[diskléim]

부인하다, 거절하다, 거부하다
to deny or renounce any claim to or connection with; disown

discombobulate
[diskəmbábjuəlèit]

혼란시키다, 당황스럽게 하다
to confuse, disconcert

discompose
[dìskəmpóuz]

마음의 평정을 없애다, 동요시키다
to disturb the composure or calm of; perturb

discrete
[diskrí:t]

불연속의, 분리된, 별개의
constituting a separate entity

discretion
[diskréʃən]

자유재량, 신중함
the quality of being discreet; power of free decision or latitude of choice

discretionary
[diskréʃənèri]

재량껏 할 수 있는
giving somebody authority to decide

discursive
[diskə́:rsiv]
주제를 벗어난, 산만한, 논증적인
digressing from subject to subject

disembark
[dìsimbá:rk]
하선하다, 상륙하다, 비행기에서 내리다
to leave a vehicle or aircraft

disembarrass
[dìsembǽrəs, -im-]
(짐, 장애, 걱정 등에서) 해방하다, 안심시키다
to free from something bothersome or encumbering; relieve

disentangle
[disintǽŋgl]
얽힘을 풀리다, (다툼, 분규 등에서) 해방하다
to extricate from entanglement or involvement; free

dishevel
[diʃévəl]
난잡하게 하다, 헝클어놓다
to loosen and let fall (hair or clothing) in disarray

disillusion
[dìsilú:ʒən]
(몽상, 잘못된 믿음 등을) 깨우치게 하다; 환상에서 깨어나기
to cause (someone) to realize that a belief or an ideal is false

disimpassioned
[dìsimpǽʃənd]
냉정한, 침착한
without being filled with passion

disinclined
[disinkláind]
하고 싶지 않은, 마음이 내키지 않는
unwilling or reluctant

disjunction
[disdʒʌ́ŋkʃən]
분리, 분열
a difference between two things that you would expect to be in
agreement with each other

dismal
[dízməl]
음산한, 음울한, 참담한, 매우 안 좋은, 서투른
showing or causing gloom or depression

disparage
[dispǽridʒ]
깎아내리다, 비난하다
to regard or represent as being of little worth

dispirit
[dispírit]
(열정, 사기, 희망 등을) 잃게 하다
to cause (someone) to lose enthusiasm, morale or hope

disposition
[dìspəzíʃən]
기질, 취향, 배치, 처리
a person's inherent qualities of mind and character, temperament

dissimulate
[disímjulèit]
(감정 등을) 숨기다, 겉꾸려서 숨기다, 체하다
to disguise (one's intentions, for example) under a feigned appearance

dissipate
[dísəpèit]
흩어지게 하다, 낭비하다
to disperse or scatter

divulge
[divʌ́ldʒ, dai-]
누설하다, 폭로하다
to make known (private or sensitive information)

docile
[dá:sl]
순한, 고분고분한, 다루기 쉬운, 길들이기 쉬운
yielding to supervision, direction, or management; tractable

dogged
[dɔ́(:)gid]
끈질긴, 끈덕진
having or showing tenacity and grim persistence

dole
[dóul]
슬픔, 고통, 시주, 분배; 주다, 베풀다
sorrow, grief, or pain

domineering
[dáməníəriŋ]
오만한, 거만한
asserting one's will over another in an arrogant way

dote
[dóut]
맹목적으로 좋아하다
to be lavish or excessive in one's attention

draconian
[dreikóuniən, drə-]
가혹한, 아주 엄격한
(of laws or their application) excessively harsh and severe

dross
[drɔ:s]
찌끄러기, 가치 없는 것
worthless, commonplace, or trivial matter

dulcet
[dʌ́lsit]
(소리가) 감미로운
(esp. of sound) sweet and soothing (often used ironically)

dupe
[dju:p]
곧잘 속아넘어가는 사람
an easily deceived person

dwindle
[dwíndl]
점차 줄어들다
diminish gradually in size, amount, or strength

ecclesiastical
[iklì:ziǽstikəl]
교회의, 성직자의
of or pertaining to the church or the clergy; churchly; clerical; not secular

ecumenical
[èkjuménik(əl)]
보편적인, 전반적인
representing a number of different Christian churches; worldwide or general in extent, influence, or application

edacious
[idéiʃəs]
게걸스럽게 먹는, 대식하는, 식욕이 왕성한, 소모하는
characterized by voracity; devouring

edify
[édəfài]
교화하다
to instruct and improve especially in moral and religious knowledge

effectual
[iféktʃuəl]
효과적인, (행위, 수단이 목적에 대하여) 알맞은, 적절한
producing or sufficient to produce a desired effect; fully adequate

efficacious
[èfəkéiʃəs]
효과적인, 효험 있는
having the power to produce a desired effect

effrontery
[ifrʌ́ntəri]

뻔뻔스러움, 염치 없음, 후안구치
brazen boldness; presumptuousness

effuse
[ifjúːz]

발산하다, (감정 등을) 억제 없이 표현하다
to radiate; diffuse

effusive
[ifjúːsiv]

(즐거움, 감사의 감정이) 억제 없이 표현하는, 용암분출의
expressing feelings of gratitude, pleasure, or approval in an
unrestrained or heartfelt manner; of or relating to the eruption of
large volumes of molten rock

egress
[íːgres]

밖으로 나감, 출구
exit

elicit
[ilísit]

이끌어내다, 도출하다
to call forth or draw out

embolden
[imbóuldən, em-]

대담하게 하다
to give (someone) the courage or confidence

embryonic
[èmbriánik]

미발달의
(of a system, idea, or organization) in a rudimentary stage with
potential for further development

empirical
[impírikəl, em-]

경험상의, 실험적인
based on observation or experience

emulate
[émjulèit]

모방하다, 경쟁하다, 애쓰다, 겨누다, 필적하다
to try to equal or excel; imitate with effort to equal or surpass

encapsulate
[inkǽpsjulèit]

요약하다
to enclose in or as if in a capsule; epitomize, summarize

encomium
[enkóumiəm]
찬사, 칭찬하는 말
a speech or piece of writing that praises someone or something highly

engrossed
[ingróus, en-]
몰두한, 열중한
having all one's attention or interest absorbed by someone or something

enhearten
[inháːrtn, en-]
용기를 북돋우다
to hearten

enigmatic
[ènigmǽtik(əl)]
수수께끼 같은, 난해한
difficult to interpret or understand; mysterious

enjoin
[indʒɔ́in]
명령하다, 이르다
to direct or order to do something

enmity
[énməti]
적대감
the feeling of being hostile to someone or something; hostility

ennui
[aːnwíː]
권태
a feeling of listlessness and dissatisfaction arising from a lack of occupation or excitement

enraptured
[inrǽptʃərd, en-]
기뻐서 어쩔 줄 모르는
given intense pleasure or joy

enthrall
[inθrɔ́ːl, en-]
마음을 사로잡다, 노예로 만들다
to capture the fascinated attention of; enslave

entrance
[éntrəns]
매료시키다; 들어가기, 입구
to fill (someone) with wonder and delight, holding their entire attention

envision
[invíʒən]

상상하다, 그리다
to picture mentally, especially some future event or events

ephemeral
[ifémərəl]

일시적인, 덧없는; 단명한 것
lasting for a very short time

epicure
[épəkjùər]

세련된 감각의 소유자, 미식가, 쾌락주의자
a person with refined taste especially in food and wine

epitome
[ipítəmi]

전형 본보기, 요약
a representative or an example of a class or type

epitomize
[ipítəmàiz]

요약하다, 전형이 되다
to make an epitome of, sum up; to be a typical example of

eschew
[istʃúː]

피하다, 삼가하다
deliberately avoid using; abstain from

esoteric
[èsətérik]

난해한, 소수만 아는
likely to be understood by only with a specialized knowledge or interest; difficult to understand

espouse
[ispáuz]

지지하다, 신봉하다
to take up and support as a cause; become attached to

essay
[ései]

논평, 수필, 시도, 기도; 시도하다, 꾀하다
to make an attempt at; try

ethereal
[iθíəriəl]

천상의, 영적인, 가볍고 섬세한
extremely delicate and light in a way that seems too perfect for this world; heavenly, spiritual

ethos
[íːθas]

(한 국민, 사회, 제도 등의) 기풍, 정신
the distinguishing character, sentiment, moral nature, or guiding beliefs of a person, group, or

evanescent
[èvənésnt]

사라져가는, 덧없는
fleeting, passing away

evocative
[ivάːkətiv]

(감정을) 불러일으키는
tending or having the power to evoke

exceptionable
[iksépʃənəbl]

반대 받을 만한, 비난해야 할, 바람직하지 않은
open or liable to objection or debate; objectionable or debatable

excise
[éksaiz, -sais]

잘라내다, 삭제하다, 소비세를 부과하다; 소비세, 물품세, 면허세
to cut out surgically; to remove (a section) from a text or piece of music

excrete
[ikskríːt]

배설하다, 분비하다
to separate and discharge (waste matter) from the blood, tissues, or organs

execrable
[éksikrəbl]

혐오스러운, 형편없는
odious, detestable, abominable; extremely bad or unpleasant

exemplar
[igzémplər]

전형, 모범
a person or thing serving as a typical example or excellent model

exhort
[igzɔ́ːrt]

강력하게 권고하다, 간곡히 타이르다
to encourage strongly or urge (someone) to do something

exigency
[éksədʒənsi]

위급, 긴급함
a state of affairs that makes urgent demands

expatiate
[ikspéiʃièit]

자세히 설명하다
to speak or write at length

expiate
[ékspièit]

보상하다, 죄를 속죄하다, 벌충하다
to make amends or reparation for; atone

explicate
[ékspləkèit]

설명하다, 전개하다, 분석하다
to make plain or clear; explain; interpret

exponent
[ikspóunənt]

해설자, 설명이 되는 것
a person who believes in and promotes the truth or benefits of
an idea or theory

expository
[ikspázitɔːri]

설명적인, 해설의
intended to explain or describe something

expound
[ikspáund]

(남에게) 소상하게 설명하다, 상술하다
to give a detailed statement of; set forth

expressly
[iksprésli]

명백히, 확실히, 특별한 목적으로
explicitly, particularly, specifically

extant
[ékstənt, ikstǽnt]

현존하는
(esp. of a document) still in existence; surviving

extemporaneous
[ekstèmpəréiniəs, iks-]

즉흥적인, 계획 없이 이루어진
spoken or done without preparation

extemporize
[ikstémpəràiz]

즉석에서 이야기하다, 즉흥적으로 연설하다, 임시변통하다
compose, perform, or produce something such as music or
a speech without preparation; to improvise

extirpate
[ékstə:rpèit]
멸종시키다, 뿌리채 뽑다
to pull up by the roots

extrapolate
[ikstrǽpəlèit]
(기지의 사실로 부터의) 추정하다
to infer (values of a variable in an unobserved interval) from values within an already observed

extricate
[ékstrəkèit]
(위험, 곤란에서) 벗어나게 하다, 구해내다, 빼내주다
to free (someone or something) from a constraint or difficulty

exude
[igzú:d, iksú:d]
스며 나오게 하다, 발산시키다
to discharge or emit (a liquid or gas, for example) gradually

exultant
[igzʌ́ltənt]
매우 기뻐하는
triumphantly happy

facetious
[fəsí:ʃəs]
익살스런, 웃기는, 가벼운
treating serious issues with deliberately inappropriate humor; flippant

faction
[fǽkʃən]
파벌, 분파
a group within a larger group, party, government, organization, or the like

factious
[fǽkʃəs]
당파적인
relating or inclined to a state of faction

faint-hearted
[feinthá:rtid]
소심한, 자신이 없는
deficient in conviction or courage; timid

fallow
[fǽlou]
묵어 있는, 경작하지 않은, 개간하지 않은; 휴한지, 휴경; (논, 밭, 등을) 묵히다
characterized by inactivity

falter
[fɔ́:ltər]
주저하다, 비틀거리다; 비틀거리기, 머뭇거리기
to move unsteadily or in a way that shows lack of confidence

farcical
[fá:rsikəl]
우스꽝스런
of or resembling a farce, esp. because of absurd or
ridiculous aspects

far-reaching
[fá:ri:tʃiŋ]
(효과·영향 등이) 멀리까지 미치는, 폭넓은
having a wide range or effect

fashion
[fǽʃən]
만들어내다, 적응시키다; 유행, 패션
to make or construct usually with the use of imagination and
ingenuity

fastidious
[fæstídiəs, fəs-]
꼼꼼한, 까다로운
very attentive to and concernec about accuracy and detail

fathom
[fǽðəm]
헤아리다; 수심을 재다; 패덤(길이의 단위)
to understand, comprehend; to measure the depth of (water)

faultfinding
[fɔ́:ltfàindiŋ]
트집잡기; 트집을 잡는
continual criticism, typically concerning trivial things

fawn
[fɔ:n]
아부하다, (사슴이) 새끼를 낳다; 새끼 사슴
to seek or curry favor by flattery and obsequious behavior

fazed
[féiz]
(마음이) 어수선한, 당황한
disconcerted, daunted, disturbed

featureless
[fí:tʃərləs]
특색이 없는, 재미없는, 단조로운
lacking distinguishing characteristics or features

feckless
[féklis]

무책임한, 쓸모 없는
lacking in efficiency or vitality; irresponsible

fecund
[fí:kənd, fék-]

비옥한, 생산력이 있는, 풍성한
capable of producing an abundance of offspring or new growth

feign
[féin]

가장하다, 꾸미다, 속이다
to give a false appearance of; pretend

felicitous
[filísitəs]

적절한, 들어맞는, 멋들어진
admirably suited; apt

fetid
[fétid]

악취가 나는, 고약한 냄새가 나는
having an offensive odor

fetter
[fétər]

족쇄를 채우다, 구속하다; 족쇄, 속박, 구속물
to restrain with chains or manacles, typically around the ankles

feud
[fjú:d]

(두 집안 사이의 또는 여러 대에 걸친) 불화, 반복, 다툼; 싸우다
a bitter, often prolonged quarrel or state of enmity, especially
such a state of hostilities between two families or clans

fickle
[fíkl]

변덕스런, 불안정한
changing frequently, esp. as regards one's loyalties, interests,
or affection

filibuster
[fíləbʌstər]

의사진행 방해 (긴 연설 등); 의사 진행을 방해하다
an action such as a prolonged speech that obstructs progress in a
legislative assembly while not technically contravening the
required procedures

filigree
[fíləgriː]

필리그리, 금 또는 은 선(線)세공, 매우 섬세한 무늬, 매우 정교한 것:
금 또는 은 선 세공의, 섬세한, 우아한; 세공으로 장식하다
delicate and intricate ornamental work made from gold, silver,
or other fine twisted wire

finicky
[fíniki]

몹시 까다로운
extremely or excessively particular, exacting, or meticulous

fitful
[fítfəl]

불규칙적인, 발작적인, 변하기 쉬운, 변덕스런
recurring irregularly or intermittently

flabby
[flǽbi]

살이 축 늘어진, 허약한
soft, loose, and fleshy; not powerful or effective

flag
[flǽg]

약화되다, 축 늘어지다, 기를 게양하다, 깃발로 신호를 보내다; 기, 국기
to decline in vigor or strength

flagitious
[fládʒíʃəs]

흉악한, 파렴치한, (죄 등이) 극악한, 악명 높은
characterized by extremely brutal or cruel crimes; vicious

flagging
[flǽgiŋ]

(힘, 권한, 결심 등이) 약해지는, 축 늘어진
declining; weakening

flaunt
[flɔ́ːnt]

자랑하다, 과시하다
to display ostentatiously or impudently; to treat contemptuously

fledge
[flédʒ]

(새끼가) 깃털이 다 자라다, 둥지를 떠나다, 키우다
to grow the plumage necessary for flight

fledgling
[flédʒliŋ]

풋나기(의), 애송이(의), 어린 새
young, new, or inexperienced

fling
[flíŋ]
거칠게 내던지다, 버리다; 내던지기, 돌진, 방종
to throw with violence; to put or send suddenly or unexpectedly; to cast aside; to discard

flip
[flip]
(손가락으로) 튀기다, 재빨리 넘기다; 가볍게 치기, 갑자기 움직이기
to throw with a light motion

flippant
[flípənt]
경박한, 성의 없는, 무례한
not showing a serious or respectful attitude

floppy
[flápi]
(옷이) 펄럭이는, 늘어진, 느슨한
tending to hang or move in a limp, loose, or ungainly way

florid
[flɔ́(:)rid]
불그레한, 혈색이 좋은, 장밋빛의, 화려한, 화사한
flushed with rosy color; ruddy

flounder
[fláundər]
간신히 나아가다, 버둥거리다, 몸부림치다; 버둥 거림, 몸부림, 허둥댐
to proceed or act clumsily or ineffectually; to struggle or stagger helplessly or clumsily in water or mud

flout
[fláut]
경멸하다, 비웃다, 멸시하다; 경멸적인 말, 모욕
to disregard (a rule, law or convention) openly; to mock, scoff

flux
[flʌks]
흐름, 끝없는 변동; 녹이다, 흘리다
action or process of flowing; continuous change

foil
[fɔil]
방해하다, 막다; 좌절, 방해
to prevent from succeeding

folly
[fáli]
어리석음, 우둔
lack of good sense; foolishness

foment
[foumént]

선동하다, 자극하다
to instigate or stir up

foot-dragging
[fútdræ̀giŋ]

지체, 더딤, 주저
reluctance or deliberate delay concerning a decision or action

footloose
[fútlù:s]

마음대로 할 수 있는, 구속 없는
having no attachments or ties; free to do as one pleases

ford
[fɔ:rd]

얕은 곳, 여울; 얕은 곳을 따라 걸어서 건너다, 강을 건너다
a shallow place in a body of water, such as a river, where one can cross by walking or riding on an animal or in a vehicle

forswear
[fɔ:rswέər]

포기하다, 그만두다, 부정하다, 위증하다
to agree to give up or do without (something); swear falsely; to commit perjury

forestall
[fɔ:rstɔ́:l]

선 손써서 막다, 기선을 제압하다
to exclude, hinder, or prevent by prior occupation or measures; to get ahead of

forgo
[fɔ:rgòu]

무시하다, 경시하다, 없이 지내다
to abstain from; relinquish

forsake
[fərséik]

버리다, 그만두다
to renounce or turn away from entirely

fortuitous
[fɔ:rtjú:ətəs]

우연한
happening by accident or chance rather than design

foul
[faul]

불쾌하고 역겨운, (날씨가) 사나운, 나쁜 (사람, 언행 등이) 사악한, 부도덕한, 저속한; 싫은 일, 더러운 것; 더럽히다, 불결하게 하다
very disagreeable or unpleasant; (of the weather) wet and stormy; wicked or immoral

founder
[fáundər]
침몰하다, 실패하다; 창설자, 기부자
(of a ship) to fill with water and sink; to fail

fracas
[fréikəs]
싸움판, 야단법석, 소동
a noisy, disorderly fight or quarrel; a brawl

fractious
[frǽkʃəs]
짜증 잘 내는, 다루기 힘든
easily irritated; bad-tempered; difficult to control; unruly

frantic
[frǽntik]
광란의, 정신 없는, 미쳐날 뛰는
wild or distraught with fear, anxiety, or other emotion

frequent
[frí:kwənt]
자주 들르다, 늘 할께 있다; 자구 일어나는, 간격이 짧은, 상습적인, 흔한
to visit (a place) often or habitually

fretful
[frétfəl]
안달하는, 초조해하는, 화내는, 언짢아하는
feeling or expressing distress or irritation

frivolous
[frívələs]
가벼운, 경박한, 하찮은
carefree and not serious

forward
[fróuwərd]
앞으로; 앞에 있는, 진척된, 주제넘은; 나아가게 하다, 발송하다, 촉진하다
located ahead

fruition
[fru:íʃən]
성취, 실현, 달성, 성취의 순간
the realization of a plan or project; the point at which a plan or project is realized

full-bodied
[fulbádid]
뚱뚱한, 힘센, (내용이) 풍부한, 뜻있는, 중요한, (술이) 감칠 맛이 있는
having richness and intensity of flavor or aroma; rich and intense

full-fledged
[fulfléʤd]
완전한, 성숙한
completely developed or established; of full status, full-blown

fulsome
[fúlsəm]
(찬양 따위가) 지나쳐 역겨운, 불쾌한
excessively or insincerely lavish

fumble
[fʌ́mbl]
서툴게 다루다, 더듬어 찾다, 말을 더듬거리다; 어색한 손돌림, 실수
to use the hands clumsily while doing or handling something

furtive
[fə́ːrtiv]
은밀한, 수상쩍은
attempting to avoid notice or attention; secretive

gaffe
[gǽf]
(사교상의) 실수, 결례
a clumsy social error; a faux pas; a blatant mistake

gainsay
[gèinséi]
반박하다, 부인하다, 반대하다
to deny or contradict, speak against, oppose

gall
[gɔːl]
화나게 하다, 스쳐 벗겨지다; 찰과상, 화남, 쓸개즙, 증오
to make (someone) feel annoyed

gallant
[gǽlənt]
용감한; 정중한, 기사도적인; 용감한 남자; (여성에게) 친절하게 하다
(of a person or their behavior) brave; heroic;
(of a man or his behavior) giving special attention and respect to
women; chivalrous

gambol
[gǽmbəl]
뛰놀다, 까불다; 뛰놀기, 장난
to run or jump about playfully

garish
[gɛ́əriʃ]
(옷 등) 지나치게 화려한, 너무 요란한
obtrusively bright and showy; lurid

garner
[gáːrnər]
저장하다, 축적하다, 모으다; 저장, 비축
to gather and store in or as if in a granary

gauche
[góuʃ]
서투른, 세련되지 않은, 솜씨 없는
lacking social polish; tactless; lacking ease or grace;
unsophisticated and socially awkward

gaudy
[góːdi]
(옷, 장식 등이) 지나치게 화려한, 세련되지 못한
showy in a tasteless or vulgar way

gawky
[góːki]
서투른, 어색한
nervously awkward and ungainly

germane
[dʒə(ː)rméin]
관련 있는, 적절한
relevant to a subject under consideration

gibberish
[dʒíbəriʃ]
이해할 수 없는 말, 횡설수설
unintelligible or nonsensical talk or writing; highly technical or
esoteric language; unnecessarily pretentious or vague language

giddy
[gídi]
경솔한, 진지하지 못한, 현기증 나는, 아찔한
excitable and frivolous; having a sensation of whirling and
a tendency to fall or stagger; dizzy

glib
[glíb]
(깊이 없이) 말만 유창한, 입심 좋은
fluent and voluble but insincere and shallow

goad
[goud]
자극하다, 부추기다, 선동하다, 막대기로 찌르다;(가축을 몰 때 쓰는) 막대기,
찌르는 기구, 자극
to prod or urge with or as if with a long pointed stick

gorge
[góːrdʒ]
(게걸스럽게) 먹다, 삼키다; 폭식, 과식
to stuff with food; glut

gossamer
[gásəmər]
매우 얇은, 섬세한; 공중에 뜬 거미줄, 얇고 가벼운 천
used to refer to something very light, thin, and insubstantial
or delicate

gouge
[gaudʒ]
바가지 씌우다, (돈을) 사취하다, 속이다, 후벼파다; 둥근 끌로 판 홈, 갈취, 강탈
to overcharge; to swindle

grandiose
[grǽndiòus]
(겉모습, 외양 등이) 웅장한, 장엄한, 거창한
impressive or magnificent in appearance or style, esp.
pretentiously so; excessively grand or ambitious

grandstand
[grǽndstænd]
(관객, 미디어로 부터) 주목 받으려 하다, (관객을 의식하여) 화려한 플레이를 하다;
특별 관람석의 구경꾼을 흥분시키는; 특별 관람석
to perform ostentatiously so as to impress an audience

grate
[gréit]
삐걱거리게 하다, (남을) 신경질 나게 하다, 감정을 해치다
to make a harsh rasping sound by or as if by scraping or grinding

gratify
[grǽtəfài]
만족시키다
to give (someone) pleasure or satisfaction

grating
[gréitiŋ]
삐걱거리는, (소리가) 신경에 거슬리는
sounding harsh and unpleasant; irritating

green
[grí:n]
경험이 없는, 미숙한, 초목이 우거진
lacking training or experience; abounding in or covered with
green growth or foliage

grim
[grím]
엄격한, 단호한, 잔인한, 무서운, 섬뜩한, 무시무시한
unrelenting, rigid; ghastly, sinister; gloomy, dismal; ferocious,
savage

grouse
[graus]
투덜대다, 불평하다; 불평
to complain; grumble

groveling
[grʌ́vəliŋ, gráv-]
비굴한, 아첨하는, 기는
acting in an obsequious manner in order to obtain someone's forgiveness or favor; creeping in a prostrate position

grumble
[grʌ́mbl]
투덜거리다; 불평, 불만
to complain or protest about something in a bad-tempered but typically muted way

guffaw
[gʌfɔ́ː, gə-]
파안대소
loud, unrestrained burst of laughter

guile
[gàil]
속임수, 꾀, 술책
sly or cunning intelligence, trick

hackneyed
[hǽknid]
진부한
lacking significance through having been overused; unoriginal and trite

hairbreadth
[hέərbrèdθ]
털끝만한 간격, 폭; 가까스로(의)
a very small amount or margin

haggard
[hǽgərd]
몹시 수척한, 초췌한, 말라빠진
appearing worn and exhausted; gaunt

halcyon
[hǽlsiən]
평온한, 평화로운, 행복한, 즐거운
denoting a period of time in the past that was idyllically happy and peaceful

hale
[héil]
튼튼한, 원기 왕성한; 힘껏 잡아당기다, 끌어내다
sound, strong and healthy

halfhearted
[hæfháːrtid]
열성이 없는, 내키지 않는
without enthusiasm or energy

hallow
[hǽlou]
거룩히 여기다, 신성하게 하다
to honor as holy

ham-handed
[hæmhǽndid]
서투른, 실수하는
clumsy; bungling

hangdog
[hǽŋdɔ:g]
처량한, 부끄러워하는; 아무 쓸모없는 사람, 비열한 사람
having a dejected or guilty appearance; shamefaced

hapless
[hǽplis]
운없는
(esp. of a person) unfortunate

harangue
[hərǽŋ]
장광설, 비난, 질책; 장광설을 늘어놓다, 비난하다, 질책하다
a long pompous speech; a tirade; deliver a harangue

hardheaded
[há:rdhédid]
완고한, 고집센, 현실적인
practical devoid of sentimentality; tough, callous

hard-nosed
[há:rdnóuzd]
현실적인, 실제적인, 다루기 어려운, 고집센
being tough, stubborn, or uncompromising

harrow
[hǽrou]
괴롭히다, 못살게 굴다
to cause distress to; to disturb, violate, despoil

harry
[hǽri]
괴롭히다, 못살게 굴다, 황폐하게 하다, 약탈하다; 침략, 약탈, 고통
persistently carry out attacks or; persistently harass

haughty
[hɔ́:ti]
(사람, 말, 태도 등이) 거만한, 오만한, 불손한
scornfully and condescendingly proud

havoc
[hǽvək]
대파괴, 황폐, 대혼란; 파괴하다, 엉망진창을 만든다
widespread destruction; confusion or disorder

headlong
[hédlɔ:ŋ]
무모한, 성급한, 거꾸로의
without deliberation, in a rush, with reckless haste

headstrong
[hédstrɔ:ŋ]
고집센
self-willed and obstinate

hearten
[há:rtn]
기운을 북돋아 주다, 격려하다
to make more cheerful or confident

heavy-handed
[hevihǽndid]
서투른, 솜씨 없는, 고압적인, 포악한
clumsy or insensitive; overly forceful

hegemony
[hidʒémǝni]
헤게모니, 주도권 맹주권
the predominant influence of one state over others

heinous
[héinǝs]
(행동이) 극악한
(of a person or wrongful act, esp. a crime) utterly odious or
wicked

heresy
[hérǝsi]
이단
belief or opinion contrary to orthodox religious (esp. Christian)
doctrine

heretic
[hérǝtik]
(일반적인 믿음을) 따르지 않는 사람, 이단자
a dissenter from established religious dogma; one who dissents
from an accepted belief or doctrine; nonconformist

heretical
[hǝrétikǝl]
이단의, 이설의, 이교도의
characterized by, revealing, or approaching departure from
established beliefs or standards

hermetic
[hǝ:rmétik]
밀봉, 밀폐된, 난해한
insulated or protected from outside influences; esoteric, cryptic

histrionic
[hìstriánik]

배우의, 연기의, 지나치게 감정적인
of or relating to actors or acting; excessively dramatic or emotional; affected

hoary
[hɔ́:ri]

백발의, 나이든, 오래된, 진부한
(of a person) having gray or white hair; aged

hobble
[hábl]

절뚝거리다, 어색한 방법을 쓰다; 발을 절기, 곤경
to move along with difficulty

homily
[háməli]

설교, 지루한 도덕적 훈계
sermon; tedious moralizing discourse

hoodwink
[húdwiŋk]

속이다, 눈가림을 하다
to take in by deceptive means; deceive

hubris
[hjú:bris]

지나친 자신감, 오만함
excessive pride or self-confidence

husband
[hʌ́zbənd]

아껴 쓰다, 절약하다, 관리하다; 남편
to use (resources) economically; conserve

idyllic
[aidilik]

목가적인, 소박하고 아름다운, 시적이고 아름다운
of or having the nature of an idyll; simple and carefree

ignoble
[ignóubl]

비천한, 비열한, 야비한
dishonorable, unworthy, base, shameful, contemptible, despicable

ignominy
[ígnəmìni, ignáməni]

불명예, 치욕, 굴욕
public shame or disgrace

imbroglio
[imbróuljou]

복잡한 사태, 난국, 복잡한 오해, 분규
a difficult or intricate situation; an entanglement

imbue
[imbjú:]
(생각 등을) 주입시키다, 스며들게하다, (색깔 등을) 물들이다
to inspire or permeate with a feeling or quality; permeate or saturate; to tinge or dye

immaterial
[imətíəriəl]
중요하지 않은, 관련 없는, 영적인, 비물질적인
unimportant under the circumstances; irrelevant; spiritual rather than physical

immeasurable
[iméʒərəbl]
잴 수 없는, 무한한
impossible to measure; vast; limitless

immemorial
[ìməmɔ́:riəl]
옛날의, 태고적의
reaching beyond the limits of memory, tradition, or recorded history

impassive
[impǽsiv]
무정한, 비정한, 무표정한, 냉담한, 무감각한
not feeling or showing emotion

impel
[impél]
강요하다, 강제하다
to drive, force, or urge (someone) to do something

imperative
[impérətiv]
꼭 해야 하는, 필수적인, 명령조의, 명령문의; 긴급한 명령, 의무, 필요, 명령문 동사
expressive of a command, entreaty, or exhortation

imperious
[impíəriəs]
오만한, 고압적인, 긴박한
assuming power or authority without justification; arrogant and domineering

impetuous
[impétʃuəs]
충동적인, 성급한, 격렬한
acting or done quickly and without thought or care

importune
[impɔ:rtjú:n, impɔ:rtʃən]
성가시게 졸라대다
to ask (someone) pressingly and persistently for or to do something

impressionable
[impréʃənəbl]
영향을 잘 받는, 감수성이 예민한
easily influenced because of a lack of critical ability

impunity
[impjú:nəti]
형벌을 면하기, 손실을 면하기, 무사
exemption from punishment, penalty, or harm

impute
[impjú:t]
돌리다, 지우다, 전가하다, 귀속시키다
to charge with the fault or responsibility for

inadvisable
[ìnədváizəbl]
현명하지 못한, 부적당한
unwise, ill-advised, imprudent, ill-judged, ill-considered, injudicious, impolitic

inalienable
[inéiljənəbl, -liə-]
양도할 수 없는, 빼앗을 수 없는
not alienable; unable to be taken away from or given away by the possessor

inane
[inéin]
무의미한, 어리석은
lacking significance, meaning, or point; silly, stupid

inattentive
[inəténtiv]
무관심한, 부주의한, 배려하지 않는, 태만한, 무뚝뚝한
exhibiting a lack of attention; not attentive; not assiduously attending to the comfort or wishes of others

inauspicious
[inɔ:spíʃəs]
불행한, 불운한, 불길한
not favorable; not auspicious

inception
[insépʃən]
시작, 개시
the establishment or starting point of an institution or activity

inchoate
[inkóuit]
방금 시작한, 갓 시작한, 초기의, 불완전한; 시작하다
in an initial or early stage; incipient

incinerate
[insínərèit]
소각하다, (시체를) 화장하다
to cause to burn to ashes

incipient
[insípiənt]
시작단계의, 초기의, 발단의
in an initial stage; beginning to appear or develop;
not fully realized

incise
[insáiz]
새기다, 새겨 만들다, 파다
to carve figures, letters, or devices into

incisive
[insáisiv]
예리한, 날카로운, 통렬한
penetrating, acute, sharp, sharp-witted, trenchant, astute,
discerning

incite
[insáit]
자극하다, 선동하다
to encourage or stir up (violent or unlawful behavior)

inconsonant
[inkánsənənt]
조화되지 않은, 일치되지 않는
not in agreement or harmony; not compatible

incontrovertible
[inkàntrəvó:rtəbl]
논박의 여지가 없는, 명백한
not able to be denied or disputed

incorrigible
[inkó:ridʒəbl]
고칠 수 없는, 완고한; 교정할 수 없는 사람, 다루기 힘든 사람
(of a person or their tendencies) not able to be corrected,
improved, or reformed

incriminate
[inkrímənèit]
죄를 씌우다, 고소하다
make (someone) appear guilty of a crime or wrongdoing; strongly
imply the guilt of (someone)

indecipherable 해독할 수 없는, 판독할 수 없는
[ìndisáifrəbl] impossible to decipher

indefatigable 지치지 않는, 끈기 있는
[ìndifǽtigəbl] (of a person or their efforts) persisting tirelessly

indefeasible 무효화할 수 없는
[ìndifíːzəbl] not able to be lost, annulled, or overturned

indelible 지울 수 없는, 제거할 수 없는
[indéləbl] (of ink or a pen) making marks that cannot be removed;
not able to be forgotten or removed

indigent 궁핍한, 결핍된
[índidʒənt] poor, needy

indignation 분노, 분개
[ìndignéiʃən] anger aroused by something unjust, unworthy, or mean

indivisible 분할할 수 없는, 불가분의; 분할 할 수 없는 것, 극소량
[ìndivízəbl] incapable of undergoing division

indomitable 불굴의, 꿋꿋한, 굴복하지 않는
[indámətəbl] impossible to subdue or defeat

industrious 근면한, 부지런한
[indʌ́striəs] assiduous in work or study; diligent

ineptitude 부조리, 어리석음
[inéptituːd] display of a lack of judgment, sense, or reason; being foolish

inequity 불공정, 불공평
[inékwəti] lack of fairness or justice

inexhaustible
[ìnigzɔ́:stəbl]
다 쓸 수 없는, 무진장의, 지칠 줄 모르는, 끈기 있는
incapable of being used up

inexplicable
[inéksplikəbl]
설명될 수 없는, 난해한
incapable of being explained, interpreted, or accounted for

infecund
[infí:kənd]
새끼를 낳지 않는, 열매 맺지 않는, 불모의
incapable of producing offspring or vegetation

infelicitous
[infəlísətəs]
불행한, 불운한, 적절하지 않은, 서투른
inappropriate; ill-chosen

infinitesimal
[ìnfinətésəməl]
극소의, 매우 작은; 극미량
immeasurably or incalculably minute

inflate
[infléit]
부풀게 하다, 확장시키다, 팽창시키다, 부당하게 인상하다
to increase (something) by a large or excessive amount

infraction
[infrǽkʃən]
(법률, 약속 등의) 위반
a violation or infringement of a law, agreement, or set of rules

infrangible
[infrǽndʒəbl]
부서지지 않는, 위반해서는 안 되는, 불가침의
unbreakable; inviolable

infuriate
[infjúərièit]
몹시 화나게 하다, 분노케 하다
to make (someone) extremely angry and impatient

infuse
[infjú:z]
채우다, 주입하다
to fill; to pervade, instill

ingrained
[ingréind]
(기질, 습관) 뿌리깊은, 깊이 박힌
to fix or establish firmly (a habit, belief, or attitude) in a person

ingratiate
[ingréiʃièit]
환심을 사기 위해서 비위를 맞추다
to bring (oneself, for example) into the favor or good graces of
another, especially by deliberate effort

inimitable
[inímitəbl]
흉내낼 수 없는, 비길 데 없는, 모방할 가치 없는
defying imitation; matchless

iniquitous
[iníkwitəs]
매우 부정한, 사악한, 무도한
characterized by iniquity; wicked

iniquity
[iníkwəti]
부도덕함, 사악함, 극악함
immoral or grossly unfair behavior

inkling
[íŋkliŋ]
어렴풋이 알고 있음, 넌지시 비침, 암시
a slight knowledge or suspicion; a hint

innervate
[inə́:veit]
자극하다, 신경을 발달시키다
to supply (an organ or a body part) with nerves

insalubrious
[insəlú:briəs]
건강에 해로운, 건강치 못한
not promoting health; unwholesome

insentient
[insénʃiənt, -ʃənt]
무감각한, 비정한, 생명 없는
incapable of feeling or understanding things; inanimate

insolent
[ínsələnt]
무례한, 불손한; 오만한 사람
showing a rude and arrogant lack of respect

insouciant
[insú:siənt]
태평한, 근심이 없는
marked by blithe unconcern; nonchalant

instate
[instéit]
(지위, 직무에) 임명하다, 취임시키다
to establish in office; install

instigate
[ínstəgèit]
부추기다, 선동하다
to incite someone to do something, esp. something bad

insular
[ínsələr, -sju-]
섬의, 고립된, 편협한; 섬사람
being, having, or reflecting a narrow provincial viewpoint

insurgent
[insə́:rdʒənt]
반란을 일으킨 사람, 반군, 폭도; 반란을 일으킨, 밀려오는
a rebel or revolutionary

intemperance
[intémpərəns]
과음; 무절제, 방종
lack of temperance, as in the indulgence of an appetite or
a passion

intemperate
[intémpərit]
무절제한, 방탕한, 폭음하는, 과격한
having or showing a lack of self-control; immoderate

interminable
[intə́:rmənəbl]
끝없는, 그칠 줄 모르는, 무기한의, 지겨운
endless (often used hyperbolically)

intermittent
[ìntərmítnt]
때때로, 가끔 발생하는, 간헐적인, 일시적으로 멈추는
occurring at irregular intervals; not continuous or steady

interpose
[ìntərpóuz]
삽입시키다, 양자 사이에 개입하다
to place or insert between one thing and another;
intervene between parties

intertwine
[ìntərtwáin]
얽히게 하다
to unite or be united by twisting or twining together

intransient
[intrǽnʃnt]
영원한
for everlasting time; eternally

invective
[invéktiv]
욕설, 모욕적인 말; 비난의, 욕설의
insulting, abusive, or highly critical language

inveigh
[invéi]
심하게 항의하다, 매도하다, 욕설하다, 몹시 책망하다
to give vent to angry disapproval; protest vehemently

inveigle
[invéigl]
유인하다, 교묘하게 속이다, 빼앗다
to win over by coaxing, flattery, or artful talk

invert
[invə́:rt]
거꾸로 하다, 뒤집다
to reverse in position, order, or relationship

inveterate
[invétərət]
만성적인
long-established and unlikely to change

invidious
[invídiəs]
시샘나게 하는, 비위에 거슬리는, 불공정한, 불쾌한
tending to rouse ill will, animosity, or resentment

invigorate
[invígərèit]
기운 나게 하다, 격려하다
to give strength or energy to

invincible
[invínsəbl]
이길 수 없는, 무적의
too powerful to be defeated or overcome

irascible
[iræsəbl, ai-]
화를 잘 내는, 성미 급한
easily made angry

irate
[airéit]
성난
extremely angry; enraged

irk
[ə́:rk]
짜증나게 하다, 화나게 하다, 얀날나게 하다, 안절부절 못하게 하다
to irritate; to annoy

irreverent
[irévərənt]
불손한, 불경스런
showing a lack of respect

irrevocable
[irévəkəbl]
돌이킬 수 없는, 취소할 수 없는
not able to be changed, reversed, or recovered; final, permanent

issue
[íʃuː]
나오다, 흘러나오다; 방출하다, 지급하다, 발표하다; 논점, 문제점, 발행
to spring or proceed from a source; to cause to flow out; emit; to
circulate or distribute in an official capacity; to publish

jaundice
[dʒɔ́ːndis]
편견을 가지게 타다; 편견, 비뚤어짐
to distort or prejudice, as by envy or resentment

jovial
[dʒóuviəl]
쾌활한, 명랑한, 재미있는, 즐거운
marked by hearty conviviality and good cheer

juxtaposition
[dʒʌ̀kstəpəzíʃən]
병렬, 병치
the act or an instance of placing two or more things
side by side

kudos
[kjúːdou]
영광, 명성, 찬양
praise and honor received for an achievement

labile
[léibàil]
변화하기 쉬운, 변하기 쉬운, 불안정한, 유연한, 적응성 있는
open to change; adaptable

labyrinth
[lǽbərìnθ]
미로, 미궁, 매우 복잡한 사정
a complicated irregular network of passages or paths in which it is
difficult to find one's way; a maze

lachrymose
[lǽkrəmòus]
눈물이 가득한, 눈물 나게 하는
tearful or given to weeping; inducing tears, sad

laconic
[ləkánik]

간결한, 과묵한, 무뚝뚝한
using very few words

lag
[læg]

꾸물거리다, 처지다, 시들다; 지연, 지체, 시간적 경과
to fall behind in movement, progress, or development; not keep
pace with another or others

lambaste
[læmbéist]

심하게 비난하다
to criticize (someone or something) harshly

languid
[lǽŋgwid]

늘어진, 나른한, 기력 없는
displaying or having a d sinclination for physical exertion or effort;
slow and relaxed

languish
[lǽŋgwiʃ]

기력을 잃다, 쇠약해지다, 비참하게 살다, 버림받고 살다; 쇠약
to fail to make progress or be successful; (of a person or other
living thing) to lose or lack vital ty; to grow weak or feeble

languor
[lǽŋgər]

쇠약, 무기력, 권태, 무관심; 약해지다
the state or feeling, often pleasant, of tiredness or inertia

largesse
[la:rdʒés]

후함
generosity in bestowing money or gifts upon others

lassitude
[lǽsətjù:d]

무기력, 피곤, 나른함
a state of physical or mental weariness; lack of energy

laudable
[lɔ́:dəbl]

칭찬할 만한, 칭찬해야 할, 훌륭한
deserving commendation; praiseworthy

lax
[lǽks]

축 늘어진, 엄하지 않은, 관대한, 부주의한
(of the limbs or muscles) relaxed, loose; lenient, not sufficiently
strict or severe

laxity
[lǽksəti]
느슨함, 트릿함, 방종
the state or quality of being lax

lenient
[líːniənt]
관대한, 인정이 많은, 자비심이 많은
inclined not to be harsh or strict; merciful, generous, or indulgent

lethargic
[ləθáːrdʒik(əl)]
무기력한, 활발하지 못한
of, causing, or characterized by lethargy

lethargy
[léθərdʒi]
무기력, 권태, 혼수상태
a lack of energy and enthusiasm

libel
[láibəl]
문서에 의한 명예훼손; (문서로) 명예를 훼손하다
a published false statement that is damaging to a person's reputation; a written defamation; make a false and malicious statement about

lighthearted
[láitháːrtid]
걱정이 없는, 쾌활한, 명랑한
cheerful and carefree

limn
[lim]
그림을 그리다, 묘사하다
to depict

limpid
[límpid]
(액체 등이) 깨끗한, 맑은, 명쾌한
free of anything that darkens; completely clear

lionize
[láiənàiz]
명사로 대접해주다, 치켜세우다
to give a lot of public attention and approval to (someone); to treat as a celebrity

lissome
[lísəm]
나긋나긋한, 유연한, 민첩한, 날렵한
easily bent; supple; having the ability to move with ease; limber

list
[list]

표, 목록; 기입하다, 일람표를 만들다, 기울이다, 기울다
to lean or cause to lean to the side

lithe
[làið]

유연한, 우아한
characterized by easy flexibility and grace

livid
[lívid]

(타박상, 충혈로) 납빛인, 검푸른, 격노한, (죽은 듯이) 창백한
discolored, as from a bru se; black-and-blue; ashen or pallid;
extremely angry; furious

lubricate
[lú:brəkèit]

기름칠하다, 매끄럽게 하다, 원활하게 하다
to make (something) slippery or smooth by applying an
 oily substance

lucidity
[lu:sídəti]

명석, 명쾌, 통찰력, 바른 정신, 광휘, 밝음, 맑음, 투명
being easily understood; ntelligible

ludicrous
[lú:dəkrəs]

웃기는, 익살스런
amusing or laughable through obvious absurdity, incongruity

lugubrious
[lugjú:briəs]

침울한, 슬픈
looking or sounding sad and dismal

lukewarm
[lú:kwɔ́:rm]

(물이) 미지근한, 열의 없는
moderately warm; half-hearted

lumber
[lʌ́mbər]

나무를 벌채하다, 육중하게 움직이다, 돌아다니다; 제재목
to walk or move with heavy clumsiness

lurid
[lúərid]

무시무시한, (색깔이) 매우 밝은 선정적인, 타는 듯이 붉은
causing shock or horror, gruesome; very vivid in color, esp. so as
 to create an unpleasantly harsh or unnatural effect

lurk
[lə́:rk]

잠복하다, 숨어서 기다리다, 살금살금 다니다
(of a person or animal) to be or remain hidden so as to wait in ambush for someone or something

luxuriant
[lʌɡʒúəriənt]

무성한, 비옥한, 풍성한
(of vegetation) rich and profuse in growth; lush

maculate
[mǽkjulèit]

반점이 있는, 더러워진; 반점을 찍다, 더럽히다
spotted or stained; to stain, make impure

malady
[mǽlədi]

질병, 병폐
a disease or ailment

malinger
[məlíŋɡər]

꾀병을 부리다, (의무를) 회피하다
to exaggerate or feign illness in order to escape duty or work

malleable
[mǽliəbl]

(금속 등이) 변형이 잘되는, 적응성 있는, 유순한
figurative easily influenced; pliable

mar
[má:r]

망치다, 손상하다; 손상시키는 것, 결점, 흠
to impair the quality of; to spoil

marbled
[má:rbld]

대리석 무늬의, 대리석으로 만든
having markings or coloration suggestive of marble

martinet
[má:rtənét]

엄격한 규율가, 엄격한 교관
a strict disciplinarian, esp. in the armed forces

maunder
[mɔ́:ndər]

두서 없이 말하다, 두서 없이 푸념하다, 맥없이 걷다
to talk or act incoherently or aimlessly

maven
[méivən]

전문가, 박식한 사람, 통달해 있는 사람
a person who has special knowledge or experience; an expert or connoisseur

maverick
[mǽvərik]

독불장군, 어느 파에도 속하지 않는 사람, 소유자 표시의 낙인이 없는 소
a person who refuses to conform to a particular party or group

mean
[mí:n]

질이 떨어지는, 가치가 없는, 양이 적은, 시시한; 의미하다, 짐심으로 -할 작정이다
low in quality or grade; inferior; low in value or amount; paltry

meander
[miǽndər]

정처 없이 거닐다, (강) 굽이굽이 흐르다; 꼬불꼬불한 길, 미로, 우회
(of a speaker or text) proceed aimlessly or with little purpose

melancholy
[mélənkàli]

우울, 침울; 우울한, 음침한, 울적한
sadness or depression of the spirits; gloom

meld
[méld]

혼합하다, 병합하다
blend, combine

mellifluous
[melífluəs]

(소리, 말 등이) 감미로운, 달콤하게 흐르는
(voice, words) sweet or musical; pleasant to hear

menace
[ménis]

위협하는 것(사람); 위협하다
a person or thing that is likely to cause harm; a threat or danger; threaten, esp. in a malignant or hostile manner

mendicant
[méndikənt]

거지, 비렁뱅이, 구걸하는, 거지의
a beggar

mercurial
[mərkjúəriəl]

변덕스런, 경박한, 활발한, 명랑한, 수은의, 수은을 함유 하는; 수은제
(of a person) subject to sudden or unpredictable changes of mood or mind

meretricious
[mèritríʃəs]
야하게 차려서 남의 이목을 끄는, 저속한, 겉치레만의, 성실성이 없는
attracting attention in a vulgar manner

metamorphose
[mètəmɔ:rfous]
변형하다
to change completely in form or nature

meteoric
[mi:tió:rik]
유성같이 빠른, 밝은, 금방 사라지는
similar to a meteor in speed, brilliance, or brevity; very fast, brilliant or temporary

methodical
[məθádikəl]
질서정연한, 꼼꼼한, 공들인
arranged, characterized by, or performed with method or order

meticulous
[mətíkjuləs]
매우 꼼꼼한, 지나치게 소심한, 정확한
showing great attention to detail; very careful and precise

mettle
[métl]
용기, 원기, 기개
courage and fortitude, spirit

mettlesome
[métlsəm]
원기 있는, 용기 있는
full of mettle; spirited and plucky

militate
[mílitèit]
작용하다, 영향을 주다, 싸우다
to have force or influence; bring about an effect or a change

minatory
[mínətɔ:ri]
위협하는
expressing or conveying a threat

mint
[mínt]
대량, 다량, 화폐 주조소, 조폐국, 박하; 화폐를 주조하다
a vast sum or amount; a place where money is coined, esp. under state authority

minute
[mainjú:t, mínit]

즉석으로 만든, 미세한, 상세한; (시간) 분, 잠깐, 초고; 시간을 정확히 재다, 초고를 작성하다, 의사록에 기록하다
prepared in a very short time; extremely small

minutia
[minjú:ʃiə]

작고 사소한 세부사항
the small, precise, or trivial details of something

misanthrope, misanthropist
[mísənθròup]

인간을 싫어하는 사람, 염세가
one who hates or mistrusts humankind

mitigate
[mítəgèit]

완화시키다
to make less severe, serious, or painful

modicum
[mádikəm]

소량
a small quantity of a particular thing, esp. something considered desirable or valuable

morbid
[mó:rbid]

병의, 병적인
of, relating to, or characteristic of disease, abnormally susceptible to or characterized by gloomy or unwholesome feelings

mordant
[mó:rdənt]

신랄한, 독설적인, 부식성의
(esp. of humor) having or showing a sharp or critical quality; biting

muddle
[mʌdl]

혼동시키다, 흐리게 하다, 무디게 하다; 혼란 상태, 난잡
to mix confusedly; confuse, mix up, disarrange, disorganize, disorder

mulish
[mjú:liʃ]

노새 같은, 고집스런
resembling or likened to a mule in being stubborn

multifaceted
[mʌltifæsitid]

다면적인
having many facets or aspects

multifarious
[mʌltəfɛriəs]
다양한, 다채로운, 다방면에 걸친
having great variety; diverse

mundane
[mʌndéin]
평범한, 흔한; 세속적인
ordinary, routine; worldly, secular, temporal

munificent
[mju:nífəsnt]
돈을 후하게 쓰는
(of a person) very generous

myopia
[maióupiə]
근시안 , 통찰력의 결여
near-sightedness; lack of imagination, foresight, or
intellectual insight

myriad
[míriəd]
수많은, 다수, 1만; 무수한, 1만의
countless or extremely great in number

nadir
[néidər, -diər]
천저, 밑바닥, 절망상태
the point on the celestial sphere directly below an observer;
the lowest point in the fortunes of a person or organization

natty
[nǽti]
말끔한
(esp. of a person or an article of clothing) smart and fashionable

nefarious
[nifέəriəs]
사악한, 범법의
(typically of an action or activity) wicked or criminal

negate
[nigéit]
무효로 하다, 취소하다, 부정하다, 부인하다
to make ineffective or invalid; nullify; to rule out; deny

nepotism
[népətìzm]
친족등용, 족벌주의
favoritism shown or patronage granted to relatives, as in business

nerve
[nə:rv]
격려하다, 용기를 북돋우다; 신경, 체력, 활력, 용기
to give strength or courage to

nettle
[nétl]
화나게 하다, 안절부절 못하게 하다; 쐐기풀
to irritate or annoy (someone); a herbaceous plant that has
jagged leaves covered with stinging hairs

nice
[nais]
철저한, 꼼꼼한, 정확한 , 유쾌한, 다정한
fastidious; scrupulous, exacting n requirements or standards,
punctilious

nimble
[nímbl]
민첩한, 영리한
quick and light in movement or action, agile; quick to understand

nitpick
[nítpìk]
트집잡다
to be concerned with or find fault with insignificant details

nocturnal
[naktə́:rnl]
밤의, 야행성의 , 밤에 활동하는 사람, 밤을 다룬 작품
done, occurring, or active at night

noisome
[nóisəm]
불쾌한, 해로운, 악취가 나는
disagreeable; unpleasant; having an extremely offensive smell

nominal
[ná:minl]
명목상의, 명의상의, 명색 뿐인
of, resembling, relating to, or consisting of a name or names

nonchalant
[nánʃəlá:nt]
태연한, 무관심한
(of a person or manner) casually calm and relaxed; not displaying
anxiety, interest, or enthusiasm

nonplus
[nanplʌ́s]
혼란스럽게 하다, 난처하게 하다; 당황, 난처한 지경
to surprise and confuse (someone) so much that they are unsure
how to react

nonplussed
[na:nplʌst]

당황한, 혼란스런
to put at a loss as to what to think, say, or do; bewilder

nostrum
[nɔ́strəm]

엉터리약, (사회, 정치 문제 해결을 위한) 특효약, 묘약
a medicine whose effectiveness is unproved and whose ingredients are usually secret; a quack remedy; a favorite but untested remedy for problems or evils.

nugatory
[njú:gətɔ:ri]

중요하지 않은, 하찮은
of no value or importance, futile

oaf
[óuf]

바보, 멍청이
a stupid person, lout

oafish
[óufiʃ]

어리석은
stupid

obfuscate
[ábfəskèit]

애매하게 하게 하다, 어리둥절하게 하다
to render obscure, unclear, or unintelligible; to bewilder

oblique
[əblí:k]

기울어진, 비스듬한, 완곡한, 모호한, 부정한, 잘못된; 경사지다; 경사져 있는 것
sloping, slanting; indirect and evasive; devious, underhanded

obtrusive
[əbtrú:siv]

돌출한, 눈에 거슬리는, 나서는, 주제넘은
noticeable or prominent in an unwelcome or intrusive way

obviate
[abvièit]

불필요하게 하다, 예방하다, 제거하다
to remove (a need or difficulty); avoid, prevent

occlude
[əklú:d]

닫다, 가두다, 막다
to stop, close up, or obstruct, to shut in

odious
[óudiəs]
몹시 불쾌한, 혐오스런
extremely unpleasant; repulsive

officious
[əfíʃəs]
참견이 심한, 주제넘게 나서는
objectionably eager in offering one's unrequested and unwanted
services, help, or advice; meddlesome

ominous
[ɔ́mənəs]
불온한, 험악한, 심상치 않은, 흉조를 보이는, 불길한
menacing; threatening

omnipotent
[amnípətənt]
전능한; 전능자
(of a deity) having unlimited power; able to do anything

opine
[oupáin]
의견을 말하다, 생각하다
to hold or state as an opinion

opprobrium
[əpróubriəm]
불명예, 비난, 비난의 대상
harsh criticism or censure; the public disgrace arising from
someone's shameful conduct

orator
[ɔ́rətər]
웅변가, 대중 연설가
a public speaker, esp. one who is eloquent or skilled

oscillate
[ásəlèit]
진동하다, 주저하다, 흔들리다
to move or swing back and forth at a regular speed; to waver
between extremes of opinion, action

ossify
[ásəfài]
골화되다, 경화시키다
to change into bone, become bony; to become set in a rigidly
conventional pattern

ostensible
[asténsəbl]
표면상의, 겉보기만의, 명백한, 명료한
pretended or seeming; apparent or evident

ostentation
[à:stentéiʃn]
자랑해 보이기, 허식
pretentious display meant to impress others; boastful showiness

ostentatious
[ástentéiʃəs]
자랑하는, 과시하는, 허세부리는, 저속하게 화려한
characterized by vulgar or pretentious display; designed to impress or attract notice

ostracize
[ástrəsàiz]
추방하다
to exclude (someone) from a society or group

outlandish
[àutlǽndiʃ]
별난, 기이한, 희한한, 이국적인
looking or sounding bizarre or strikingly unfamiliar; foreign, alien

outlaw
[àutlɔ:]
범법자, 무법자; 금하다, 불법화 하다, 사회에서 추방하다
a person who has broken the law, esp. one who remains at large or is a fugitive

outstrip
[àutstríp]
능가하다, 뛰어나다
to get ahead of, exceed

outwit
[àutwit]
계략으로 앞서다, 한 수 위이다
to surpass in cleverness or cunning; outsmart

overbearing
[òuvərbéəriŋ]
횡포한, 고압적인, 거만한, 압도적인
domineering in manner, arrogant; overwhelming in power or significance, predominant

overhaul
[òuvərhɔ:l]
정밀점검하다, 정비하다; 분해수리, 점검 정비
to examine or go over carefully for needed repairs; to make extensive renovations or revisions on; to renovate

overt
[ouvé:rt]
공공연한, 명백한, 숨김없는
done or shown openly; plainly or readily apparent, not secret or hidden

overweening
[òuvərwíːniŋ]
자만심이 강한, 잘난 체하는, 우쭐대는, 과장된, 도가 지나친
presumptuously arrogant, overbearing

overwhelming
[òuvərhwélmiŋ]
압도적인
tending or serving to overwhelm, great

paean
[píːən]
찬가
a song of praise or triumph

palatable
[pǽlətəbl]
맛있는, 기분 좋은, 마음에 드는
(of food or drink) pleasant to taste

palatial
[pəléiʃəl]
궁전같이 웅장하고 멋진
resembling a palace in being spacious and splendid

palliate
[pǽlièit]
(증상을) 완화시키다, 변명하다, 꾸며대다
to make (a disease or its symptoms) less severe or unpleasant without removing the cause

palpable
[pǽlpəbl]
만져서 알 수 있는, 명백한, 뚜렷한
able to be touched or felt; clear to the mind or plain to see

paltry
[pɔ́ːltri]
시시한, 하찮은
(of an amount) small or meager; petty or meager

pan
[pǽn]
심하게 비난하다, 냄비로 익히다; 냄비, 접시 모양의 것
to criticize severely

panache
[pənǽʃ]
당당한 태도, 품격, 기백, 과시, 깃털 장식
flamboyant confidence of style or manner

paramount
[pǽrəmàunt]
가장 중요한, 최고의; 대군주 최고권자-
more important than anything else; supreme

parity
[pǽrəti]
동등, 동격, 동량
the state or condition of being equal

parry
[pǽri]
(대답 등) 회피하다, 받아 넘기다; 받아넘기기, 발뺌, 핑계
to ward off (a weapon or attack), esp. with a countermove; answer (a question or accusation) evasively

parse
[pa:rs]
구성 요소로 분석하다, 세밀히 조사하다
to examine closely or subject to detailed analysis, especially by breaking up into components

parsimony
[pá:rsəmòuni]
인색함
the quality or state of being stingy

partisan
[pá:rtisən]
열렬한 지지자(당원); 당파심이 강한
a strong supporter of a party, cause, or person

passé
[pá:sei]
시대에 뒤진, 구식인, 쇠퇴한
no longer current or in fashion; out-of-date

patent
[pǽtnt]
명백한, 눈에 띄는, 특허의, 특허권이 있는; 특허, 인가
obvious, conspicuous

peccadillo
[pèkədílou]
가벼운 죄, 사소한 실수
a small, relatively unimportant offense or sin

peeve
[pí:v]
화나게 하다, 약올리다, 안달나게 하다; 불쾌한 기분, 화남, 불평
to annoy; irritate

peevish
[pí:viʃ]
투정을 부리는, 성미 까다로운, 토라진, 성마른, 화 잘 내는
easily irritated, esp. by unimportant things, querulous

pejorative
[pidʒɔ́ːrətiv]

경멸적인, 비난적인, 가치를 덜어뜨리는; 경멸어 , 비방어
expressing contempt or disapproval

pell-mell
[pélmél]

뒤죽박죽의, 황급한, 허둥지둥의; 뒤죽박죽으로, 황급히; 혼잡, 뒤섞임, 황급
in a confused, rushed, or disorderly manner

penchant
[péntʃənt]

강한 기호, 경향, 좋아함
a strong or habitual liking for something or tendency to do something

penitent
[pénətənt]

참회하는, 뉘우치는; 참회자, 후회하는 사람
feeling or showing sorrow and regret for having done wrong; repentant

penurious
[pənjúəriəs]

몹시 가난한, 인색한
extremely poor; poverty-stricken; parsimonious; mean

peremptory
[pərémptəri]

단호한, 지엄한, 위압적인, 독단적인
insisting on immediate attention or obedience, esp. in a brusquely imperious way

perennial
[pəréniəl]

지속적인, 영구적인
lasting or existing for a long time; enduring

perfidy
[pə́ːrfədi]

배신
deceitfulness; untrustworthiness

perfunctory
[pərfʌ́ŋktəri]

형식적인, 기계적인, 무관심한
(of an action or gesture) carried out with a minimum of effort or reflection

perimeter
[pərímətər]

주변, 주위, 한계, 한도
the boundary of a closed plane figure

peripatetic
[pèrəpətétik]
순회하는, 돌아다니는, 아리스토텔레스 학파의, 아리스토텔레스 학파의 사람, 떠돌아 다니는 사람
traveling from place to place, esp. working or based in various places for relatively short periods

peripheral
[pərífərəl]
주변부의, 중요하지 않은, 본질적이 아닌
of, relating to, or situated on the edge or periphery of something; of secondary or minor importance; marginal

permissive
[pərmísiv]
허용하는, 관대한
granting or tending to grant permission

permute
[pərmjú:t]
변경하다, 순서를 바꾸다
to change the order or arrangement of

pernicious
[pərníʃəs]
해로운
having a harmful effect, esp. in a gradual or subtle way

perpetual
[pərpétʃuəl]
영원한; 다년생 식물
never ending or changing

perpetuate
[pərpétʃuèit]
영속하게 하다, 불멸하게하다
to make something continue indefinitely

perplex
[pərpléks]
혼란스럽게 하다
to make unable to think logically

perquisite
[pə́:rkwəzit]
(직위로 인해 얻는) 특권, (급료 이외의) 임시 수입, 팁
a privilege, gain, or profit incidental to regular salary or wages

persecute
[pə́:rsikju:t]
학대하다, 박해하다, 압박하다, 벌하다
to oppress or harass with ill-treatment, especially because of race, religion, sexual orientation, or beliefs

personable
[pə́:rsənəbl]
잘생긴, 매력적인
(of a person) having a pleasant appearance and manner

pertinacious
[pə:rtənéiʃəs]
완고한, 끈질긴
holding firmly to an opinion or a course of action

peruse
[pərú:z]
정독하다, 숙독하다, 자세히 조사하다
to read or examine, typically with great care

petrify
[pétrifài]
굳어지게 하다, 딱딱해지게 하다, 무감각하게 하다, 석화하다
to cause to become stiff or stonelike; deaden

petrous
[petrəs]
돌같이 단단한
of, relating to, or resembling rock, especially in hardness; stony

petulant
[pétʃulənt]
성마른, 안달하는, 초조해하는
insolent or rude in speech or behavior

philistine
[fílistàin]
펠리시테인, 고대 팔레스티나 남해안의 필리스티아(Philistia)인; 속물의, 교양없는 사람의, 문외한
boorish, barbarous

phlegmatic
[flegmǽtik(əl)]
점액질의; 무감한, 무기력한
(of a person) having an sluggish, unemotional and stolidly calm disposition

piddling
[pídliŋ]
사소한, 하찮은
so trifling or trivial as to be beneath one's consideration

pied
[paid]
얼룩인, 잡색인, 다색의
patchy in color; splotched or piebald

pillory
[píləri]
칼을 씌워 구경거리로 만들다, 웃음거리로 만들다; 형틀, 칼, 오명, 조롱
a wooden framework on a post, with holes for the head and hands, in which offenders were formerly locked to be exposed to public scorn as punishment

pinion
[pínjən]
손발을 묶다, 속박하다
to tie or hold the arms or legs of (someone)

pinnacle
[pínəkl]
절정, 전성기, 정상; 높은 곳에 두다
the highest point of development or achievement; acme

piquant
[píːkənt]
자극적이고 맛있는, (분위기, 태도) 자극적이고 적극적인
having a pleasantly sharp taste or appetizing flavor; engagingly provocative

pique
[píːk]
화나게하다, 자극하다; 화, 분개
to arouse anger or resentment in, irritate; excite or arouse especially by a provocation, challenge, or rebuff

pith
[piθ]
진수, 요점, 중요성
the essential or central part; the heart or essence

pithy
[píθi]
간결한, 뜻이 깊은, 명쾌한, 날카로운
succinct; full of vigor, substance

plaintive
[pléintiv]
슬픈, 불쌍한, 애처로운
sounding sad and mournful

plangent
[plǽndʒənt]
밀려오는, 구슬프게 울리는, 울려 퍼지는
loud and resounding; expressing or suggesting sadness; plaintive

platitude
[plǽtətjùːd]
진부한 말, 진부함
a trite or banal remark or statement, especially one expressed as if it were original or significant; lack of originality, triteness

platitudinous
[plǽtətjúːdənəs]
진부한, 단조로운
having the characteristics of a p atitude: full of platitudes

pliable
[pláiəbl]
모양이 잘 휘는, 고분고분한
easily bent; flexible; easily influenced

pliant
[pláiənt]
유연한, 고분고분한
pliable

plod
[plɑːd]
무거운 발걸음으로 힘들게 걷다, 천천히 나아가다; 무거운 발걸음, 터벅터벅 걷기, 꾸준히 하기, 고달픈 일
to move or walk heavily or laboriously; trudge

pluck
[plʌk]
용기, 결단, 뽑아내기, 홱 당기기; 깃털을 잡아 뽑다, 잡아 당기다
spirited and determined courage, guts

plumb
[plʌm]
면밀히 조사하다, 수직으로 하다, 깊이를 재다; 수직으로, 정확히; 수직인, 철저한; 추
to explore or experience fully or to extremes

plunder
[plʌ́ndər]
약탈하다, 훔치다; 약탈, 강탈
to take by force or wrongfully

poised
[pɔ́izd]
차분한, 침착한, 균형이 잡힌
marked by balance or equilibrium

polymorphous
[pàːlimɔ́ːrfəs]
여러 형태의, 다양한
of the occurrence of different forms, stages, or types in individual organisms or in organisms of the same species, independent of sexual variations

pompous
[pámpəs]
(태도, 말 등이) 오만한, 거만한, 과장된
affectedly and irritatingly grand, solemn, or self-important

pontificate
[pantífikit]
오만하고 독단적으로 말하다, 주교의 직무를 수행하다; 주교의 임기, 주교의 직위
to express one's opinions in a way considered annoyingly pompous and dogmatic

porous
[pɔ́:rəs]
다공성의, (기체, 액체) 쉽게 통과하는, 침투하기 쉬운
full of or having pores; admitting the passage of gas or liquid through pores or interstices; easily penetrated

portentous
[pɔ:rténtəs]
전조의, 불길한, 흉조의, 중대한, 놀라운, 이상한
inauspicious, unpropitious; grave or serious; eliciting amazement or wonder

posit
[pázit]
가정하다, 당연하게 여기다
to assume or affirm

postulate
[pástʃulèit]
가정하다, 요구하다; 자명한 일, 가정, 기본원리
to make claim for, demand; to assume or assert the truth, reality, or necessity of, especially as a basis of an argument; to take for granted, presume

potable
[póutəbl]
마시기에 적당한; 음료, 술
safe to drink; drinkable

potentate
[póutntèit]
권세가, 강대한 힘의 소유자
a monarch or ruler, esp. an autocratic one

precarious
[prikɛ́əriəs]
위태로운, 불확실한
not securely held or in position; dangerously likely to fall or collapse; dependent on chance, uncertain

precept
[prí:sept]
가르침, 교훈, 훈계
a rule or principle prescribing a particular course of action or conduct

precipitous
[prisípətəs]

급경사의; 성급한
dangerously high or steep; (of a change to a worse situation or condition) sudden and dramatic

predilection
[prèdəlékʃən]

편애, 좋아함
a partiality or disposition in favor of something; a preference

preemptive
[priémptiv]

선제적인, 선매의, 선매권이 있는
serving or intended to preempt something, esp. to prevent attack by disabling the enemy; relating to the purchase of goods or shares before the opportunity is offered to others

preen
[príːn]

치장하다, 자기만족을 드러내다, 새가 부리로 날개를 다듬다
to devote effort to making oneself look attractive and then admire one's appearance

prepossessing
[príːpəzésiŋ]

매력 있는
tending to create a favorable impression

preposterous
[pripástərəs]

비상식적인, 터무니없는
contrary to reason or common sense; utterly absurd or ridiculous

prescience
[préʃəns]

예지력, 통찰력
knowledge of actions or events before they occur; foresight

prevaricate
[privǽrəkèit]

얼버무리다, 둘러대다, 속이다
to speak or act in an evasive way; to palter, equivocate

prize
[práiz]

소중히 여기다, 평가하다; 상, 목적물, 귀중한 것; 입상한, 상품으로 주어진
to value highly, esteem

probe
[proub]

철저히 조사하다, 정밀 조사하다; 정밀조사
to delve into; investigate

prod
[pra:d]
(자극을 주어) 불러 일으키다, 격려하다, 자극하여 시키다, 쑤시다, 찌르다;
자극, 격력, 쑤시기, 찌르기
to goad to action; incite

prodigal
[prɔ́digəl]
낭비하는; 낭비가, 난봉꾼, 방탕아
spending money or resources freely and recklessly; wastefully
extravagant

profane
[prouféin]
불경스러운, 세속적인, 거룩하지 않은 더러운; 남용하다, 천하게 하다,
신성을 더럽히다
not concerned with religion or religious purposes: secular not
holy because unconsecrated, impure, or defiled

profligate
[prafligèit]
탕진하는, 낭비하는, 부도덕한, 품행이 나쁜 사람, 방탕아, 낭비가
recklessly extravagant or wasteful in the use of resources

profuse
[prəfjú:s]
많은, 풍부한, 낭비하는, 너그러운
(esp. of something offered or discharged) exuberantly plentiful;
abundant; (of a person) lavish; extravagant

prolix
[proulíks]
장황한, 지루하게 긴
(of speech or writing) using or containing too many words,
tediously lengthy

promulgate
[práməlgèit]
공표하다, 알리다, 선포하다
to make known; to publish

propitiate
[prəpíʃièit]
달래다, 비위를 맞추다, 진정시키다
to conciliate an offended power, appease

propitiatory
[prəpíʃiətɔ:ri]
달래는
intended to reconcile or appease

propitious
[prəpíʃəs]

유리한, 형편이 좋은, 기분이 좋은, 길조의
giving or indicating a good chance of success; favorable

proponent
[prəpóunənt]

지지자, 제안자
one who argues in favor of something

propriety
[prəpráiəti]

행동의 적절함, 예의바름
appropriateness, suitability

protuberance
[proutjú:bərəns]

돌출, 돌기, 융기
a thing that protrudes from something else

provender
[právəndər]

여물, 꼴, (사람의) 식량
food or provisions

providential
[právədénʃəl]

시기 적절한, 운이 좋은, 섭리의, 신의 뜻에 의한
occurring at a favorable time, opportune; involving divine
foresight or intervention

provincial
[prəvínʃəl]

지방의, 촌스러운, 세련되지 못한, 시야가 좁은, 편협한; 지방출신 사람,
투박한 사람, 편협한 사람
of or characteristic of people from the provinces, not fashionable
or sophisticated; limited in perspective, narrow and self-centered

provocative
[prəvá:kətiv]

자극하는, 유발하는; 자극물, 유인
tending to provoke

prudent
[prú:dnt]

현명한, 신중한, 절약하는
acting with or showing care and thought for the future

prude
[prú:d]

숙녀인체, 고상한척하는 여자
a person excessively concerned about propriety and decorum

prudish
[prú:diʃ]
고상한 체하는, 새침한, 몹시 얌전 빼는
marked by or exhibiting the characteristics of a prude; priggish

prurient
[prú:riənt]
호색한, 외설한
lascivious

puerile
[pjú:əril]
유치한, 미숙한
childishly silly and trivial

pulverize
[pʌ́lvəràiz]
분쇄하다
to reduce to fine particles

pundit
[pʌ́ndit]
대학자, 권위자, (미디어에 출연해서 의견을 말하는) 전문가
an expert in a particular subject or field who is frequently called on to give opinions about it to the public

putative
[pjú:tətiv]
추정의, 소문에 들리는
generally regarded as such; supposed

quaff
[kwa:f]
벌컥 벌컥 마시다, 한숨이 들이키다; 쭉 들이킴
to drink heartily

quail
[kweil]
질리다, 움츠리다 겁먹다; 메추라기
to shrink back in fear; cower

quaint
[kwéint]
(특이하거나 옛스런 정취로 인해) 흥미로운, 이상한, 특이한
unusual or different in character or appearance

qualm
[kwá:m, kwɔ:m]
불안, 걱정, 양심의 가책, 꺼림직함
an uneasy feeling of doubt, worry, or fear, esp. about one's own conduct; a misgiving

quandary
[kwándəri]
난처함, 궁지
a state of perplexity or uncertainty over what to do in a difficult situation

quench
[kwéntʃ]
불을 끄다, 억제하다, 갈증을 해소하다, 관족시키다
to put out (a fire, for example), extinguish; to suppress; to squelch; to slake, satisfy; to cool (hot metal) by thrusting into water or other liquid

querulous
[kwérjuləs]
불평이 많은, 징징거리는
complaining in a petulant or whining manner

query
[kwíəri]
질문하다, 캐묻다; 의문, 질문, 의심
to ask a question about something

quibble
[kwíbl]
둘러대기, 발뺌, 트집잡기; 사소한 문제에 트집잡다, 논의의 주제를 회피하다
a slight objection or criticism; to evade the point of an argument by caviling about words

quiescence
[kwaiésns(i)]
무활동, 정지, 고요
a state or period of inactivity or dormancy

quirky
[kwéːrki]
별난, 특이한
a peculiar trait

quixotic
[kwéːrki]
지나치게 이상적인; 비현실적인, 돈 키호테식인
exceedingly idealistic; unrealistic and impractical

rabid
[rǽbid]
과격한, 광신적인, 맹렬한
having or proceeding from an extreme or fanatical support of or belief in something

ragged
[rǽgid]

(옷이) 낡고 헤진, (표면이) 울퉁불퉁한, 손질하지 않은
(of cloth or clothes) old and torn; having a rough, irregular, or uneven surface, edge, or outline

rail
[réil]

몹시 비난하다, 철도로 여행하다; 울타리, 철로
to complain or protest strongly and persistently about

rake
[reik]

방탕자, 난봉꾼, 도락가, 갈퀴, 써레; 갈퀴로 긁어모으다, 긁어내다, 제거하다
an immoral or dissolute person; a libertine

rakish
[réikiʃ]

방탕한, 바람난, 난봉부리는, 음탕한, 세련된, 맵시 있는, 화려한
of the character of a rake; dissolute

rally
[rǽli]

세를 규합하다, 집회로 모이다, (사기를) 진작시키다, (건강, 기세를) 회복시키다; 재집합, 회복, 집회, 궐기대회
(of troops) to come together again in order to continue fighting after a defeat or dispersion; to come together fcr a common purpose; to arouse for action; revive (a person or their health or spirits)

ramble
[rǽmbl]

산책하다, 거닐다, 어슬렁거리다, 장황하게 이야기 하다; 산책
to move about aimlessly

ramshackle
[rǽmʃækl]

(집 등) 쓰러져가는, 상태가 매우 안 좋은, 금방이라도 무너질 듯한
carelessly or loosely constructed

rancid
[rǽnsid]

(부패로) 악취 나는
smelling or tasting unpleasant as a result of being old and stale

rancor
[rǽŋkər]

원한, 악의
long-standing bitterness or resentfulness

rancorous
[rǽŋkərəs]

원한에 사무친
variant of rancor

rapacious
[rəpéiʃəs]

약탈하는, 강탈하는, 착취하는, 탐욕스러운
taking by force; plundering, greedy

rarefy
[rɛ(:)ərəfài]

희박하게 하다, 순화하다, 정화하다
to make thin, less compact, or less dense, to purify or refine

raucous
[rɔ́:kəs]

(소리가) 거슬리는, 불쾌한
making or constituting a disturbingly harsh and loud noise

ravenous
[rǽvənəs]

게걸스러운, 몹시 굶주린, 탐욕스러운, 걸신들린
extremely hungry; voracious; rapacious; predatory

reassure
[rì:əʃúər]

안심시키다
to say or do something to remove the doubts and fears of someone

rebuff
[ribʌ́f]

퉁명스럽게 거부하다, 거절하다; 단호한 거절, 퇴짜, 방해
to reject (someone or something) in an abrupt or ungracious manner

rebuke
[ribjú:k]

심하게 꾸짖다, 몹시 비난하다; 심한 비난, 질책
to criticize, reprove sharply

rebut
[ribʌ́t]

반박하다, 논박하다
to claim or prove that (evidence or an accusation) is false

recalcitrant
[rikǽlsitrənt]

권위에 저항하는, 다루기 힘든; 다루기 어려운 사람, 고집불통의 사람
having an obstinately uncooperative attitude toward authority or discipline

recant
[rikǽnt]

(주장을) 철회하다, 부정하다
to say that one no longer holds an opinion or belief, esp. one considered heretical; to withdraw or repudiate (a statement or belief) formally and publicly

recapitulate
[rìːkəpítʃulèit]
요약하다, 개괄하다
to repeat in concise form

recapitulation
[rìːkəpìtʃuléiʃən]
요약, 개요
an act or instance of summarizing and restating the
main points of something

recidivism
[risídəvìzm]
상습적 범행
tendency to relapse into a previous condition or mode of
behavior

reckless
[réklis]
무모한, 무분별한
marked by lack of proper caution: careless of consequences

recluse
[rékluːs, riklúːs]
은둔자
a person who withdraws from the world to live in seclusion and
often in solitude

recondite
[rékəndàit]
난해한
(of a subject or knowledge) little known; abstruse

recourse
[rikɔ́ːrs]
의지하기, 의지가 되는 것
a turning to someone or something for help or protection

recuse
[rikjúːz]
(법관·배심원 등을) 기피하다 , 회피하다
to disqualify or seek to disqualify from participation in a decision
on grounds such as prejudice or personal involvement

redolent
[rédələnt]
향기로운, 생가나게 하는
strongly smelling of something; fragrant or sweet smelling

redoubtable
[riːdàutəbl]
두렵고 존경스러운, 가공할 만한, 강력한
formidable; inspiring fear or respect through being impressively
large, powerful, intense, or capable

| **redress**
[ríːdres] | (부정 행위 등을) 고치다, 바로잡다, 교정하다; 교정, 구제, 보상
to set right; remedy or rectify |

| **refractory**
[rifrǽktəri] | 고집불통의, 다루기 힘든
stubborn or unmanageable |

| **regale**
[rigéil] | 충분히 기분 좋게 대접하다, 즐겁게 하다
to provide with great enjoyment; entertain |

| **regiment**
[rédʒəmənt] | 연대, 큰 떼, 다수; 연대로 편성하다, 엄격히 관리하다
organize according to a strict, sometimes oppressive system or pattern |

| **regimental**
[rèdʒəméntl] | 획일적인, 통제된
of a regiment |

| **regression**
[rigréʃən] | 회귀, 복귀, 퇴화
a return to a former or less developed state |

| **remold**
[riːmóuld] | (모양, 구조, 특징 등을) 바꾸다, 개조하다
to change or refashion the appearance, or character of |

| **remonstrate**
[rimánstreit] | 항의하다, 이의를 제출하다
to make a forcefully reproachful protest |

| **renegade**
[rénigèid] | 배교자, 변절자, 반역자; 배반하다
one who rejects a religion, cause, allegiance, or group for another, a deserter; an outlaw, a rebel |

| **renege**
[riníg] | 약속을 이행하지 못하다, (약속, 계약) 폐기시키다
to fail to carry out a promise or commitment; to go back on a promise, undertaking, or contract |

renounce
[rinàuns]

공식적으로 포기하다, 철회하다, 거부하다
formally declare one's abandonment of (a claim, right, or possession); reject and stop using or consuming

repeal
[ripí:l]

취소하다, 철회하다; 취소, 철회
to revoke or rescind, especially by an official or formal act

repel
[ripél]

물리치다, 불쾌감을 주다
to drive or force (an attack or attacker) back or away; to be repulsive or distasteful to

repellent
[ripélənt]

불쾌감을 주는, 혐오감을 주는; 반발력, 다가오지 못하게 하는 것
repelling, repugnant, repulsive

repine
[ripáin]

투덜거리다, 안달하다, 불평하다, 푸념을 늘어놓다, 한탄하다
to be discontented or low in spirits; complain or fret

replenish
[ripléniʃ]

다시 채우다
to fill (something) up again; to restore (a stock or supply of something) to the former level or condition

repose
[ripóuz]

휴식, 고요한, 침착; 휴식하다, 평온하다
rest, tranquility

reprehensible
[rèprihénsəbl]

비난 받아 마땅한
deserving censure or condemnation

repress
[riprés]

억압하다, 억제하다
to subdue (someone or something) by force; to restrain or prevent (the expression of a feeling)

repressive
[riprésiv]

억압적인, 탄압적인, 진압하는
causing or inclined to cause repression

reproachable
[ripróutʃ]
비난할 만한
deserving disapproval or disappointment

reproach
[ripróutʃ]
비난하다, 책망하다, 비난의 원인이 되다; 비난, 질책, 치욕, 불명예
to address (someone) in such a way as to express disapproval or
disappointment

repudiate
[ripjú:dièit]
부인하다, 거절하다
to refuse to accept or be associated with; deny the truth or
validity of

repugnance
[ripʌ́gnəns]
혐오함, 적대감, 반감
intense disgust; inconsistency or incompatibility of ideas or
statements

repute
[ripjú:t]
믿다, 간주하다; 평판, 명성
to consider, believe

rescind
[risínd]
폐지하다, 철회하다
to revoke, cancel, or repeal (a law, order, or agreement)

resignation
[rèzignéiʃən]
사퇴; 체념, 포기, 단념
an act of retiring or giving up a position; the acceptance of
something undesirable but inev table

resort to
[rizɔ́:rt]
의지하다, 호소하다 , 자주가다; 휴양지, 자주 가는곳, 호소하기, 의지할 것
to turn to and adopt (a strategy or course of action, esp. a
disagreeable or undesirable one) so as to resolve a difficult
situation

restive
[réstiv]
안절부절 못하는, 고집부리는 다루기 힘든
unable to keep still or silent and becoming increasingly difficult to
control, esp. because of impatience, dissatisfaction, or boredom;
resisting control; difficult to control, refusing to move

retention
[riténʃən]

보존, 보유, 유지, 기억력
the continued possession, use, or control of something

retrench
[ritréntʃ]

삭감하다, 줄이다, 제거하다
to reduce costs or spending in response to economic difficulty

revere
[rivíər]

깊이 존경하다
to feel deep respect or admiration for (something)

reverence
[révərəns]

공경, 존경, 숭배, 경의
honor or respect felt or shown

reverent
[révərənt]

공경하는, 숭배하는
marked by, feeling, or expressing respect

revert
[rivə́:rt]

되돌아 가다, 복귀하다, 회고하다, 되돌아가는 것
to come or go back

revulsion
[rivʌ́lʃən]

역겨움, 혐오감, 급변, 격변
a sense of disgust and loathing

ribald
[ríbəld]

무례한, 음담패설을 해대는, 상스러운; 점잖지 못함 사람
referring to sexual matters in an amusingly rude or irreverent way

risible
[rizəbl]

웃음을 자아내는, 우스운, 익살스런
relating to laughter or used in eliciting laughter

riveting
[rívitiŋ]

대단히 매력적인, 푹 빠지게 하는
wholly absorbing or engrossing one's attention; fascinating

robust
[roubʌ́st]

건강한, 건장한
strong and healthy; vigorous

roil
[rɔil]

화나게 하다, 초조하게 만들다, 액체를 휘저어 흐리게 하다
to rile, stir up, disturb, disorder; to make (a liquid) muddy or cloudy by stirring up sediment

rowdy
[ráudi]

소란스러운, 난폭한; 난폭한 사람, 싸움쟁이
noisy and disorderly

rubicund
[rú:bikənd]

(얼굴 등이) 붉은, 불그레한, (사람이) 붉은 얼굴의, 혈색이 좋은, 홍조를 띤
inclined to a healthy rosiness; ruddy

ruse
[rú:z]

계략, 책략, 음모
trick, subterfuge

salacious
[səléiʃes]

외설스런, 저속한, 추접스런
appealing to or stimulating sexual desire; lascivious

salient
[séiliənt]

돌출한, 눈에 띄는, 유명한; 돌출부, 철각
prominent; conspicuous; most noticeable or important

sap
[sæp]

(토대 밑을 파서) 쇠약하게 만든다, 무너뜨리다; 수액, 체액, 활기, 생기
to weaken gradually or destroy (a person's strength or power)

saturnine
[sǽtərnàin]

침울한, 우울한, 납중독에 걸린, 납의
(of a person or their manner) slow and gloomy

schism
[sízm]

(교회) 분열, 분파
a split or division between strongly opposed sections or parties, caused by differences in opinion or belief

scintillate
[síntəlèit]

불꽃이 너울거리다, 기지가 번뜩이다, 번쩍이다
to emit flashes of light; sparkle; to be lively or brilliant or exhibit virtuosity

scoff
[skɔ(ː)f]
조롱하다; 비웃음, 조롱
to speak to someone or about something in a scornfully derisive or mocking way

score
[skɔːr]
악보, 총보(악보모음), 배경음악, 득점, 성적; 득점하다, 평가하다, 작곡하다
a written representation of a musical composition showing all the vocal and instrumental parts arranged one below the other; the music composed for a movie or play

scorn
[skɔːrn]
업신여기다, 깔보다, 경멸하다, 무시하다, 비웃다; 경멸, 냉소
to reject or refuse with derision

scourge
[skə:rdʒ]
괴로움의 원인, 고민거리, 사회악, 회초리, 벌주는 것; 매질하다, 호되게 비판하다
a source of widespread, dreadful affliction and devastation such as that caused by pestilence or war; a means of

scrimp
[skrímp]
매우 아끼다, 인색하게 굴다
to be thrifty or parsimonious; economize

scruple
[skrú:pl]
양심, 주저함, 거리낌; 망설이다, 주저하다
an uneasy feeling arising from conscience or principle that tends to hinder action

scrupulous
[skrú:pjuləs]
양심적인, 세심한, 꼼꼼한, 면밀한
diligent, thorough, and extremely attentive to details; very concerned to avoid doing wrong

secretive
[síːkritiv]
비밀의, 숨기려 하는
inclined to conceal feelings and intentions or not to disclose information

secular
[sékjulər]
세속적인
denoting attitudes, activities, or other things that have no religious or spiritual basis; mundane, worldly, temporal

sedulous
[sédʒuləs]

근면 성실한, 주의 깊고 부지런한
(of a person or action) showing dedication and diligence; assiduous

self-abasement
[sélfəbéismənt]

자기비하, 자기 경멸, 겸손
the belittling or humiliation of oreself

self-effacing
[sélfiféisiŋ]

삼가는, 겸손한, 과시하지 않는
not claiming attention for oneself; retiring and modest

sententious
[senténʃəs]

경구가 많은, (표현이) 경구적인, 경구를 즐겨 쓰는
terse and energetic in expression; pithy

sequester
[sikwéstər]

고립시키다
to isolate or hide away (someone or something)

sere
[siər]

시든, 말라 빠진
very dry

servile
[sə́:rvail]

노예 상태의, 노예 특유의, 노예 근성의, 천한, 비굴한, 굽실거리는, 아첨하는, 맹종하는, 주체성이 없는
abjectly submissive; slavish

servitude
[sə́:rvətjù:d]

노예상태, 예속, 징역, 강제 노등
a condition in which one lacks liberty especially to determine one's course of action or way of life

shackle
[ʃǽkl]

족쇄를 채우다, 구속하다; 수갑; 족쇄, 속박, 구속
to chain with shackles; to limit, restrain

shard
[ʃá:rd]

(도자기, 유리, 바위 등의) 파편조각
a piece of broken ceramic, metal, glass, or rock, typically having sharp edges

shiftiness
[ʃífti]
교활함, 속임수, 간사함; 이동하는, 바뀌는, 계략을 쓰는, 속임수의
appearance of deceitful or evasive

shiftless
[ʃíftlis]
목표 없는, 게으른, 무능한
lacking ambition or purpose; lazy

shifty
[ʃífti]
수단이 좋은, 속임수가 많은, 교활한, 간사해 보이는
having, displaying, or suggestive of deceitful character; evasive or untrustworthy

shipshape
[ʃípʃèip]
정연한, 잘 정리된, 말쑥한, 다듬은; 정연하게, 깔끔하게
marked by meticulous order and neatness; tidy

shirk
[ʃə́:rk]
회피하다; 회피하는 사람, 게으름쟁이, 꾀부리는 사람
to avoid or neglect (a duty or responsibility); a person who shirks

shoddy
[ʃádi]
(물건 등) 질 떨어지는, 볼품없는, 모조품의; 겉만 번지르르한 물건, 가짜, 싸구려, 겉치레, 허울
cheaply imitative; vulgarly pretentious

shore up
[ʃɔ́:rʌp]
지지하다, 버팀목을 괴다; 지주, 버팀목
to support or hold up (something) with such props or beams

shun
[ʃʌn]
기피하다
persistently avoid, ignore, or reject (someone or something) through antipathy or caution

sieve
[siv]
체로 치다, 체질하다, 체로 거르다; 체
to use a sieve; sift

simper
[simpər]
선웃음 짓다, 억지 웃음 짓다; 바보 같은 선웃음
to smile in a silly, self-conscious way

sinewy
[sínjui]

힘찬, 활발한, 건장한
tough, muscular

skew
[skju:]

비스듬한, 경사진, 비뚫어진; 비뚫어짐, 비스듬한 움직임; 빗나가다, 왜곡하다
to take an oblique course or direction

skimp
[skímp]

아까워하다, 인색하게 굴다, 절약하다; 부족한, 인색한
to use less time, money, or material on something than is
necessary in an attempt to economize

skittish
[skítiʃ]

잘 놀라는, 겁 많은, 변덕스런, 활발한
unpredictably excitable (especially of horses); characterized by
nervousness and quickness to take fright; unpredictable, playful

slacken
[slǽkən]

느슨하게 만들다, 느슨해지다, (속도 등을) 줄이다
to make or become slack

slake
[sléik]

갈증을 해소하다, 만족시키다
to quench or satisfy (one's thirst)

slant
[slǽnt]

기울다, 기울어지게 하다, 왜곡하다, 편향된 시각을 보여주다; 경사, 편향
to give a direction other than perpendicular or horizontal to;
make diagonal, to cause to slope; to present so as to conform to a
particular bias or appeal to a certain audience

slipshod
[slípʃàd]

칠칠치 못한, 대충하는, 단정하지 못한, 닳아빠진 옷이나 신발을 신은
marked by carelessness, sloppy or slovenly; slovenly in
appearance, shabby or seedy

slothful
[slɔ́:θfəl]

게으른
lazy; inactive; sluggish; indolent; idle; tending to sloth

slovenly
[slʌ́vənli]

지저분한, 단정치 못한, 되는대로 하는, 날림의; 단정치 못하게, 되는 대로
(esp. of a person or their appearance) messy and dirty; careless, excessively casual, slipshod

sluggish
[slʌ́giʃ]

둔한, 활력 없는, 게으른
slow-moving or inactive

smattering
[smǽtəriŋ]

피상적인 지식, 적은 양, 소수; 천박한, 어설픈
a slight superficial knowledge of a language or subject; a small amount of something

sneer
[sníər]

비웃다, 조롱하다, 조소하다; 냉소, 조소, 경멸
to smile or speak in a contemptuous or mocking manner

snub
[snʌb]

타박 주다, 핀잔 주다; 냉대하여 (어떤 상태에) 이르게 하다; 모욕, 경시, 거절
to ignore or behave coldly toward; slight

sodden
[sádən]

흠뻑 젖은, 흠뻑 스며든; 흠뻑 적시다
thoroughly soaked

solder
[sóldər]

납땜질하다, 밀착시키다, 친밀하게 하다; 땜납, 결합시키는 것, 유대
to serve as a bond between; join

solemn
[sá:ləm]

엄숙한, 무게 있는, 진지한 체하는, 우울한, 장엄한
deeply earnest, serious, and sober; somberly or gravely impressive

solicit
[səlísit]

요청하다, 구하다, 간청하다
to try to obtain by usually urgent requests; to entice or lure

solicitous
[səlísətəs]

염려하는, 간절히 원하는
expressing concern and care

solitude
[sάlətjùːd]
고독, 외로움
the state or situation of being alone

solvent
[sάlvənt]
지급 능력이 있는, 녹이는, 용해력 있는, 약화시키는; 용매, 해결, 약화시키는 것
having assets in excess of liabilities; able to pay one's debts; able to dissolve   other substances

soporific
[sòupərífik]
수면성의, 잠이 오게 하는, 졸리는; 수면제, 최면제, 마취제
tending to induce drowsiness or sleep; sleepy, drowsy

sordid
[sɔ́ːrdid]
추잡스런, 더러운, 비열한
involving ignoble actions and motives; arousing moral distaste and contempt

spendthrift
[spéndθrift]
낭비하는, 방탕의; 낭비자, 방탕아
wasteful or extravagant

spent
[spént]
(힘, 에너지가) 소진된, 낭비된, 다 써버린
having no power or energy left

spirited
[spíritid]
활기(용기, 열의) 넘치는
full of energy

spleen
[splíːn]
울화, 악의
anger, ill will, bad temper, spite

splenetic
[splinétik]
비장의; 까다로운, 성깔 있는, 짓궂은; 성깔 있는 사람
of or relating to the spleen; affected or marked by ill humor or irritability

splurge
[splέːrdʒ]
(돈을) 펑펑 쓰기, 과시; (돈을) 펑펑 쓰다, 과시하다, 자랑하다
an act of spending money freely or extravagantly; to spend (money) freely or extravagantly

sporadic
[spərǽdik]
간헐적인, 이따금 일어나는
occurring occasionally

sprightly
[spráitli]
활발한, 씩씩한, 쾌활한; 활발하게
full of spirit and vitality; lively; brisk

spur
[spə́:r]
박차를 가하다, 독려하다, 자극하다; 박차, 자극, 격려
to give an incentive or encouragement to (someone); to cause or
promote the development of; to stimulate

spurious
[spjúəriəs]
가짜의, 허위의
lacking authenticity or validity in essence or origin; not genuine;
false

spurn
[spə́:rn]
경멸하다, 딱 거절하다; 퇴짜, 일축
to reject with disdain or contempt

squalid
[skwálid]
더러운, 지저분한, 누추한, 비참한, 비열한
dirty and wretched, as from poverty or lack of care

squash
[skwaʃ]
진압하다, 억압하다, 짓누르다; 짓눌림, 혼잡, 군중
to put down or suppress; quash; silence or fluster, as with crushing
words

staid
[stéid]
조용한, 진지한
sedate, respectable, and unadventurous

stalwart
[stɔ́:lwərt]
충성된, 튼튼한, 건장한; 충성된 사람, 건장한 사람
loyal, reliable, and hardworking; strongly built and sturdy; one who
steadfastly supports an organization or cause; one who is
physically and morally strong

stanch
[stǽntʃ]
흐름을 막다, 지혈하다
to check or stop the flowing of

standoffish
[stǽndɔ:fiʃ]

쌀쌀맞은, 마음을 잘 열지 않는, 무뚝뚝한
aloof or reserved

stasis
[stǽs-]

정지상태, 균형상태
a period or state of inactivity or equilibrium

stench
[sténtʃ]

악취
a strong and very unpleasant smell

stentorian
[stentɔ́:riən]

(소리가) 우렁찬, 울리는
(of a person's voice) loud and powerful

stickler
[stíklər]

끝까지 주장하는 사람, 까다로운 사람
one who insists on something unyieldingly; something puzzling or difficult

stigmatize
[stígmətàiz]

낙인을 찍다, 비난하다, 오명을 씌우다
to characterize or branc as disgraceful or ignominious; to mark with stigmata or stigma

stint
[stint]

줄이다, 절감하다, 제한하다; 제한, 한정, 정량, 할당
to restrict or limit, as in amount or number; be sparing with

stolid
[stálid]

둔감한, 무감한
calm, dependable, and showing little emotion or animation

stray
[stréi]

(있어야할 곳을 벗어나) 헤매다, 벗어나다; 길 잃은 가축, 일행을 놓친 사람; 길 잃은, 빗나간
to deviate from the direct course, leave the proper place, or go beyond the proper limits, esp. w thout a fixed course or purpose; ramble

strident
[stràidnt]

(소리가) 불쾌한, 귀에 거슬리는, 삐걱거리는
loud and harsh, grating, jarring

strut
[strʌt]
거만하게 걷다; 뽐내며 걷기, 버팀목
to walk with a stiff, erect, and apparently arrogant or conceited gait; a rod or bar forming part of a framework and designed to resist compression

stultify
[stʌ́ltəfài]
활력을 없애다, 바보로 만들다; 무효로하다
to cause to lose enthusiasm and initiative, esp. as a result of a tedious or restrictive routine; to render useless or ineffectual

sturdy
[stə́:rdi]
튼튼한
(of a person or their body) strongly and solidly built

stymie
[stáimi]
방해하다, 좌절시키다; 어려운 상태, 어려운 문제
to prevent

subjugate
[sʌ́bdʒugèit]
굴복시키다, 지배하다
to bring under domination or control, esp. by conquest

sublime
[səblàim]
숭고한, 탁월한, 숭고한 것, 최고, 극치; 고상하게 하다
of such excellence, grandeur, or beauty as to inspire great admiration or awe

submissive
[səbmísiv]
순종하는, 순응하는
ready to conform to the authority or will of others; meekly obedient or passive

subordinate
[səbɔ́:rdənət]
종속적인, 부하의, 아래의; 하위에 놓다, 종속시키다
to make subject or subservient; to treat as of less value or importance

subservient
[səbsə́:rviənt]
굴종하는, 비굴한, 부차적인, 부수적인
prepared to obey others unquestioningly; less important; subordinate

subterfuge
[sʌ́btərfjùːdʒ]
핑계, 구실, 속임수
deceit used in order to achieve one's goal

subvert
[səbvə́ːrt]
전복시키다
to undermine the power and authority of (an established system or institution); overturn

succinct
[sʌksíŋkt]
간결한
briefly and clearly expressed

succor
[sʌ́kər]
원조하다; 원조, 구조
to give assistance or aid to

sumptuous
[sʌ́mptʃuəs]
호화로운, 사치스러운, 비싸 보이는
splendid and expensive-looking

sunder
[sʌ́ndər]
분리하다, 절단하다
to break apart or in two, using violence

sundry
[sʌ́ndri]
여러 가지의, 갖가지의
various; miscellaneous

supplant
[səplǽnt]
(자리 등) 찬탈하다, 대신하다
to take the place of another especially using underhanded tactics

supple
[sʌ́pl]
나긋나긋한, 잘 휘는, (운동, 동작 등이) 유연한; 유연하게 하다
moving and bending with agility; limber

surreptitious
[səːrəptíʃəs]
은밀한, 비밀리의, 부정한
kept secret, esp. because it would not be approved of

svelte
[svelt]
(특히 여성이) 날씬한, 유연한, (사람이) 온화한, 세련되고 품위 있는
slender or graceful in figure or outline; slim

sway
[swéi]
흔들리다, 동요하다; 흔들림, 동요
(to cause) to fluctuate or vacillate, as in opinion

swerve
[swə́:rv]
(진로에서) 벗어나다, 이탈하다, 방향을 갑자기 바꾸다; 빗나가기, 탈선
to change or cause to change direction abruptly

sybarite
[síbəràit]
쾌락주의자
voluptuary, hedonist

sycophant
[síkəfənt]
아첨꾼
a servile self-seeker who attempts to win favor by flattering influential people

symbiosis
[sìmbióusis, -bai-]
공생
interaction between two different organisms living in close physical association

tactile
[tǽktil]
촉각의
of or connected with the sense of touch

tailor
[téilər]
(필요, 목적에 맞게) 변경하다, 맞추다
a person whose occupation is making fitted clothes such as suits, pants, and jackets to fit individual customers

tame
[teim]
길 들여진, 사람을 따르는; 길 들이다, 복종시키다, 제어하다
brought from wildness into a domesticated or tractable state

tangential
[tændʒénʃəl]
주변의, 핵심에서 벗어난, 접선의
hardly touching a matter; peripheral

tantamount
[tǽntəmàunt]
비슷한, 동등한
equivalent in seriousness to; virtually the same as

tantrum
[tǽntrəm]
역정, 울화
an uncontrolled outburst of anger and frustration, typically in a young child

tatty
[tǽti]
낡고 초라한, 넝마를 걸친
worn and shabby; in poor condition

taunt
[tá:nt]
조롱하다, 비웃다; 비웃음, 비꼼
to provoke or challenge (someone) with insulting remarks

tawdry
[tɔ́:dri]
장식만 번지르르하고 싸구려의; 야한 장식의 옷
showy but cheap and of poor quality

teem
[tí:m]
가득하다, 풍부하다
to be full of or swarming with

telling
[téliŋ]
효과적인, 의미 있는, 설득력 있는; 말하기, 진술하기
having a striking or revealing effect; significant

temerity
[təmérəti]
지나친 자신감, 무모함
excessive confidence, boldness, audacity

temper
[témpər]
기분, 기질, 화, 성미, 평정, 침착; 누그러뜨리다, 완화시키다
to adjust or attuned by add a counterbalancing element

temperance
[témpərəns]
자제, 절제
moderation or self-restraint, esp. in eating and drinking

tempestuous
[tempéstʃuəs]
폭풍우 치는, 격정적인
very stormy; characterized by strong and turbulent or conflicting emotion

tenable
[ténəbl]
(반대, 공격을) 방어할 수 있는, 견뎌내는, 유지 할 수 있는
able to be maintained or defended against attack or objection

tendentious
[tendénʃəs]
편향적인, 명확한 의도를 지닌, 선정적인
expressing or intending to promote a particular cause or point of view, esp. a controversial one

tender
[téndər]
제공하다, 입찰하다, 부드럽게 하다, 소중히 다루다; 부드러운, 약한
to offer or present (something) formally; to make a formal written offer to carry out work

tepid
[tépid]
미지근한, 열정이 거의 없는
(esp. of a liquid) only slightly warm; lukewarm; showing little enthusiasm

terrestrial
[təréstriəl]
지구의, 세속적인, 땅의; 지구에 사는 것, 인간
of or relating to the earth or its inhabitants; having a worldly, mundane character or quality; of, relating to, or composed of land

terse
[tə́:rs]
간결한
sparing in the use of words; concise

testy
[tésti]
조급한, 쉽게 화내는
easily irritated; impatient and somewhat bad-tempered

thorny
[θɔ́:rni]
가시가 많은; 어려운, 곤란한
having many thorns or thorn bushes; causing distress, difficulty, or trouble

threadbare
[θrédbɛ̀ər]
옷이 해어지고 낡은; 진부한
having the nap worn down; frayed or shabby; hackneyed

thwart
[θwɔ:rt]

막다, 좌절시키다
to prevent (someone) from accomplishing something; to oppose successfully

timeworn
[táimwɔ:rn]

너무 오래 입어서 해어진, 너무 많이 써먹은, 진부한
showing the effects of long use or wear; used too often; trite

tirade
[táireid]

장광설, 신랄한 공격
a long, angry speech of criticism or accusation

toady
[tóudi]

아첨하는 사람; 아첨하다
a person who behaves obsequiously to someone important

tonic
[tánik]

힘을 주는, 원기 왕성하게 하는 강장제, 원기를 돋우는 것
giving a feeling of vigor or well-being; invigorating

toothsome
[tú:θsəm]

맛있는, 매력적인
temptingly tasty; attractive, good-looking

topsy-turvy
[tàpsité:rvi]

거꾸로, 머리를 아래로, 뒤죽박죽
upside down; in a state of confusion

torpid
[tɔ́:pid]

움직이지 않는, 둔한, 활발하지 못한, 둔감한, 무기력한
lethargic; apathetic

torrid
[tɔ́:rid]

매우 더운, 열정적인
very hot and dry; full of passionate or highly charged emotions arising from sexual love

tout
[tàut]

성가시게 조르다, 강매하다; 성가시게 조르는 사람
to solicit customers or voters in a brazen way

tractable
[træktəbl]
다루기 쉬운, 유순한
easy to control or influence; easy to deal with

trammel
[træməl]
얽히게 하다, 방해하다, 막다; 방해, 장애, 제약, 속박
to deprive of freedom of action

treacherous
[trétʃərəs]
배신하는
guilty of or involving betrayal or deception; (of ground, water, conditions, etc.) hazardous because of presenting hidden or unpredictable dangers

tremulous
[trémjuləs]
(손발이) 떨리는, 겁 많은, 소심한
shaking or quivering slightly; timid, nervous

trenchant
[tréntʃənt]
(표현이) 신랄한, 날카로운, 명쾌한, 효과적인
(comment, criticism) vigorous, clear, effective, forceful; distinct, clear-cut

trite
[trait]
진부한
(of a remark, opinion, or idea) overused and consequently of little import; lacking originality or freshness

truculent
[trʌ́kjələnt]
싸우기 좋아하는, 호전적인, 공격적인, 신랄한
eager or quick to argue or fight; aggressively defiant

trudge
[trʌdʒ]
걷다, (특히) 무거운 발걸음으로 터벅터벅 걷다
to walk in a laborious, heavy-footed way; plod

truism
[trúːizm]
자명한 이치, 뻔히 아는 일
a self-evident truth; cliché

truncate
[trʌ́ŋkeit]
길이를 줄이다
to shorten (something) by cutting off the top or the end

tumid
[tjúːmid]

부푼, 과장된
swollen, distended

tumultuous
[tju(ː)mʌltʃuəs]

요동하는
making a loud, confused noise; uproarious

turbid
[tə́ːrbid]

흐린, 불투명한
having sediment or foreign particles stirred up or suspended; muddy

turgid
[tə́ːrdʒid]

과장된, 허풍 떠는, 부푼, 팽창한, 부어 오른
excessively ornate or complex in style or language; grandiloquent; swollen or distended, as from a fluid, bloated

turpitude
[tə́ːrpitjùːd]

야비함, 비열함
baseness

tyro
[táiərou]

초보자, 초심자
a beginner in learning something

unabated
[ʌnəbéitid]

줄어들지 않는, 감퇴하지 않는, 약해지지 않는
sustaining an original intensity or maintaining full force with no decrease

unaccountable
[ʌnəkàuntəbl]

설명되지 않는, 불가사의한, 책임이 없는
unable to be explained

uncouth
[ʌnkúːθ]

(사람, 행동 등이) 무례한, 거친, (외모가) 세련되지 못한, 꼴사나운
(of a person or their appearance or behavior) lacking good manners, refinement, or grace

unctuous
[ʌŋktʃuəs]

(사람이) 지나치게 아부하는, (물질이) 미끈미끈한, 기름기 있는
(of a person) excessively or ingratiatingly flattering, oily; (chiefly of minerals) having a greasy or soapy feel

undaunted
[ʌndɔ́:ntid]

풀죽지 않은, 대담한
not intimidated or discouraged by difficulty, danger, or disappointment

underscore
[ʌndərskɔ́:r]

밑줄 그어 강조하다
to underline

unequivocal
[ʌnikwívəkəl]

애매하지 않은, 명확한
admitting of no doubt or misunderstanding; clear and unambiguous

unfathomable
[ʌnfæðəməbl]

이해하기 힘든, 측정하기 힘든
difficult or impossible to understand; incomprehensible; difficult to measure

unfeigned
[ʌnféind]

꾸밈 없는, 진실한, 성실한
genuine, sincere

unfettered
[ʌnfétərd]

구속 없는, 자유로운
free, unrestrained

unflappable
[ʌnflǽpəbl]

침착한
persistently calm, whether when facing difficulties or experiencing success; not easily upset or excited

ungainly
[ʌngéinli]

(외모, 행동, 솜씨 등이) 서툴고 어색한, 보기 흉한; 꼴사납게, 보기 흉하게
(of a person or movement) awkward; clumsy

unkempt
[ʌnkémpt]

(외모 등이) 흐트러진, 단정하지 못한
(esp. of a person) having an untidy or disheveled appearance

unprepossessing
[ʌnpri:pəzésiŋ]

매력 없는, 호감을 주지 못하는
failing to impress favorably; nondescript

unpropitious
[ʌ̀nprəpíʃəs]
흉조의
unfavorable; inauspicious

unremitting
[ʌ̀nrimítiŋ]
끊임없는, 계속적인
continuing without interruption

unrepentant
[ʌ̀nripéntənt]
후회하지 않는, 회개하지 않는
showing no regret for one's wrongdoings

unscathed
[ʌ̀nskéiðd]
상처 없는
wholly unharmed; not injured

unscrupulous
[ʌ̀nskrú:pjələs]
거리낌 없는, 조심성 없는, 비양심적인
devoid of scruples; oblivious to or contemptuous of what is right
or honorable

untenable
[ʌnténəbl]
(논리가) 방어되지 않는
not able to be maintained or defended against attack or objection

untold
[ʌntóuld]
셀 수 없을 만큼 많은, 무수한, 말로 나타낼 수 없는, 밝혀지지 않은
too much or too many to be counted or measured

untoward
[ʌntóuərd]
적당치 않는, 곤란한, 불리한
unexpected and inappropriate or inconvenient

unwitting
[ʌnwítiŋ]
무의식적인, 고의가 아닌, 우연적인
(of a person) not aware of the full facts; not done on purpose;
unintentional

upbraid
[ʌpbréid]
(몹시) 나무라다, 비난하다
to find fault with (someone); scold

usurp
[juːsə́ːrp]
권력을 불법적으로 찬탈하다, 강탈하다
to take (a position of power or importance) illegally or by force

usury
[júːʒəri]
고리, 고리대금
the practice of lending money and charging the borrower interest, especially at an exorbitant or illegally high rate

vacillate
[væsəlèit]
주저하다, 망설이다, 흔들리다
to alternate or waver between different opinions or actions; be indecisive

vanquish
[væŋkwiʃ]
정복하다, 항복시키다, 이겨내다, 극복하다
to defeat thoroughly

vapid
[vǽpid]
맛없는, 재미없는
lacking flavor; offering nothing that is stimulating or challenging

variable
[vέəriəbl]
가변적인; 변하기 쉬운 것, 변수
able or apt to vary: subject to variation or changes

variegation
[vὲəriəgéiʃən]
얼룩덜룩함, 다양화 하기, 다양성
state of exhibiting different colors, esp. as irregular patches or streaks

vault
[vɔːlt]
금고, 아치형 천장; 둥근 천장을 만들다
a secure room in a bank in which valuables are stored

vaunt
[váːnt]
자랑하다, 허풍 떨다; 자랑, 호언장담
to boast about or praise (something), esp. excessively

vehement
[víːəmənt]
격렬한, 열정적인
showing strong feeling; forceful, passionate, or intense

veiled
[véild]
숨겨진, 감추어진 , 베일에 가려진, 흐릿한
obscured as if by a veil

venal
[víːnl]
매수되기 쉬운, 타락한
showing or motivated by susceptibility to bribery

venerable
[vénərəbl]
공경 받는; 존경할 만한 사람, 존귀한 사람
accorded a great deal of respect, esp. because of age, wisdom, or character

venerate
[vénərèit]
깊이 존경하다, 우러르다
to regard with great respect; to revere

veneration
[vènəréiʃən]
존경
the condition or status of one who is venerated

verdant
[vэ́ːrdnt]
초목이 무성한, 경험적은, 미숙한
green with grass or other rich vegetation

vernacular
[vərnǽkjulər]
사투리, 방언, 일상어, 전문어; 그 고장 그유의, 일반 서민의 일상어를 쓰는
using a language or dialect native to a region or country rather than a literary, cultured, or foreign language

versed
[vэ́ːrst]
경험이 있는, 잘 알고 있는, 술달된
experienced or skilled in knowledgeable about

vestigial
[vestídʒiəl]
흔적의, 자취의, 잔존적인, 퇴화한
of, relating to, or constituting a vestige

vex
[véks]
짜증나게 하다, 귀찮게 하다
to make (someone) feel annoyed, frustrated, or worried, esp. with trivial matters

vexation
[vekséiʃn]
짜증나게 하기, 괴롭히기, 신경질남, 귀찮음, 낭패, 난처, 화남
the quality or condition of being vexed; annoyance

vexatious
[vekséiʃəs]
귀찮은, 성가신, 짜증나는, 무질서한
full of annoyance or distress; harassed

vicarious
[vaikέəriəs]
대리의, 대행의
experienced in the imagination through the feelings or actions of
another person

vindicate
[víndəkèit]
옹호하다, 무죄 방면하다, 의혹을 풀다
to defend, justify, clear (someone) of blame or suspicion

vindictive
[vindíktiv]
복수심이 불타는, 앙심을 품은
having or showing a strong or unreasoning desire for revenge

virtuosity
[vé:rtʃua:səti]
탁월한 기량, 명인의 솜씨
the technical skill, fluency, or style exhibited by a virtuoso;
an appreciation for or interest in fine objects of art

virtuoso
[və:rtʃuóusou, -zou]
명인, 대가
a person highly skilled in music or another artistic pursuit

visceral
[vísərəl]
내장의, 이성보다는 감정에서 비롯되는, 거친, 노골적인, 본능적인
deep, not intellectual, dealing with crude emotions

vitiate
[víʃièit]
손상시키다, 망치다, 무효화하다
to spoil or impair the quality or efficiency of; to destroy or impair
the legal validity of

vitriol
[vítria:l]
황산염, 반류, 황산, 통렬한 비평, 신랄한 반어, 비꼼
any of various sulfates of metals, such as ferrous sulfate, zinc
sulfate, or copper sulfate; bitterly

vitriolic
[vitriálik]

신랄한, 황산염의
very caustic; scathing

vituperate
[vitjú:pərèit]

욕설하다, 몹시 비난하다
blame or insult (someone) in strong or violent language

vivify
[vívəfài]

생기를 주다, 기운 차리게 하다
to enliven or animate

voracious
[vɔ:réiʃəs]

식욕이 왕성한, 게걸스러운
wanting or devouring great quantities of food

waffle
[wáfl]

장황하게 말을 늘어놓다, 모호한 태도나 입장을 취하다; 와플;
격자 모양의 무늬가 있는
to speak or write, esp. at great length, without saying anything
important or useful

waft
[wa:ft]

떠돌게 하다, 가볍게 나르다; 부유, 떠돌기
to cause to go gently and smoothly through the air or over water

wane
[wéin]

작아지다, 약해지다, 달이 기울다; 쇠퇴, 감퇴
to decrease in size or power

wanting
[wántiŋ]

부족한
lacking in a certain required or necessary quality

wanton
[wá:ntən; wɔ́:n-]

악의에 의한, 터무니없는, 부정한, 호색적인, 외설스런, 음탕한; 낭비하다,
탕진하다
immoral or unchaste; unrestrainedly excessive

wax
[wǽks]

커지다, 강해지다, 밀랍 왁스를 바르다; 증대, 강화, 밀랍, 왁스
to become larger and stronger

wayward
[wéiwərd]

통제할 수 없는, (행동이) 어디로 튈지 모르는
difficult to control or predict because of unusual or perverse behavior

weather
[weðə(r)]

(폭풍우, 위험, 어려움 등을) 뚫고 나가다, 극복하다; 날씨, 기상; 비바람을 맞는
to come through (something) safely; survive

wheedle
[wí:dl]

(남을) 그럴 듯한 말로 속이다, 술술 구슬리다, 감언으로 꾀어 시키다
to persuade or attempt to persuade by flattery or guile; cajole

wilt
[wílt]

시들다, 약해지다
to become limp through heat, loss of water, or disease; droop

winning
[wíniŋ]

매력적인, 승리의; 승리, 성공
attractive; endearing

winsome
[wínsəm]

매력적인, 쾌활한
attractive or appealing in appearance or character

withered
[wíðərd]

쭈글쭈글한, 쇠약한, 시든
shrunken or wrinkled from age or disease

woe
[wóu]

비통, 고뇌, 비통의 원인, 어려움
a condition of deep suffering from misfortune, affliction, or grief

yoke
[jouk]

결합하다, 함께 있게 되다, 함께 일하다, (소나 말에) 멍에를 메우다, 멍에를 잇다; 멍에, 양쪽에 짐을 걸고 메는 막대기
to join securely as if with a yoke; bind

yokel
[jóukl]

시골뜨기
a rustic; a bumpkin